THE MANAGERIAL LEADERSHIP BIBLE

Learning the Strategic, Organizational, and Tactical Skills Everyone Needs Today

Jeffrey Magee, PDM, CSP, CMC

Publisher: Paul Boger
Editor-in-Chief: Amy Neidlinger
Acquisitions Editor: Charlotte Maiorana
Operations Specialist: Jodi Kemper
Cover Designer: Alan Clements
Managing Editor: Kristy Hart
Senior Project Editor: Betsy Gratner
Copy Editor: Geneil Breeze
Proofreader: Paula Lowell
Indexer: Erika Millen
Compositor: Nonie Ratcliff
Manufacturing Buyer: Dan Uhrig

© 2015 by Jeffrey Magee
Published by Pearson Education, Inc.
Upper Saddle River, New Jersey 07458

For information about buying this title in bulk quantities, or for special sales opportunities (which may include electronic versions; custom cover designs; and content particular to your business, training goals, marketing focus, or branding interests), please contact our corporate sales department at corpsales@pearsoned.com or (800) 382-3419.

For government sales inquiries, please contact governmentsales@pearsoned.com.

For questions about sales outside the U.S., please contact international@pearsoned.com.

Company and product names mentioned herein are the trademarks or registered trademarks of their respective owners.

Printed in the United States of America

First Printing April 2015

ISBN-10: 0-13-409754-8
ISBN-13: 978-0-13-409754-1

Pearson Education LTD.
Pearson Education Australia PTY, Limited
Pearson Education Singapore, Pte. Ltd.
Pearson Education Asia, Ltd.
Pearson Education Canada, Ltd.
Pearson Educación de Mexico, S.A. de C.V.
Pearson Education—Japan
Pearson Education Malaysia, Pte. Ltd.

Library of Congress Control Number: 2015930431

Contents

ACCESS TO THE FINAL EXAMINATION

The Final Examination is an online-only element. To access it, please go to www.ftpress.com/title/9780134097541 and click the Downloads tab.

Course CPE Information

Course Expiration Date

AICPA and NASBA standards require all self-study courses to be completed and the final exam submitted *within one year from the date of purchase as shown on your invoice*. No extensions are allowed under AICPA/NASBA rules.

Field of Study

Management Advisory Services. Some state boards may count credits under different categories—check with your state board for more information.

Course Level

Intermediate.

Prerequisites

There are no prerequisites.

Advanced Preparation

None.

Course Description

The traditional top-down style of management is proving to be less and less effectual and efficient. This four-part course gives you the tools you need to succeed as a manager and a leader and tells you how to apply them to get the most out of the people around you. Some of the topics covered include mission statements, organizational structures, and management intervention styles; steps to tactical leadership; how to improve communication, develop good habits, and convert negatives to positives; and leadership pitfalls to avoid.

About the Author

Dr. Jeffrey Magee, PDM, CSP, CMC, has been called one of today's leading leadership and marketing strategists. Jeff is the author of more than 20 books, including two college textbooks and four bestsellers, and is the publisher of *PERFORMANCE/ P360 Magazine* (www.Professional PerformanceMagazine.com). He also is the former co-host of the national business entrepreneur program on Catalyst Business Radio and human capital developer for more than 20 years with www.JeffreyMagee.com.

Raised on a farm, Jeff started his first business at age 15 and sold it before going to college. By age 24, he was recognized by American Home Products, a Fortune 500 company, as its top salesman in the nation, while at the same time becoming the youngest certified sales instructor for the Dale Carnegie Sales Course. After experiencing downsizing in 1987, he went on to work as a sales associate for the nation's largest educational and youth advertising/ marketing firm, Target Marketing, and was promoted to vice president of sales and chief operating officer within two years.

Magee's credentials are significant. He is a certified speaking professional, a certified management consultant, and a certified professional direct marketer. He has been recognized as one of the Ten Outstanding Young Americans (TOYA) by the U.S. Junior Chamber of Commerce and twice selected to represent the United States at the World Congress as a leadership speaker (Cannes, France, and Vienna, Austria). Magee is a three-term president of the Oklahoma Speakers Association and was twice awarded its Professional Speaker Member of the Year. Today, the chapter's outstanding member of the year is awarded the Jeff Magee Member of the Year Award. Jeff served for four years as an appointed civil service commissioner (judge) for the city/ county of Tulsa, Oklahoma, before relocating to Montana.

Today, Magee is the author of the nationally syndicated "Leadership" column appearing in local business newspapers. His books on leadership, performance, and sales have been translated into multiple languages. In fact, his text, *Yield Management* has been a #1 selling graduate management school textbook with CRC Press, while *The Sales Training Handbook* published by McGraw-Hill was an instant bestseller and has been translated into more than 20 languages. His newest books *It! How to Find It, Get It, Keep It, and Grow It* and *Performance Execution* are currently bestsellers as well, and *The Line: Your Trajectory Code* is being released January 2015 by John Wiley.

Many Fortune 100 firms today use Jeff for Performance Execution® in the areas of managerial-leadership effectiveness, human capital performance, and sales training and coaching. He also been invited to be the keynote speaker at many major associations in America and to speak at West Point Military Academy on leadership.

Magee was commissioned to design, train, and present a new series of national leadership and sales recruitment programs for the more than 5,000 professional sales recruiters and sales managers with the U.S. Army National Guard. For this he has subsequently received the prestigious Commander's Coin of Excellence.

In 2010 while merging his business Jeff Magee International (Tulsa, Oklahoma) of 20 years with WesternCPE (Bozeman, Montana) he simultaneously was recognized with the U.S. Small Business Commerce Association (SBCA) 2010 Best of Business Award in the Lecture bureau category.

In 2011 Magee unmerged from WesternCPE to continue with his own firm JeffreyMagee.com (Leadership Training & Technology/What You Need To Succeed!) and has been a regular content provider to AICPA, WesternCPE, Boomer Consulting, iShade, CPELink, and many Fortune 500 firms and government agencies, as well as appearing regularly at major conventions and conferences around the world.

Today, Magee is the architect and lead facilitator of the Leadership Academy of Excellence managerial leadership series, which engages leaders and executives for a 12-month intensive program to elevate their business knowledge around strategy, operational, and tactical skill abilities. For the past 20 years the federal government, the United States Army National

Guard, Fortune 100 firms, entrepreneurial organizations, and the CEOs of billion dollar businesses have sought out Jeff and his managerial-leadership acumen for their use.

To reach the author, go to www.JeffreyMagee.com or email at DrJeffSpeaks@aol.com

Preface

Bi-ble, n. A book held to be authoritative in its field.

Lead, v. To direct the performance or activity of; to be ahead or at the head of.

Man-age, v. i. To direct or carry on business affairs; to achieve one's purpose; to exercise executive, administrative, and supervisory direction of a business.

A company's ability to gain a marketable and manageable advantage in today's business environment is critical to both its survival and its growth. This book, *The Managerial Leadership Bible,* focuses on how individuals within organizations manage resources and develop leadership skills to lead people on their teams and within their spheres of influence.

It is about three forces that can be understood and leveraged for constructive gains, and if misunderstood and ill-utilized will spell organizational chaos:

1. Strategy

2. Operations

3. Tactics

At the end of the day, as managers, leaders, and executives, it is about your ability to understand these three elements and how they work and serve an organization, the marketplace, and the individuals within them for sustained success. These three must ebb and flow and serve as the architectural framework from which everything takes place.

Sadly, most organizational leadership and business texts, business schools, and graduate-level courses in management still profess the ways of days gone by. This may be due in part to the fact that many of the individuals professing to know the business climate today have never signed the front of a paycheck!

Strategy—Having the strategic focus driven by the key stakeholders' and the organization's values and vision to drive what an organization is and is not is the essence and foundation of the organization. Strategy provides the direction of how an organization enters the marketplace or remains relevant within a marketplace. Strategy is the framework that dictates the trajectory of all resources—every endeavor, every action, and the final essence for why an organization is what it is. Strategy directs what one must adhere to in administrating a business enterprise. Strategies serve as your GPS system.

Operations—In the context of this book, having the operational systems to bring strategy to life is critical to everything you do. The operational systems, processes, and architecture from a proprietary perspective to any individual organization is not what this book addresses. It addresses operational systems from the perspective of the human capital component to your organization and as the managerial-leader. The operational systems should be appropriate to ensure that individuals and business units are at all times trending in the trajectory necessary for the health and wealth of the enterprise. These ops serve as the dashboard in essence to allow you to calibrate in real-time, 24/7, every human capital factor to know when you are or are not on trajectory for return on investment (ROI). (The trajectory model concept is discussed at the end of this book.)

Tactical—The tactical actions, behaviors, and engagements necessary to fulfill the operational systems that are born out of the strategies to generate the multiple levels of ROI for an organization and that the managerial leader needs for success will be addressed. How one does what he does is tactics. The tactics of individuals can also be benchmarked to ensure that the trajectory of success is in fact being executed or to discover whether an individual is going rogue and actually steering an entity off the desired trajectory for success and actually on a trajectory toward disaster.

Gaining a better understanding of what does and doesn't work requires neither an advanced degree nor a high-profile celebrity consultant. It only takes eyes open to success and an avoidance of patterns that have led others to bankruptcy. Whether your business is local market centric or global, virtual or traditional brick-and-mortar, you must keep a *globocal* (global and local) perspective to everything you do as the managerial-leader.

Take a look at the stewardship of leading businesses around your community, across the nation and globe to gain valuable best practice clues.

Some firms, and some managers and leaders, though, are steadfast in their resistance to change. Instead, they expect others to change to fit and meet their styles and needs. This resistance to change compounds stress, anxiety, and failures that otherwise could be avoided within work environments. Consider some large firms and their styles of management—and the executive-level influences that mentally support the negative behaviors. These behaviors ultimately may have led to the collapse of institutional leaders: command-and-control style; layered, hierarchical structures. Witness the migration of some of the fired CEOs of Fortune 500 firms in the past decade. Many serve/served on one another's boards of directors. It is just now becoming an operational trend for better corporate governance to actually give a capability test to a candidate before placing him or her on a board.

Passage of new corporate governance laws (by the federal government) to ensure better administrative reporting and board membership has merely made the complexion of boards adhere more to an EEOC checklist of acceptability, rather than a competency checklist for success. Succession planning is more about succession management at every level within an organization to remain market ready and market creators.

Let me use a horrific leadership example from my early days of being a human capital development specialist to illustrate my point. A great example of this is the post-9/11 airline industry. Many in that industry use this tragic date's events as the reason for their financial collapse, as if to say that on September 10, 2001, they were profitable!

What's amazing is that in each of the past four decades the signposts to managerial leadership ineffectiveness seem to repeat themselves.

In the technology world, Amazon.com, in the first decade-and-a-half of its existence, created enormous wealth for its founder and CEO yet never reported a profit. Or consider a more traditional business of the last century, such as aviation. American Airlines/AMR illustrates the good-old-boy network and old-school mindset that this book exposes. This book shines a light on what works—as well as what doesn't. A look at the AMR board in 2004 reveals something more like an EEOC checklist for "nice-nice" than a board of individuals in tune with present-day realities and profitable business practices. In some alarming cases, a review of the board would reveal individuals who, while personally "nice," are professional case studies in how not to do business.

In 2004, Southwest Airlines had just posted its fiftieth consecutive quarter of profitability *(Wall Street Journal)*. AMR, in contrast, had just posted a $1.8 billion debt, while publicly saying things were getting better (see *Risky Business: A Primer on Wise Organizational Decision-Making at the C-Level, How Smart People Make Them and What Happens When Dumb People Try!* by Jeffrey L. Magee and Leland Harty, Performance Publishing, 2004). A critical component to Southwest's sustained success is the No Policy that Herb Kelleher (founding CEO) and his early president Howard Putnam created and instituted and which to this day influences their managerial leadership styles—most business management consultants and authors are unaware of this, and that, too, illustrates lack of leadership acumen.

Imagine the level of performance output individuals and organizations could yield, if only capable individuals were involved.

—Jeff Magee

Truly successful individuals and leaders recognize that they cannot always have the answer themselves and that it is unrealistic for any one person to be the expert on everything. Truly great leaders, though, understand that they may not have to be the answer themselves. They merely need to be the catalyst for others to generate the answers, as well as to create a safe culture and environment for such energies to come forth. Leaders ask questions; answers will reveal themselves. Thus they serve as a conduit to harness the collective spirit and energies of their organization for a common goal.

How can you identify signs of a decaying organizational structure and leadership? How can you initiate change patterns and institute winning management ways?

I have purposefully chosen many examples, writings, and subject matter experts from the past 50 years as a beacon for our next 50 years. These all have a direct footprint ROI on every person and organization today to the learned mind. In doing so, on purpose I've tried to avoid the more popular cultural options that many in management may be familiar with and subsequently could be grossly misguided to what really makes for ROI!

The answer is not as difficult as some would have you believe. Consider some of the following warning signs and note which ones sound like an organization you know, have participated in as a customer, or have worked in during your past career, or even, perhaps, in your present environment.

Warning Signs of Decaying Managerial Leadership Effectiveness

- Only senior management can call meetings.
- Only senior management initiates new policies, procedures, and directives.
- Only senior management initiates training and educational development.

- Senior management initiates training programs for staff and doesn't participate themselves.
- A tendency to deny problems or unpleasant situations exists.
- There is an excessive need for controls.
- A tendency exists toward secrecy and mid-level manager controls on information and access to materials necessary for successful development, unless managers are involved.
- Compulsive behavior is rampant.
- Autocratic leadership and thinking dominates.
- Inconsistent moods (mood swings) and emotions are evident.
- An overriding loyalty to the organization leads to maintaining the status quo at all costs.
- Employees exhibit the inability to successfully address critical issues.
- An overriding tendency to involve emotions in issues stalls communication.
- A protective attitude guards against discussing certain topics.
- Strict lines of authority and power abide. Little vertical or horizontal movement occurs.
- Defined lines of bureaucracy and layers of management may outweigh workers on the staff.
- Layers of mid-level managers may equal one manager for as few as 5-to-20 rank-and-file workers.

Did you note several signs present in your environment? Whether your management style resembles anything in the previous chart, alternative managerial leadership styles can be used to instill self-confidence in individuals for performance improvement within your organization.

Reflect upon the changing environment in which you live and work. Consider the chaos the market stimulates, and you in turn have to operate in. With changing markets, increased competition (locally, regionally, nationally, and internationally), and changing needs among the players on your team, your ability to manage with alternative styles and techniques is fundamental to your success and ability to provide world-class products or services to your internal and external customers.

Why This Book, *The Managerial Leadership Bible*? The Answer Is Easy!

Today, literally hundreds of management and leadership books are on the market, yet none of these new gospels arm individuals with the actual strategies, operational direction, or tactical ideas, techniques, formulas, and actual how-to tools necessary to attain and sustain peak performance. Many books by some of today's leading authors don't even offer the educated reader anything more than the current litany of existing leading business names and a profile of what these individuals are either doing or have done. There are no step-by-step tools, maps or chronological strategies, operational systems, or tactical interactions in these books. And yet, it doesn't take a rocket scientist to search for, identify, and profile today's excellent companies!

The Managerial Leadership Bible is your field book, your playbook, and your blueprint for building your success behaviors and those of others. This book looks at organizational dynamics unlike any text before it. First, it focuses on ideas, methodologies, and strategies that impact strategic planning (SP) activities and efforts. Next, the foundations of managerial leadership illustrate the nine immediate application techniques necessary for organizational development (OD) to become your daily success reality. Consider this section your playbook on how to engage and stimulate maximum performance from everyone within your realm or sphere of influence. Then the managerial leader moves beyond the nine commonalities of any and every great leader and what each will continually be absorbed in on a daily basis. Tools for articulating, measuring, and addressing the operational challenges are detailed. Finally, the book details the legacy a managerial leader creates, nurtures, and leaves.

The design of these four parts requires that successful leaders and management personnel incorporate ideas from the first two parts through individual efforts, and then apply them as detailed in the last two parts.

Today's business environment emphasizes both organizational and corporate cultures (what some may call the organization's DNA) and the evolutionary changes companies are experiencing. In an attempt to design environments that foster and promote dynamic interactions and growth, this book explores numerous ways in which success and effective interactions can be attained. *We are no longer in a professional marketplace of "heads" versus "hands" management mentality.*

To be successful, today's management leader must enable people to feel powerful rather than helpless. This book shows how to become a value-added leader with alternative management skills.

As Aristotle said, we are what we repeatedly do. Excellence, then, is not an act, but a habit.

Now, learn how to use alternative styles of management with each interaction to attain maximum results and stimulate maximum performance from each person you come into contact with as a leader. Here is your *Managerial Leadership Bible,* your step-by-step management-to-leadership user's guide to serve as the skill development map for emerging leaders. Become a manager and leader for tomorrow, today!

Dr. Jeffrey L. Magee, PDM, CSP, CMC

What lies in front of you and what lies behind you, pales in significance when compared to that which lies within you.... Unless you try to do something beyond what you have already mastered, you will never grow.

—Ralph Waldo Emerson

1

Ground Zero, All Factors Being Equal

Management today is reactive behavior. You put your hand on a hot stove and yank it off. A cat would know to do as much.

—W. Edwards Deming

The operational mindset of "heads" versus "hands" in an organization can no longer be allowed to exist. Every "hand" within an organization has a "head," and all players have to be cultivated and empowered to take ownership and use their heads while using their hands to make things happen!

—Jeff Magee

Learning Objective

After completing this section of the course, you will be able to discuss changing leadership styles to match contemporary business needs.

Traditional business school doctrine for decades professed lines of authority and responsibility, layers of bureaucracy, and lines of top-down accountability. Upper management layers were reserved for analysis and direction. Lower levels of management needed the hand and guidance of upper management; likewise, rank-and-file workers needed the hand and guidance of middle managers for productivity, implementation, and success.

In today's climate, the managerial leadership style needed to be effective must be fluid, one of strategic collaboration yet decisive execution. This flexibility allows organizations to adapt to changing business cycles; the influx of differing genders, generations, ethnicity, education, and professional backgrounds; variances in individuals' socioeconomic backgrounds, lifestyle, and personal aspirations; and elasticity within ethics, morals, standards-of-excellence, values, vision, and cultures. This flexibility, coupled with the following three forces, can be understood and leveraged for constructive gains, and if misunderstood and ill-utilized will spell organizational chaos:

1. **Strategy**—The where we are going and why factors
2. **Operations**—The who, when, and what factors
3. **Tactics**—The how factors

The style of management that worked or appeared to work for decades across the globe, especially during the post-World War II era that gave rise to the industrial complex and then to the information age, no longer works in today's service and technology world. The old models of management and leadership actually stifle growth and productivity in workers today. Studies of traditional management styles and hierarchies—bureaucratic and autocratic—that are imposed ("heads" versus "hands") show them doing more damage to overall organizational growth in the long term today than alternative styles of managerial leadership.

To illustrate this management trend, consider that the traditional and "old school" management styles resemble a pyramid. Front-line workers and entry-level positions are at the bottom of the pyramid (typically closest to daily realities and customers). Mid-level managers and supervisors are in the middle (typically facing daily operational issues and becoming removed from the daily pulse of reality). Finally, senior-level managerial leaders or executive-level functionaries are at the top (typically concentrating on the future direction of the organization and industry and, unfortunately, extremely removed from the actual daily realities of the front line). At the top of this model place a large letter "M" as your symbol for where "management" is located. Does your organization resemble this model?

The Wharton School of Business studied this traditional format and organizational structure and found a wide range of awareness levels among individuals and their ability to pinpoint the challenges and problems facing an organization.

They found that the rank-and-file workers could identify roughly 44 percent of the challenges and problems facing an organization on a regular daily basis.

Upper layers of management break down dramatically. Middle and upper levels of management could identify roughly 14 percent of the challenges and problems facing an organization. Senior management could identify roughly 4 percent.

Traditional organizational structure breeds contempt, apathy, and lower levels of participation. It also stifles communication of upward ideas and concerns. The lines of authority were/are well defined, and individuals are often in a position of seeking permission to be real implementers of success.

A study by USA Today and Gallup also revealed in the workplace today that the demographic breaks down into three influence groups as well, and any organization can experience this manifestation if it is not consciously engaged 24/7:

- Fifty-six percent of workers indicated that they are "disengaged" today—that is, complacent. Managerial leadership effectiveness can address this.

- Fifteen percent are "actively disengaged" and are so bitter and narcissistic that they poison the efforts of others and can derail an entire organization, further eroding culture and the foundations of survival.

- Twenty-nine percent are "engaged" and serve as the catalyst to daily return on investment (ROI) and actually produce the work that job description and job expectations indicate.

How can a company turn around or redirect this flow of percentages and stimulate inner activity among players for greater success and rewards? Consider the new view of organizational culture and climate, or the DNA of dynamics. Consider the need for each of the previously mentioned layers (senior management, mid-level management, staff) as still relevant to an organization, but imagine four circles on a page, connected with lines indicating their fluid ability to interface with one another, as needed for ultimate organizational effectiveness and success.

What the new view of organizational structure (whether called teams, work groups, self-directed work groups, total quality management, empowerment, strategic business units, and so on) advocates is an image of team and player equality with respect to the need for profitability of the organization. This image sends the visual message of player equality. The traditional diagram of organizational structure holds that an individual is equal only to his colleagues' level and subordinate to those players above him (see previous discussion). Many times this is a challenging situation, due to age, tenure, skill level, and accomplishment differences of individuals, even at a similar function level.

To illustrate this new managerial leadership effectiveness model, consider four simple circles on a sheet of paper (or computer screen) placed in a manner that forms a square, as shown in Figure 1.1. In essence, the new view allows for an equal-sized circle for each player. Notice that the need for management is still present; therefore one of the circles could have a letter "M." Only now you are telling players that "management" has the job of ensuring results and that a manager will assist players in performing their functions. However, management will not be ultimately responsible for a player's position. Old-time traditional management sent that message, which is why many times at the end of the day, workers would be gone and management would still be there—completing others' jobs!

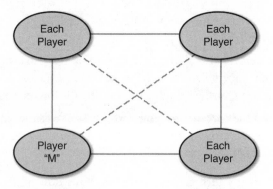

Figure 1.1 New management model

The new view of management sends the signal that all players in a winning and thriving organization are accountable and responsible for both their own actions and the performance of the team overall.

If the team wins, each player wins. If the team loses, ultimately each player loses. Characteristics of the new view of organization imply that some of the following ingredients are present:

- Each player is accountable to one another and to himself or herself, with ultimate authority still going to the one player who is responsible and leads the team in a mutually agreed upon direction. But specific key performance indicators (KPIs) must always be identified and assigned.

- Cross-training and functional awareness are both initiated at all levels and fostered among all players and the now-flattened hierarchical layers.

- Interactive and nonconfrontational communication occurs among players and teams (of departments, units, layers, regions and geographies, vendors, customers, and players), both internally and externally in an organization, in a fluid manner.

- Interdependence develops among players so they become proactive and not reactive.

- Vertical and horizontal movement and advancement occur within the organization between the players and the management team.

- Lateral, vertical, and horizontal synergy and development occur on a regular basis.

- Teams (departments, lines, and so on) are lean, yet they generate a high yield factor.

- Everyone understands that his or her operational center must be highly effective and efficient, and thus must be a stand-alone profit center for the organization as well (whether a not-for-profit business or a commercial enterprise).

- Management and labor are blended, and no one is allowed to excuse away low or poor performance.

- The rule book is constantly being written and revised for success. No one is allowed to justify slow performance or apply excessive man-hours (personnel) to any one task simply because the book says they must do so.

Ultimate advancement of an organization focuses on management ground zeros. An organization today cannot afford to have its marketable advantages rest on traditional business-school organizational resources: structure, financial budgets, and products/resources. Management by these three factors alone will lead to "dead zones" far more often than any other single factor.

Let's back up and look at some historical facts with present-day implications. As Peter Drucker warned in his 1973 classic *Management: Tasks, Responsibilities, Practices,* in a ground zero market, any of these three major resources can be attained, refined, and even expanded upon by your organization. Yet a competitor can—and many times will—attain and deliver better on these three than you. Many times a traditional management structure works to protect these three factors at the expense of the customers—the people on the team on the inside and those on the outside who make your existence possible.

Therefore, the only truly marketable and lasting advantage point is not just how you enter a marketplace with your "deliverables" or what "distribution channels" you deploy to reach and own a market, it is the unique leveraging and unleashing of your "people factor" today.

As some entrepreneurs and business leaders evaluate other market entrants or leaders to discover what their secret sauce to success is, the reality is that it is always based within the following:

- **Strategy**—Driven by core stakeholders' values and vision to set the direction of opportunities

- **Operations**—The systems for advancing that strategy and the interlinked KPIs and more importantly accountability mechanisms to attain and measure success

- **Tactics**—The actual behaviors and actions in motion to make your market actualize

The basic theme of Jim Collins's popular book *Good to Great* is "Get the right people on your bus, the wrong ones off, and then put people in the right place," regardless of other temptations to place people into positions of incompetency. This is known as the Peter Principle, whereby some individuals rise to a level and position beyond their skill set and beyond their will to perform, thereby becoming a derailment to others' effectiveness and organizational success. This book focuses on developing and maximizing that resource—the "people" factor.

Given the need for flexibility in the midst of the chaos and professional challenges facing you daily, you must have immediate alternatives for improving employee interactions and for leading the company to greater efficiency and profitability. Cutting staff and making only gradual quality improvements as a business map to greater profitability and growth is a dangerous road to travel.

Let's look at what happened during the late 1990s and first quarter of the new century on the American and the global marketplace. In 2000, the dot-com "phantom" industry arrived, only to implode as fast as it came.

We could study business phenomena such as KODAK, Krispy Kreme Donuts, Starbucks, Southwest Airlines, Google, Facebook, Amazon.com, Howard Johnson's, Alibaba, Tesla Motors, Holiday Inn, and a host of others. The historical trends of these brands—some alive and thriving and others dead and gone—all provide the managerial leader of today with powerful clues from yesterday to set a trajectory for tomorrow.

The examples of global businesses, national businesses, regional businesses, and even your own business can be seen within the pages of this text; my examples don't matter. Success leaves clues and so too does failure. Recognize, analyze, learn, and chart your course for sustained success.

In almost every business failure, the key factor management fails to pay attention to is the people factor.

Jack Welch at GE taught the world in the last century the science of and necessity for leadership development as well. By designing the on-boarding process, career pathway development track, and talent management environment, Jack Welch build a leadership development system and machine.

The ability to strike when opportunity knocks is critical to management and organizational success. To empower themselves and those within their organizations to take calculated initiatives and to advance causes, the front-line leaders within an organization (managers, supervisors, team leaders, work group facilitators, executive staffers, owners, and so on) have to understand what the organization is about and how the players fit into that picture. Individuals placed in leadership and management positions need to realize there are a lot of techniques and strategies to be incorporated in people management.

Traditional management focused upon the effective use of resources in its environment to accomplish desired results. For management to do this, there has to be new vitality within the leadership of an organization. Traditional management and traditional management-school ideology taught that management's function in an organization is to maintain primary participation in *five key areas:*

- Controlling
- Coordinating
- Directing
- Organizing
- Planning

From the traditional, five-key management responsibilities, management today must focus on additional factors and empower those around it to assume both responsibility and accountability for the preceding five areas, as well as other directional maps. Among these interaction maps (habits, styles, techniques, strategies, purpose, values, mission, culture, generationally influenced approaches to work, and so on) is the need for developed and understood mission statements. The fastest way to growth and productivity is a well-defined mission statement. Within organizations today, there must be several different yet interlinked mission statements (see Chapter 2, "Five Mission Statements for Ultimate 'New View' Success"). The new view of management incorporates flexibility and a willingness and ability to make adjustments in how one interacts, motivates, and thus manages the only true management advantage—the people.

The starting point for managing winning teams is to gain a better understanding of how people interact with one another and how mission statements impact their interaction.

Sidney Yoshida, a guidance quality expert in Japan, invested a significant amount of his life studying the structure of business organizations and the interaction abilities of players within the group. Yoshida's studies also include the awareness of players—at all levels in an organization—regarding problems, customer concerns, growth concerns, and overall challenges.

Startling statistics have been garnered from focus groups regarding the level of awareness of players within these organizations and at differing levels (from rank-and-file through senior management). In many cases a culture has been created whereby many players hide from senior management the problems they experience. Yoshida found that:

- Senior management was aware of roughly **4** percent of problems.
- Upper middle management was aware of roughly **9** percent of problems.
- Middle management was aware of roughly **74** percent of daily problems.
- Rank-and-file workers could identify and were aware of roughly **100** percent of the daily problems facing an organization and its related customers.

I have found this to be true in my decades of personal work with the United States Cabinet-level departments, governors, military command structure, Fortune 100 firms, major entrepreneurial organizations and leaders, and business across the global marketplace.

All factors being equal in the global marketplace today, business leaders, managers, and individuals operating within business markets have to empower themselves and others to obtain maximum results and peak operational performance on a daily basis.

The traditional hierarchy and organizational charts of the first part of the last century must evolve into a more team-focused environment for this new century. Organizations are facing a new pattern of change from internal constituents and external constituents, traditional operating factors, and now virtual realities. And add to this the reality that every year organizations face tighter budgets and leaner staffs, while at the same time workloads increase.

The human machine is dynamic and fascinating. Given these factors of change and human capital evolution, almost every department and organization must meet these new demands for performance, but in many cases set new performance records. How do groups of people facing these factors make this happen in a sustained fashion? Teaming!

Whether you call your group of people a department, work group, quality focus group, independent work team, self-directed work group, or self-directed team, they all exhibit various dynamics of being part of a team.

The performance of people in a peak relationship is dependent upon players being able to interact and share successfully with one another without apprehension. When a player fears the outcome of interacting with another player (whether laterally or vertically), the dynamics of a team will break down, as Yoshida found in his studies.

Focusing the efforts and energies of all players, while reducing the actual interaction and hand-holding time by management, is the thrust of Chapter 2. Whether it is achieved independently of others or with others, success comes from leadership and clear vision of what each step in the business operation is, does, and should be.

Explore alternative ways for managing the resources around you, and leading the people who will be part of these interactions and successes in both your professional and personal life!

The postwar business philosophy of the 1950s and 1960s, "make it and they will buy it," doesn't apply today; it did for 50 years. Organizations today need to take into account the people factor (and generational diversity as a strategic asset has changed the landscape) as the marketable growth and success factor. People may very well be the single greatest strategic asset in the new ground zero, managerial leadership environment of the business place. For this reason management and leadership must look for and apply alternative management and leadership techniques and methodologies to survive.

The shift from product to people is illustrated throughout this book. I offer a multitude of techniques and ideas from today's most successful teams and organizations. This book serves as both your strategic and tactical playbook for essential managerial leadership effectiveness. Witness the new approaches to management and leadership across America today!

This information, field tested in the form of customized skill development training courses, is now captured in book form. Here are just some of the teams across America that are successfully incorporating these managerial leadership points:

- **Government—The United States Army National Guard** implemented a major thrust in training the senior officer corps at its national Professional Educational Center's Strength Maintenance Training Center (PEC SMTC), resulting in multiple Commander's Coin for Excellence awards for the managerial leadership lifestyle changes and positive results yielded, and within individual states on many command levels.

- **Industry—Pharmaceutical, banking, B2B, B2C, manufacturing, and associations** have recognized, adopted, and implemented this intellectual property into their respective courseware training approach for their people assets.

- **Professional certification—CPE, CLE, CUE, and others**—Hundreds of accredited hours of self-study have been drawn out from this text alone and parallel content.

As you explore each page and each idea, and the applicability to you and those you influence, consider this your *Managerial Leadership Bible*. It is continually being field tested and continually yielding significant success as a blueprint for how to manage and lead individuals and groups to greater levels of excellence.

Managerial Leadership Bible Lesson One

Successful managerial leaders realize that organizational success starts daily, by asking themselves this question: What can be done to create a lean operational structure conducive to positive attitudes, excellence in aptitude, and fluid interpersonal lines of communication and interaction among players?

Review Questions

The review questions accompanying each chapter or section are designed to assist you in achieving the learning objective stated at the beginning of each chapter. The review section is not graded; do not submit it in place of your final exam. While completing the review questions, it may be helpful to study any unfamiliar terms in the glossary in addition to course content. After completing the review questions for each chapter, proceed to the review question answers and rationales.

1. In today's climate, the managerial leadership style needed to be effective must be _____.

    A. Aggressive

    B. Flexible

    C. Rigid

    D. Simple

2. Sidney Yoshida's study of the structure of business organizations found that only _____ could identify and were aware of roughly 100 percent of the daily problems facing an organization and its related customers.

    A. Senior management

    B. Upper middle management

    C. Middle management

    D. Rank-and-file workers

3. What may very well be the single greatest strategic asset in the new ground zero?

    A. Capital

    B. People

    C. Product

    D. Marketing

4. How do groups of people facing tighter budgets, leaner staffs, and greater workloads maintain productivity in a sustained fashion?

    A. Higher wages

    B. Better computers

    C. Teamwork

    D. Temporary employees

Review Question Answers and Rationales

Review question answer choices are accompanied by unique, logical reasoning (rationales) as to why an answer is correct or incorrect. Evaluative feedback to incorrect responses and reinforcement feedback to correct responses are both provided.

1. In today's climate, the managerial leadership style needed to be effective must be _____.

   A. Incorrect. Aggressive manager-leaders can only get so far without stepping on people's toes.

   B. Correct. Flexibility allows a leader to take into account a variety of employees' needs based on gender, religion, and so on.

   C. Incorrect. This is the opposite of what a leader should be.

   D. Incorrect. If it were simple, there would be no need for books on the subject.

2. Sidney Yoshida's study of the structure of business organizations found that only _____ could identify and were aware of roughly 100 percent of the daily problems facing an organization and its related customers.

   A. Incorrect. Senior management was only aware of roughly 4 percent.

   B. Incorrect. Upper middle management was only aware of roughly 9 percent.

   C. Incorrect. Middle management was only aware of roughly 74 percent.

   D. Correct. Due to management's separation from "reality" the everyday workers were more aware of problems.

3. What may very well be the single greatest strategic asset in the new ground zero?

    A. Incorrect. While important, capital means nothing without people.

    B. Correct. In the new business world, managers cannot underestimate the power of accountable employees in all levels of employment.

    C. Incorrect. A great product cannot sell itself.

    D. Incorrect. According to the author, "organizations today need to take into account the people factor as the marketable growth and success factor."

4. How do groups of people facing tighter budgets, leaner staffs, and greater workloads maintain productivity in a sustained fashion?

    A. Incorrect. Higher wages were reserved for the top of "old school" management styles and cannot be sustained with lower budgets.

    B. Incorrect. Computers are only a tool that employees use. Thus, computers can only improve an excellent team.

    C. Correct. In the past, a top-down hierarchy required little accountability across employee levels and productivity suffered, while today, teamwork is an increasingly valuable organizational tool.

    D. Incorrect. Temporary employees cannot provide a sustained increase in productivity due to the time necessary for training and a high rate of turnover.

2

Five Mission Statements for Ultimate "New View" Success

Mission statements are like maps. With a map you can navigate every action toward a desired incremental or ultimate goal and thus: sustainable success. Without a map, you are often guessing and taking short cuts, which usually become long cuts that lead to confusion, stagnation, and ultimately failure. Your mission statement serves as the GPS to where you are and where you need to be!

—**Jeff Magee**

Learning Objective

After completing this section of the course, you will be able to explain the different types of mission statements and help the reader create them.

Great individuals can be spotted as managers and leaders in many organizations and geographical areas today. And yet, far too often, the normal path of promotion rewards individuals who have been immersed (tenured) in the institutional and technical aspects of their jobs, but who are inadequately prepared with an equal set of skills in the professional managerial leadership strategies, skills, and performance.

Becoming more efficient at what you do and understanding how to cultivate efficiency in others starts with a road map that constantly tracks what you should be doing and where everyone overall is supposed to be going. This is where most organizations and their leaders get off track in the beginning—and many times don't even realize it.

Assurance that any individual (personal, departmental, team, unit, and so on) endeavor or the overall purpose of the organization is always being addressed, and that everyone is always moving forward, is dependent upon everyone having the same road map. In business-speak, this road map would be called the company's "mission statement."

Values = Vision = Mission Statement = Return on Investment (ROI)

Your values drive the design of and/or acceptance of your professional purpose or some would call your vision. That purpose influences the makeup of the myriad of mission statements you may encounter or construct. These mission statements further enhance your belief system, commitment, and authenticity as a managerial leader. Identifying all the objectives and goals of the people involved in every organization is not easy—yet it is not impossible! Understanding these varying objectives, or missions, and how each ties into one another is critical for management success and for understanding how the differing alternative styles of managerial leadership come together. While many consultants speak of mission statements and assist in their strategic development, a shocking number of failures and bankruptcies still occur in the business world today within organizations that had "phantom" mission statements.

A phantom mission statement, while posted for all to gauge their actions by, merely serves to fill space on a wall. Members of an organization quickly learn there is no senior leadership mettle behind it.

Management icon Tom Peters widely quoted a statistic that "Only one in every ten organizations that undergoes management changes of total quality, total quality management, continuous quality improvement, etc. will survive!"

How can this be? The answer is easy to recognize. Start by evaluating the "Warning Signs of Decaying Managerial Leadership Effectiveness" inventory in the preface. Then recognize that for people to interact and integrate for success, each level of an organization must understand the others, and must know how each player, department, team, or committee impacts the big picture of success, quality, and profitable results.

In working with some of the most efficient and profitable businesses on the planet in the past two decades, it has become apparent to me that whether these organizations were trained to recognize this, were mentored to do this, or it merely became an innate operational mantra, each has had five clearly defined, understood, and adhered-to road maps (mission statements) for continued success.

Individuals' beliefs, values, vision, and cultures must be in concert with these mission statements if peak performance and interpersonal harmony are to be achieved. If individuals are not in sync with these, or if these are not in harmony with the organizational stakeholders, implosions will surely develop in the future. To maximize your position as the managerial leader and to maximize the position of each player's abilities within an organization, consider these five mission statements in the following order. Which do you have in place, and which still need to be completed for your future success?

Understand that these five mission statements need to be developed in this order for maximum success and to avoid confusion and chaos. Consider the statements and decide how many you already have identified and which ones need to be developed. Also, decide how many are not addressed by some of today's more popular consultants. Then you'll understand why many followers of these doctrine-espousing gurus are out of business today! You understand the nuances of your industry and your people better than any consultant. Therefore, prior to initiating any action, you must take the ideas presented and merge them with your common sense.

The five mission statements necessary for ultimate organizational development, productivity, and success are as follow.

The Organizational Mission Statement

The organizational mission statement is the first map to be developed. This overall road map sets the tone for where the organization is going and what needs to be achieved. This is the map by which all subsequent mission statements are gauged and measured in respect to how they either complement or detract from what the organization is supposed to be all about. This originating, first-level statement is designed only by the organization's key stakeholders and not by the team at large.

Here are some leading industry giants of the last decade and what their organizational mission statements included as they entered the new decade:

- General Electric, the only organization that could be considered a Fortune 500 firm in 1901 and is still listed on that index today, is "Boundary-less...Speed...Stretch."

- Johnson & Johnson, the healthcare leader and home care partner to families for decades, marches on with "We believe our first responsibility is to the doctors, nurses, and patients, to mothers and fathers, and all others who use our products and services."

- The explosive success and growth of Carl Sewell and his automotive dealerships across America support the power behind these mission statements as maps. Sewell has grown a small automobile dealership founded in 1968 from $10 million in business to a chain of dealerships today doing more than $250 million in annual sales, making Sewell the single largest General Motors dealer in America. Sewell's take: "There are only three reasons for having a sign: to name your business, to describe your product, or to give directions.... Signs, in a subtle way, tell the world what your values are and what kind of business you are running. Since that's true, do them right."

The Departmental Mission Statement

The departmental mission statement is the second map to be developed. Once the overall organization has developed its map—the organizational mission statement—each department, work unit, and team needs to set aside time to review this foundational statement and design its own independent statement. Each department, for example, cannot and will not be able to make the overall organizational mission statement happen. Each department only contributes a piece toward that big picture.

The departmental mission statement should be designed by all members of a specific department, team, or strategic business unit (SBU). When the members participate in it, ownership and synergy will occur. Have players assist in establishing the "how" in the plan of how their department will contribute to the organization's ultimate mission statement, and how that will be accomplished. To increase the impact of the departmental mission statement, have each player sign it and post it proudly within the department for all players and visitors to see. This regular reminder of the department's map will further foster energy and team interaction.

Another powerful by-product of having this second mission statement posted is that it will guide every individual member to recognize that his or her every decision contributes toward the overall ultimate organizational mission statement. Everyone will then understand how individuals approach their work responsibilities and how all must work in the same direction.

The Player's Mission Statement

Understanding a player's mission statement is the third step. Every person has (to some degree) a professional intention or map pointing out where he or she is aiming in life. Once you have a glimpse into what other people's personal mission statements are (especially as a manager on a team), you will better understand what is important to them. You will develop a better knowledge of how to best interact, motivate, communicate, delegate, and develop players for the overall team to be successful.

Remember in reverse, a person's mission statement is driven by the vision she has of herself, and that is driven by the values she holds. If these values are in some degree in alignment with you and your organization, you significantly increase the ability for an individual to be integrated into a team and become a peak performing contributor quickly.

Players' mission statements are derived from their values, principles, goals, and desires in life. Each person on your team has different needs in life and seeks different goals; therefore, a better understanding of the people within your department is necessary for your management success.

The Customer Mission Statement

The fourth mission statement to be developed or understood for management and organizational success is the customer mission statement. This is the map customers follow in making business decisions. Always remember that a basic psychological point of reference for people is "What's in it for me?"

By understanding what your customers' needs are and what they are striving for, you can then gauge your decisions to consider these points. Once you know what your core customers' base needs are, you will recognize multiple ways to assist customers in obtaining greater levels of success and growth through your position. Another reason for gaining some perspective on your customers' mission statements is that this insight will impact your decisions and increase your growth toward future organizational, departmental, and player mission statements.

As Stephen Covey reflects in *Seven Habits of Highly Effective People* and *Principle Centered Leadership*, "Seek first to understand, then to be understood." In detailing wildly successful organizations, I have recognized that each has written or conveyed intrinsically among all members five interconnected and interdependent mission statements that can drive every conversation, commitment, decision, action, human capital deployment, organizational deliverable, and so on. The purpose of the five core mission statements is to guide you toward understanding the forces around you that you must draw upon for ultimate success within an organization and within the competitive marketplace today.

The Self/Professional Mission Statement

The final mission statement to be designed is your self/professional mission statement (as a manager, supervisor, leader, or business owner). Until you gain some degree of understanding of the initial four mission statements, it is difficult to effectively develop your self/professional mission statement and integrate it with the other four.

By understanding the first four, you can ensure maximum integration. You then will be spending energy toward both your self/professional mission statement and the other objectives/statements. If you were to establish your mission statement prior to giving consideration to the other four, your self/professional mission statement (also known as your agenda) more than likely would not parallel the other four agendas. When you have insight to other mission statements, all five come together, and team synergy takes over.

Designing the organizational and departmental (team, business unit, line) mission statements (or purpose statements) is an involved process. Each statement should be able to address and/or identify several key issues. When designing your statements, consider how each answers or incorporates the following guideposts:

- **Six key letters: W, W, W, W, W, H**—Every mission statement should identify Who, What, When, Where, Why, and How. In school this was called the 5-W and 1-H formula.

- **Thirty words or less**—Every statement should be condensed to a few lines or a short paragraph. The longer and more involved your statements become, the more you increase the likelihood that you and others won't be able to remember them. That means your map becomes confusing.

- **Design time**—The appropriate players should come together for this strategy and brainstorming session, either offsite or in an area with limited or no distractions that could cause participants to lose focus on the purpose of the development session.

- **Involvement**—All players critical to the design and implementation of a statement must participate in the creation of its core elements. The more active participation by appropriate players at each development level, the greater the ownership level becomes; thus, increased participation, productivity, and success will take place.

- **Signatures**—Once a statement is developed, it needs to be signed by all participating players and posted as a sign of will.

- **Ultimate objective**—The final analysis of a statement is that it should serve as a clear, nondebatable map of an organization's aim. It should help players focus their efforts, provide a measurement system, and allow for celebrations of success.

You can obtain additional information for use in designing mission statements or in determining others' statements (player and customer mission statements) via these same steps and through profiling the appropriate parties. Provide information to those with vested interests, design a questionnaire, and gather these questionnaires to attain the desired information and their respective insights.

Finally, the ultimate reason for designing and implementing these sequential mission statements (as minimums within an organization today) is to empower members to focus their energies upon the same points of reference and the same goals. These statements serve as mental action plans (MAPs©), or models for individual and team effort. They serve as guideposts for individual actions, collaborative activities, and commitment toward where resources are to be applied and in what order.

Individual hesitation to commit energy in many cases is due to unclear direction and uneasiness about whether senior management (leadership) is really committed or merely paying lip service to a cause.

These factors can threaten any well-managed and well-intentioned organization and company.

Another major factor in designing these statements, both individually and as a team, is to pull together those empowered players. To empower unaligned individuals within an organization, one without these statements developed and in place, can be counterproductive.

People must share a common vision (mission) for success. Otherwise, an organization will experience increased stress, anxiety, and tension among its players. Management will carry an increased burden to maintain controls and productivity, and a slow (in some cases, quick) demise will fall upon the organization.

To facilitate a personal, departmental, or organizational statement and to aid in vision making among players and leaders, consider the following chart as a planning tool. This chart can be used as a planning worksheet for individual or group interaction.

You may want to weigh this planning chart against any existing mission statement, to determine whether the critical elements are addressed, accountability is assigned, or a present mission statement is so esoteric that it actually threatens long-term survivability and success.

If any one of the following descriptors is absent, opportunity is present for complacency, or for an individual to undermine the best intentions of a managerial leader or committed member of the team.

In using this template to design any of the previously discussed five mission statements, reflect on the 5-W and 1-H formula (Guidepost 1) as the template. This model, while simple, is powerful for designing your mission statements, whether individually or with others. As you draft your mission statement text, you are looking to clearly identify, both in your mind and on paper, the following:

- **Who**—The person who owns the category
- **What**—The tangible offering or expectation
- **When**—Immediate, intermediate, and long-term timeframes
- **Where**—The geography of design and implementation
- **Why**—The motivation, rationalization, and reasoning toward the other 4-W and 1-H objectives
- **How**—Action plans, actions, implementations

Each of these words as represented by its first letter serves to guide you and others toward a complete understanding of how you will deliver to each area. Consider as a mission statement building template, the following:

Mission Statement Planning Sheet

Editorial Explanation of Purpose or Intent:

W _____

W _____

W _____

W _____

W _____

H _____

Reminder: Now transfer the preceding information into a single coherent statement that can be seen and signed by applicable participants.

Remember, a mission statement serves as a GPS to behaviors, actions, commitments, and decisions. Here are some examples of the best in industry and their mission statements:

- **SW Airlines**—The mission of Southwest Airlines is dedication to the highest quality Customer Service delivered with a sense of warmth, friendliness, individual pride, and Company Spirit.

    —Gary Kelly, (former) CEO, SW Airlines

- **Microsoft**—At Microsoft, our Mission and Values are to help people and businesses throughout the world realize their full potential.

    —Bill Gates, (former) Chairman-of-the-Board, Microsoft

- **Zappos**—We've been asked by a lot of people how we've grown so quickly, and the answer is actually really simple.... We've aligned the entire organization around one mission: to provide the best customer service possible. Internally, we call this our WOW philosophy.

    Zappos.com was founded in 1999 with the goal of becoming the premiere destination for online shoes. Since then, we've become much more than just an online shoe store. Our unwavering focus on superior customer service has allowed us to expand our online offerings to include handbags, clothing, and so much more! If you're looking for shoes, clothing, and handbags online, compare us to other online shoe and online clothing stores, as well as online handbag stores. You'll find the absolute best service and the best selection in online shopping here at Zappos.com.

    —Tony Hsieh, CEO, Zappos

- **Harley-Davidson**—Customers for life...Harley-Davidson values the emotional connection that is created with our customers through our products, services, and experiences. We are fueled by our brand loyalty and trust that our customers place in us to deliver premium quality and the promise of fulfilling lifetime ownership experience. We exemplify the commitment by embracing a culture of personal responsibility and stewardship for quality in everything we do.

    —Keith Wandell, CEO, Harley-Davidson

- **Amazon**—At Amazon, we strive to be Earth's most customer-centric company where people can find and discover anything they want to buy online. Amazon's evolution from Web site to e-commerce partner to development platform is driven by the spirit of innovation that is part of our DNA. We hire the world's brightest minds, offering them an environment in which they can relentlessly improve the experience for customers. We do this every day by solving complex technical and business problems with ingenuity and simplicity. We're making history and the good news is that we've only just begun.

—Jeff Bezos, CEO, Amazon

Your mission statement can have as many or as few words as it takes to articulate your purpose and serve to give people a directional GPS to decisions, actions, deliverables, and future. Even if everyone can't remember word-for-word your mission statement, it is critical that everyone have the same central theme as a guiding beacon from your mission statement. Following are examples of simple and profound mission statement essence; imagine the magnitude of what these statements drive within an individual, whether a staff level member to your organization or the C-suite:

- **Ritz Carlton Hotel**—Ladies and Gentlemen serving Ladies and Gentlemen
- **Southwest Airlines**—When a plane is on the ground we are losing money.

To execute a mission statement, it takes people. You and your people. And sometimes it takes the alignment of outside vendors/partners/collaborations to actualize your mission statement. With all the people factors in play, you must understand how to read them, rally them, and ensure that they do not undermine your mission statement.

Three Subgroups in Life—Rule 80/10/10©

Because one person does not make for an entire organization and you as the managerial leader cannot be everything to all people and be in all places at all times, you need a support network to achieve greatness. In working with groups across the globe, I have recognized that any group is typically amassed from three subgroups, and understanding the demographics empowers you to know where and when an alliance and need for stakeholder buy-in is essential.

Three subgroups in life impact your mission statement development and implementation. The three also impact your people-influencing ability on a daily basis.

To design effective and applicable mission statements and thus gain a better working perspective of how an organization will develop, foster, and ultimately avoid the traps of stagnation, procrastination, apathy, and bankruptcy, consider how people come together (migration patterns) and interact (bonding patterns) with one another.

Sociology looks at groups of people, such as your organization, your department, other departments, clients, vendors, your family, social gatherings, and civic organizations you participate in. *The Managerial Leadership Bible* breaks down a group into three manageable subgroups for ultimate managerial leadership influence effectiveness. In any group dynamic, the individuals within that group have specific migration patterns and assume expected roles. Any grouping of people you come into contact with is actually comprised of three distinct subgroups. They are called the 80/10/10.

80 percent = transmitters of the norms and status quo. Eighty percent of any group tends to perpetuate the status quo it is directed to accept and support. They work and perform based upon what the influencers have conditioned them to do. These people are also known as followers. There are four types of transmitters or followers, and management's ability to recognize the subgroup a person occupies greatly directs interaction ability and reduces micromanagement likelihood. These four types are (1) *legitimate* followers are seemingly clueless, but their level of cluelessness is not implied as disrespect; they are clueless because they have never done or studied what is needed. As a managerial leader your ability to quickly assess a person also allows you to deliver the antidotes like training, educating, mentoring, showing, leading, and so on; (2) *forced* followers or clueless individuals may be due to inadvertent management pressures or feedback that may have been internalized as putdowns, which can be turned around with antidotes such as praise, self-esteem rebuilding, or delegating a task that the individual is good at doing; (3) *learned* followers or clueless people have simply learned how to play the game and systems; the antidote here is simple: Hold them accountable; (4) *traditional* followers are individuals who simply do not care either way on an issue, and they apply their energies in the direction of the most influence. Influencers are the members of the next two subgroups, who tend to dictate how the 80 percent operate.

10 percent = transformers of change and action, change agents, advocates, and allies. These are often seen as the proactive and positive members of a group, and who have strong convictions and have high levels of self-esteem. These personnel can be cultivated as strong allies and advocates for you. With them on your side, they bring the transmitter/follower subgroup into your corner.

You can recruit a transformer in one of two easy ways: First, through "people" connections that you have (these could be people you like, people who get along with you, people who like you, or maybe people who owe you a favor!); second, barring your inability to recruit a transformer in those ways, you may be able to recruit him or her through the "issue" connections you have. Evaluate your offer and ask yourself: "From the people involved in this issue whom I can engage, who has the most to gain from it because of age, gender, race, position, tenure, stature, lifestyle position, vocation, following, and so on?

10 percent = terrorists of change and positive energies. These people are often seen as the negativists, whiners, detractors, deflectors, or complainers. They are not to be confused with someone who is playing the devil's advocate, as that is someone who may oppose your position or idea, yet does have a viable an alternative solution. These people fight change for no real reason. They just don't like the idea because the idea wasn't theirs. These individuals are sometimes corrosive to your team; they are your pessimists, naysayers, criticizers, and condemners, and they live to torment and terrorize forward-moving contributors to the world. They can find fault with anyone and anything.

Your final text for each mission statement reflects your influence and how you have been conditioned by these subgroups. You can also increase your ability to persuade and influence others by expanding Rule 80/10/10 further into your own management realm. Determine whether your team is reflective as a group of all three subgroups, or if it resembles only one or two. If the latter, think about how many times you feel as though you're interacting with (and trying to motivate) a team of terrorists.

Management techniques for dealing with the three subgroups are presented later in the book, along with multiple techniques for turning your terrorists into transformers, or for converting your transmitters into proactive transformers.

An immediate way of stimulating significant organizational growth and dealing with the three subgroups comes from making a major personal management paradigm shift. Consider your normal daily office procedures. For many, they resemble the following:

- **First**—Enter office with mental plan of action established (nothing in writing) and get caught off guard by multiple urgencies, emergencies, and problem player situations (terrorists).

- **Second**—Immediately get caught up in dealing with a problem player situation (terrorist) that occupies a major portion of time: crisis management. Attitude becomes negative and stressed from this person and interaction.

- **Third**—When you finish this encounter and leave to interact with others, you notice they are not being productive. Several individuals who were put off ("Just one minute," or "Wait a second") when they tried to see you have been converted from transformers into transmitters.

Increase your organization's productivity and overall attitude by as much as 25 percent by changing your morning routine from the preceding nightmare to something new.

Whether it is for ten minutes, one hour, or is even more time-intensive, the first group of people that you interact with every morning should be your transformers. Then interact with your transmitters en route to dealing with your problems and terrorists.

Think about how this paradigm shift will impact management's attitude and productivity, as well as those of the players on the team. There are many reasons for making this conscious change in daily activity. Consider the following:

- By making your first interaction at the beginning of a working shift/day with a proactive, positive transformer, you ensure and reinforce your positive attitude and energies. You can empower these individuals to carry your message through the day to fellow transformers and, more importantly, they can assist management in motivating the transmitters with positive energies.

- Your second interaction should always be with a transmitter. There are three types: If one does not know what to do or how to do something, then he is a legitimate transmitter. If a person has been given feedback in a nonproductive manner, he will be less proactive than expected, therefore becoming a forced transmitter. Those who have learned how to play clueless or otherwise are learned transmitters. Note why a person may become a transmitter. Each of these three requires a different management interaction approach.

- Your third daily interaction should be with the terrorists unless a life is at stake. By making this your last interaction, you will find that you have more energy, a better perspective, more control, and that others on the team are working to move it forward while you are dealing with these terrorists.

Otherwise, if management interacts with terrorists at the beginning of the shift/day, management attitude is immediately zapped. Meanwhile, others on the team who need to interact with management are delayed due to the interactions with terrorists. This, in effect, neutralizes the transformers. Management is then responsible for converting transformers into transmitters. Nothing gets accomplished and tension increases. Change management habits and change organizational effectiveness.

Understanding which subgroup an individual is in at any given time or recognizing what situations or people may influence what subgroup someone may divert into is critical in determining which of the six managerial leadership engagement styles you need to administrate.

Managerial Leadership Bible Lesson Two

Successful leaders and organizations have clearly defined road maps called *mission statements* that serve to indicate where they are going. They gauge all decisions from the mission statements to know when the company is on track or off track, and when to say no to remain on course.

Your mission statement(s) serves as a road map or GPS from which you can continuously gauge where you are and maintain efficient managerial leadership stewardship for success.

With these clearly defined mission statements, leaders ensure that there is always a support network of transformers championing implementation of and adherence to the five other structured mission statements.

Review Questions

The review questions accompanying each chapter or section are designed to assist you in achieving the learning objective stated at the beginning of each chapter. The review section is not graded; do not submit it in place of your final exam. While completing the review questions, it may be helpful to study any unfamiliar terms in the glossary in addition to course content. After completing the review questions for each chapter, proceed to the review question answers and rationales.

1. The organizational mission statement is designed only by the organization's _____ and not by the team at large.

    A. Senior management

    B. Business consultant

    C. Chief executive officer

    D. Key stakeholders

2. Each department cannot and will not be able to make the overall organizational mission statement happen.

    A. True

    B. False

3. Players' mission statements are derived from their _____, principles, goals, and desires in life.

    A. Values

    B. Hobbies

    C. Education

    D. Gender

4. A basic psychological point of reference identified by the author with regard to the customer mission statement is _____.

    A. "What would the neighbors say?"

    B. "What's in it for me?"

    C. "What is everyone else doing?"

    D. "Why are we here?"

5. Every statement should be condensed to ____ words or less.

    A. 7

    B. 100

    C. 30

    D. 5

6. Individual hesitation to commit energy in many cases is due to unclear direction and uneasiness about whether leadership is really committed.

    A. True

    B. False

Review Question Answers and Rationales

Review question answer choices are accompanied by unique, logical reasoning (rationales) as to why an answer is correct or incorrect. Evaluative feedback to incorrect responses and reinforcement feedback to correct responses are both provided.

1. The organizational mission statement is designed only by the organization's _____ and not by the team at large.

   A. Incorrect. The key stakeholders can come from a variety of sources, not just management, and should design the mission statement.

   B. Incorrect. Your stakeholders understand the nuances of your industry and your people better than any consultant.

   C. Incorrect. A mission statement should not be made by an individual.

   D. Correct. This mission statement defines the rest of the mission statements, and therefore the foundational members of the organization must design it.

2. Each department cannot and will not be able to make the overall organizational mission statement happen.

   A. Correct. If this were possible, each company would only need one department.

   B. Incorrect. This is why a departmental mission statement is needed.

3. Players' mission statements are derived from their _____, principles, goals, and desires in life.

   A. Correct. Values are established early on in life and contribute to an individual's sense of direction.

   B. Incorrect. These are not a major contributing factor in a player's mission statement.

   C. Incorrect. Education does not always reflect a person's mission, as illustrated by those who choose a career unrelated to the subject of their college major.

   D. Incorrect. Gender is not a major factor in an individual's mission statement.

4. A basic psychological point of reference identified by the author with regard to the customer mission statement is _____.

  A. Incorrect. This cannot be basic because many people do not think of community first.

  B. Correct. Due to our individualistic nature, this is a person's first choice in making decisions.

  C. Incorrect. While many people are driven by trends, others are turned off by something "everybody's doing."

  D. Incorrect. While this is a common question, it has little to do with making decisions.

5. Every statement should be condensed to ____ words or less.

  A. Incorrect. Seven words would be inadequate for establishing a mission.

  B. Incorrect. One-hundred words is too long to be memorable.

  C. Correct. Thirty words equals a few sentences or a short paragraph but is not too long for people to remember.

  D. Incorrect. Five words would be inadequate for establishing a mission.

6. Individual hesitation to commit energy in many cases is due to unclear direction and uneasiness about whether leadership is really committed.

  A. Correct. If an employee thinks management is "merely paying lip service to a cause" he will not feel involved.

  B. Incorrect. Leadership is best practiced by example, thus a statement with no employee participation lets employees know that they don't have to participate in accomplishing business goals.

3

The FIST FACTOR®, Your Mental Board of Directors

Birds of a feather flock together!
—**Mrs. Murphy's Law**

Your Law of Attraction impacts your circle of influence and your capacity to lead from within your outward action.
—**Jeff Magee**

Learning Objective

After completing this section of the course, you will be able to create a mental list of those people most important in creating your attitude.

N ow you understand that the managerial leadership skills needed to be successful today include a fluid approach, as well as many skills in your mental tool belt. You also recognize that a managerial leader needs a clearly defined organizational operational map—a mission statement(s). Good managerial leaders also know they need a far better understanding of what will make or break the emerging leadership on the way to attaining the defined mission statements.

So where do you begin as a leader focused on performance? With the single area businesspeople typically spend the least amount of time discussing. In fact, consider this following mental exercise before you delve into the foundational aspects of true managerial leadership effectiveness and greatness.

Exercise: Visualize pulling a dozen books off your bookshelf right now (at home or in your office) that deal with business, management, leadership, teams, organizational effectiveness, or even managerial leadership motivation. Now visualize scanning the table of contents of each book or the glossaries of any biographies/autobiographies. Notice how many of these books single out and dedicate text to the single factor that psychology has determined is the only constant we have control over. And that factor is the only one that all human beings have in common—attitude.

Attitude (our mindsets, beliefs, self-talk, self-affirmations, inner-voice dialogues we occasionally have, and so on) is the foundational factor in life. Thus, professional success is the single factor we spend the least amount of time discussing in business circles.

In any sustained business you have ever been directly associated with or studied from afar, you will recognize that the managerial leaders of that organization have accepted as their sole and primary responsibility the daily action of creating a conducive environment for positive attitudes. To be a beacon that guides others, you need to have a basic understanding of what makes your business mind operate.

Let's gain a better understanding of how this component of our attitudes influences both us as leaders and those we employ. To create an immediate and lasting positive impact on our personal and professional lives, think about the centers of influence in our lives. The conditioning factors that hold the greatest impact and shaping power over us and our potential are tied directly to our hands—our **FIST FACTORs.**

Make a fist and shake it. Close your eyes and visualize; feel that fist. Feel the weight of your fist, and the power that your hand can make when those fingers close tightly upon one another!

Did you do this? If you did, then continue reading.

Research indicates that most of us have a nucleus of five core types of people in our lives, whom we confide in, do things with, and talk, share, and laugh with. We can refer to this nucleus as a *mental roster*. A century ago Napoleon Hill introduced the idea of a master mind within each of us, in his classic book, *Think and Grow Rich*. The evolution of that idea brings us to this mental roster (a.k.a. FIST FACTOR).

Mental implies that we can see them in our mind's eye, and *roster* implies that there are multiple names we can visualize. It is this mental roster that really serves as our mental board of directors. It influences how we see ourselves and the stimulants in our lives. This visualization that further influences how we respond or react, and thus drives our mental and physical power is the FIST FACTOR.

Now look at your fist. You see four fingers and one thumb. For the sake of this concept and exercise, consider them to be five fingers. As you look at each finger individually, associate a name from your nucleus with each. You may visualize a few less than five names or a few more than five. For most people, however, there are five fingers, and there will be just about five core (key) names.

Affix the core names of your FIST FACTOR to each finger, and shake your fist one more time. Now feel the weight of those individuals upon your body.

The fastest way to evoke a change in your behavior pattern is to adjust your FIST FACTOR!

What is the connection of your fist with *The Managerial Leadership Bible?* It's a direct connection. Think of the concept this way:

Organizations and businesses have boards of directors. The purpose of a board of directors is to guide and influence the direction of the organization or business. The board is charged with making sure that the organization or business is on track with its mission statements (another word for *mission* is goals). When an organization loses focus or needs assistance, the board is there to help. Each board is also designed to be a certain number strong. Do you agree with these two generalities?

Well, that board of directors is the same as your FIST FACTOR. Your fist is only a certain number of fingers strong, and each member you affixed to your fist (you chose consciously) has the same role and influence upon you (subconsciously) as the board does on that organization or business. When a board member no longer is serving a viable and valuable role in her respective group, the member is asked to leave or is fired.

To create a positive environment, condition an organization, or direct a business toward success, the fastest solution is to ensure that the right members make up the board. Your FIST FACTOR is the same as saying you hold your own personal board of directors within your fist. If you don't like what you see and feel, then fire a board member and replace her with someone who deserves to take up your mental space!

So, who should be on your board of directors? Think about someone who would best serve as a board member by looking into these five diverse segments listed in Table 3.1. Name only one person from each segment to your board. After all, another name for your FIST FACTOR is—your mentor(s).

Table 3.1 FIST FACTOR—Candidates/Members

Family:
Friend:
Colleague:
Super Success:
Under-Dog:

Upon reflection, this is a diverse group of individuals, who will allow you the luxury of being able to confidently and assertively interact with any one of them when the need arises. These core people have more to do with who you are and where you will go than any other single factor in life.

If your nucleus is unhealthy, you have a negative influence close to your psyche, and any outside conditioning factors can only be received negatively. Does your board make (internal) statements to you, such as

- Go for it!
- You can do that!
- Make sure that is correct, before you....
- Is there anything I can do...?
- I once did that and I found that....
- Why can't you...?

Or does your FIST FACTOR mentally hold regular board meetings to assess the state of your board and then hold out for ultimate success?

FIST FACTOR members impact how you interact with others, and how you go about designing the five core mission statements detailed in Chapter 2, "Five Mission Statements for Ultimate 'New View' Success." These personal board members also impact how effective you will be in management, as detailed in upcoming chapters. You can test the validity of this concept by considering the following memory set questions.

Memory Set Questions

- Where do you shop for groceries on a regular basis?
- What is your professional title (what do you do)?
- Where do you live?

Has your (subconscious/mental) board changed recently? You can test the validity of the FIST FACTOR and whether members of this personal motivational/attitudinal board have changed in recent memory. Consider the following three questions as points of reference, and as you reflect upon them, ask yourself whether any of your members changed within each question's scope.

> **Question One**—As you reflect upon your FIST FACTOR members you just visualized in the preceding activity, have any changed in the last three months?
>
> **Question Two**—Go back one year in your memory. Ask yourself if any members of your FIST FACTOR have changed, as you use the three memory set questions detailed previously.
>
> **Question Three**—Now, go back ten years in your memory. As you reflect upon the three memory set questions previously detailed, have any of the members of your FIST FACTOR changed?

Most people will find changes to the names of their FIST FACTOR nucleus on the first question. Others will start to see some of the names change as they reflect back from one to three years ago. When did you start to see the names change?

By using the three measurement questions within the memory set as points of reference, you can see that changing some environmental factors sometimes changes your FIST FACTOR (mental influencers). More importantly, these influence you positively or negatively.

To evoke a powerful change in yourself, your colleagues, and among teams and departments, make sure that everyone has the right FIST FACTOR members (mentors) in their makeup.

With the FIST FACTOR in mind, you can begin to see that certain individuals in your life hold the position of guiding lights. As you look inwardly upon those who comprise this select group of people, you must always pose the question as to whether they are positive influences in your life—transmitters. Even worse yet, are they a negative influence on you—terrorists?

To maintain a positive and healthy perspective, consider a board of directors for both your professional and personal life.

These groups provide you with opportunities to mentally reference what you learned from them, and ponder what they might do if placed in situations similar to what you might encounter in the future. And a board of directors also affords you opportunities to physically interact with it (or at least mentally reference it) for guidance, suggestions, and valuable input in professional and personal matters.

These people also assist in shaping your overall perspectives on management and effectively discharging the core alternate management styles detailed within *The Managerial Leadership Bible.*

Remember, you consciously picked these people for some reason important to you at some time in your past. Once chosen, they then occupy subconscious space within you, and thus influence every decision and action you make as a leader/manager for the future.

How does this concept work? Simple. There are specific influencers within us that impact our thoughts. Our thoughts impact our self-image. Our self-image impacts our self-view and inner mirror. Our inner mirror reflects to us who and what we are. This signal then gets projected outwardly to others. Our mental board of directors, therefore, directly influences what gets projected to others or what we have labeled here as our FIST FACTORS.

Of all our board members, it is typically the family category members who have the most power and influence on who we are, as they are the most deeply rooted and weigh the most on our conscious and subconscious minds.

With the precise healthy mindset or attitude, lifelong learning and development are possible. For most individuals, once they know something, the learning ends. But with these ideas frontmost in your mind, you can have the necessary mind shift to be as productive as possible yourself. The ability to guide others in their own mind shifts for peak performance can then be actualized.

Leaders must have the innate ability to mentally workshop issues, whether good or bad, efficiently and expeditiously to maintain the forward-focused momentum to gain market advantage.

You can have multiple FIST FACTORs or mental boards for differing situational needs or areas of your life. Your ability to make your mind operate bigger by elevating its associations with greater individuals than oneself, allows you to lead yourself and others to levels of greatness and legacy.

A powerful mental mind shift observation that reinforces this chapter of ideas is attributed to Einstein: "The mind that creates a problem cannot solve a problem." This implies you have to get outside yourself to see problems, challenges, issues, and even opportunities differently, and subsequently to resolve them. To validate this premise, consider a time when you were concentrating so hard on solving an issue before you that there just seemed to be no resolution. So you finally set the matter aside and focused your energies on something entirely different. While working on this second, unrelated matter, a floodgate was opened and countless ideas came rushing forth from your subconscious brain (where your FIST FACTOR is located) to your conscious brain. By having these mind shifts, you can become a whole-brain thinker, and the level of proficiency you exhibit is elevated to a new game.

Managerial Leadership Bible Lesson Three

How you see yourself, as influenced by the individuals you keep in mind, now and in the future, directly influences your self-attitude.

Attitude drives self-worth, which drives behavior—and that drives performance or lack thereof.

Successful leaders and organizations create a culture of healthy attitude for wealthy performance. What do you do daily to nurture a healthy self-attitude? What do you do daily as the leader to create environments conducive for positive, constructive attitude? Are you in someone's FIST FACTOR as a transformer or a terrorist?

Even more damaging, do you have terrorists on your mental board of directors? If so, mentally fire them from your FIST FACTOR today!

Review Questions

The review questions accompanying each chapter or section are designed to assist you in achieving the learning objective stated at the beginning of each chapter. The review section is not graded; do not submit it in place of your final exam. While completing the review questions, it may be helpful to study any unfamiliar terms in the glossary in addition to course content. After completing the review questions for each chapter, proceed to the review question answers and rationales.

1. According to the author, our_____, which he describes as our "mindsets, beliefs, self-talk, self-affirmations, inner-voice dialogues we occasionally have, and so on" is the foundational factor in life.

   A. Attitude

   B. Self-actualization

   C. Identity

   D. Upbringing

2. Why does the author use the FIST FACTOR to illustrate the core people in our lives?

   A. Because we must make a fist and be aggressive in business.

   B. Because fists represent warfare in the competitive business world.

   C. Because there are typically five core types, which correspond to fingers.

   D. Because FIST stands for Friendly Interpersonal Standard Training.

3. The three memory set questions for analyzing your FIST FACTOR people are: 1. Where do you shop for groceries on a regular basis? 2. What is your professional title (what do you do)? and 3. _____

   A. Where do you live?

   B. How many children do you have?

   C. What is your favorite color?

   D. Who is your best friend?

4. You consciously choose the people on your mental board of directors.

   A. True

   B. False

Review Question Answers and Rationales

Review question answer choices are accompanied by unique, logical reasoning (rationales) as to why an answer is correct or incorrect. Evaluative feedback to incorrect responses and reinforcement feedback to correct responses are both provided.

1. According to the author, our_____, which he describes as our "mindsets, beliefs, self-talk, self-affirmations, inner-voice dialogues we occasionally have, and so on" is the foundational factor in life.

   A. **Correct. This is why the author states that a leader must create an atmosphere for positive attitudes.**

   B. Incorrect. This is only a part of establishing our attitude.

   C. Incorrect. This is only a part of establishing our attitude.

   D. Incorrect. This is only a part of establishing our attitude.

2. Why does the author use the FIST FACTOR to illustrate the core people in our lives?

   A. Incorrect. The fist is actually about those people we are close to.

   B. Incorrect. The first is a personal reference.

   C. **Correct. A fist is also used to describe the power these people give us.**

   D. Incorrect. The author does not use FIST as an acronym.

3. The three memory set questions for analyzing your FIST FACTOR people are: 1. Where do you shop for groceries on a regular basis? 2. What is your professional title (what do you do)? and 3._____

   A. **Correct. Because the questions are about lifestyle changes, moving could affect your core members.**

   B. Incorrect. This question is irrelevant to knowing your core members.

   C. Incorrect. This question is irrelevant to knowing your core members.

   D. Incorrect. This question is only one part of establishing core members and a best friend may not even be on the list.

4. You consciously choose the people on your mental board of directors.

   A. Correct. Although in time it may be hard to remember why you did choose them.

   B. Incorrect. While their impact is often subconscious, you did purposefully choose them at one point in time in your life.

4

Six Alternative Managerial Leadership Intervention Styles

See, Say, Do—When they see, then that means we are doing it. When they say they understand, that typically means we are doing it. And when they do it, then we see and we can say they know how to do it!
—**Jeff Magee**

Learning Objective

After completing this section of the course, you will be able to explain the difference between the leadership styles and explain when and why each one should be used.

With a newly gained healthy attitude geared for peak performance, interaction with others can be elevated to a new level of effectiveness. For many managers, management deals with knowing what results need to be attained, and then focusing energies on available resources to make this magic act happen. In the course of working toward immediate, intermediate, and long-term results, traditional (old-school) management focuses upon who is most effective at barking out directions, giving orders, and maintaining significant degrees of power by controlling resources.

To truly attain peak performance personally and professionally, management in the future needs to recognize that there are six completely different ways to interact with others to facilitate (lead) the directional growth and production needed from their personnel assets on a daily basis. A better understanding of the six core styles of managerial leadership (or coaching approaches) will show a management member how to alternate these styles to obtain optimum results (from a team, individual player, and oneself), thereby becoming an effective leader and avoiding micromanagement.

The six alternative management styles are profiled on the following pages. A successful management player in a winning organization must recognize that only one style of managerial leadership intervention can be efficiently utilized at any one time.

Think of these management styles as hats on a hat rack inside your organizational walls. You must first take off your personal hat when you come in the door each morning, thereby becoming more objective and less subjective. Then assess the environment to determine which management hat to take from the hat rack and place on your head. Remember, only one hat can be on your head at a time. To maximize your management capabilities, you will continually be taking hats off and putting them on. You must become fluid in these actions. In doing so, you reduce interaction time with players, stimulate greater interactions, and ultimately, see a significant increase in team productivity and positive attitude. This means less management stress and increased management productivity during the traditional daily working hours—less pre-AM and post-PM work to maintain the status quo.

Breaking down management into six subcategories is easy when you recognize that each day management personnel participate in (or should participate in) only six activities. If management doesn't recognize its six basic alternative styles of intervention, then no matter how hard it works, managers will feel as if they are holding on for a fall (and frustration) every day.

Effective managerial leadership is in knowing when to put on the correct management hat; by doing so, the leader within you will shine. The six alternate management styles (or hats) are

1. Manager
2. Teacher
3. Coach
4. Counselor
5. Disciplinarian
6. Mentor

Prior to analyzing the six managerial leadership styles, consider the traditional dictionary definition of management. Traditional and old-style management closely resembles the following definition:

Man-age, v. i. To direct or carry on business affairs; to achieve one's purpose; to exercise executive, administrative, and supervisory direction of a business.

To better understand the roles and responsibilities of each management style, see Table 4.1. Notice the traits common to some of the styles, and the differing traits as well. Based on the leadership alternatives, you can assess the whys of some recent interactions and why those management interactions were less productive than desired.

Reduce your interaction work and increase results by using less autocratic methods of management. Consider the following six alternative styles.

Table 4.1   Six Alternative Management Styles

Management Style (Hat)	Responsibilities/Traits
Manager	Hands-on Trainer Rule(s) regulator Knowledge transfer
Teacher	Educator Appraisal evaluator Patient
Mentor	Hands-on Educator/influencer Encourager Compatibility Guider and navigator
Counselor	Hands-on One-on-one consulter Solution oriented Last intervention
Disciplinarian	Serious approach Pain factor motivator Major leverage
Coach	Hands-off Attitude adjuster Encourager/focuser Calming factor Personal cheerleader Education reminder

The power of management's effectiveness rests in your ability to determine precisely what role needs to be assumed at any given time to obtain organizational results and success from each person you engage on an individual basis. It is critical to the success, productivity, and development of the players that someone at the management level understands that the six core styles are defined and distinguishably different from one another.

For an organization to attain peak performance, management needs to assess daily environments and the players within those environments to determine how much time needs to be invested in any one specific management style.

For management to be truly effective, it needs to assume all six core management styles and alternate them routinely to obtain results. Those players vested with the six responsibilities must understand the essence of each. Explore in greater detail the thrust of each management style within your environment, and let the following six management subsections serve as a guide to effective leadership alternatives.

Manager

The *manager* is the person who watches out to ensure that organizational rules, policies, procedures, best practices, and guidelines are being followed and addressed. Within this management style, structured training and education of the players is established and executed.

The enforcement of these standards is the primary responsibility of the manager. This position is the most time-consuming. When the manager hat is being worn, the manager must avail herself to the employee, player, or other person, often becoming tied down with interaction(s) with specific players. Therefore, she has limited time available for interfacing with other players on the team, or for focusing energies on other tasks charged specifically to the manager. Traditional management focuses (and is followed up by academic disciplines that focus) efforts on a manager being merely a manager. Organizations that desire to grow and survive in the future need more than managers. Other styles of management are required.

As long as a member of the management team focuses her energies solely on being a manager, the ultimate results are a team being held back from attaining peak performance, increased player tension, organizational frustration, and higher levels of employee turnover than necessary.

In management, the role of manager is the most labor-intensive one a player can assume. As long as management focuses on being managers, there will be players on the team (transformers and even more positive transmitters/followers) who are ignored, while management is tied down with problem players (terrorists) or engaged in micromanagement of everyone's activities.

Another major drawback to the traditional manager style is that managers are charged by the organization with ensuring that things get done. This philosophy inherently holds back both organizations and players. Most managers focus their efforts on *how* things are being worked on, addressed, completed, and done. This is a dangerous word (and a management concern) for the future. Focusing on the word *how* in today's business world is a self-destructive route. Each time a manager uses the word *how* with another player, she may create an opportunity of automatically provoking a mental fight with that player. With some players this mental challenge is seen in an external outburst, tension, conflict, anger, or hostility in the workplace.

The reason for this is simple. Society has been conditioned (especially via the media for 50 years!) that it is acceptable to challenge another's intellectual position and opinion on issues and things in general. When you use the word *how*, you are challenging another person's position and asserting that yours is better and more sound than theirs—instant mental challenge and conflict!

There are times when something needs to be done a certain way (how). Successful management realizes that the best (and least threatening) way to communicate this message is to replace *how* with words, such as *what* and *why*. The word *how* sounds threatening to another person's ear. Even if management doesn't intend it to be a threat, it still is! Consider the following:

- "That is not how I asked you to...."
- "We don't do it that way. Here is how I...."
- "Let me show you how...."

All these statements are offered hundreds of times daily and more than likely are not intended to be negative or confrontational. Yet to the listener they are threatening (see Chapter 10, "Improving Interactive Communication").

To communicate the what and why requires that management flex its style and alternate styles as necessary to accomplish objectives.

Whether you are practicing the management alternative styles outlined to be a manager, teacher, mentor, counselor, disciplinarian, or coach, you can rephrase the earlier statements and substitute another word for the how, changing potentially negative interaction into educational player interaction. Consider these statements:

- "I can appreciate what you have done here. What we need to focus on is...."

- "Here is why we need to complete the project according to these specifications...."
- "To save you time, let me show you what I need...."

Other alternative management styles to adapt and adopt are teacher, mentor, counselor, disciplinarian, and coach.

Teacher

While a teacher may execute parallel actions as the manager role, this intervention style goes deeper. As a *teacher* your management style is similar in many aspects to what the manager will be doing. The critical difference is that when one deploys the teacher style, there is a greater need for deeper education and training to take place due to an individual's lack of functional knowledge to do tasks appropriate for his position. So along with the teacher needing to have a command of the "elementary knowledge" in which he will be teaching, training, and educating another, he must also be very patient in interactions with the other person. The patience is necessary. When teaching elementary knowledge, an individual can implode the interaction if he is not willing to take a calmer, more easygoing, and more patient approach to the intervention. For the Type A driver personalities, this would imply the need to take some mental Valium before engaging the other person!

Mentor

Another management style is that of *mentor*. While this is also a hands-on, labor-intensive style, it does not mean management actually serves (although it can) as the mentor. Key players on the team at any level can augment the manager's efforts by serving in this valuable position. There are some basic requirements for an effective mentor to develop within an organization to have a successful interaction and professional relationship with another colleague or team player.

The key here is to be accessible for the employee/other person, yet not be micromanaging the relationship. Here is where you default to instruments like a Performance Development Plan (PDP) to engage the mentee from where he is and chart a developmental and sequential path to his aspirations or help him grow and become a viable candidate for consideration and selection in upward movement.

Management needs to assess the ability of each player individually (via the Managerial Coaching Engagement Grid—a.k.a. SA (skill/attitude) Model©

presented later in this chapter, along with techniques presented in subsequent chapters). A primary function of individuals in managerial leadership positions is to determine which players can be assisted to greater levels of productivity by assigning mentors. When an individual or a team possesses good functional knowledge of the job and maintains a healthy attitude/perspective toward it, a mentor would be the go-to person to make the performances excel.

Players on a team that could be tapped to serve as mentors would be transformers of any age and capacity within the organization.

Mentors need to be patient, sage people who are willing to share their learned experiences and knowledge freely with wanting individuals. An effective mentor divorces emotions from the situation and serves to educate and expand a player's ability and knowledge base, through hands-on interaction (based upon the mentor's own experiences of success and failure), simple compatibility, and show-and-tell with the person being mentored. The players on the team need to know there is someone they can turn to, confide in, and gain direction and support from in the absence of their managers and coaches.

Developing players into mentors is also a powerful way to stimulate valuable interaction from senior-level players, on a team that may be burning out and slowing down. Older players can serve as great organizational champions if used genuinely and strategically within the overall management structure.

Mentors must understand the five mission (vision, purpose) statements as outlined in Chapter 2, "Five Mission Statements for Ultimate 'New View' Success." The role of mentor is a powerful one, as outlined in Table 4.2. The mentor is, in essence, shaping the life of, and building security for the future of, an organization. Choose your mentors wisely and empower them with the resources and support to accomplish your objectives.

Table 4.2 Five Different Mentor Styles/Types: The Mentor Life Cycle©

Elementary mentor	A mentor who serves as an educator and teacher to the person being mentored. This style of mentoring provides the person being mentored with the basics and "how-to's."
Secondary mentor	The person being mentored has graduated and knows the "how-to's" and now needs a motivator, encourager, or coach to show him greater functional applications of knowledge in the environment he works within.

Post-secondary mentor	The person being mentored now knows and is performing. Now he needs someone to bring him along and serve as his champion and keep building and reinforcing his confidence level(s). This level mentor serves to direct the efforts in a specialized way for peak performance and maximum contribution to an organization.
Master mentor	This mentor serves as the sponsor for the person being mentored and promotes her abilities to others. The mentor serves as the PR representative. The mentor finishes polishing the person being mentored here and prepares her for the next level or mentor life cycle.
Reverse mentoring	Now the person who was mentored pays the favor forward to someone else. The person being mentored now becomes the mentor and starts the cycle/process all over.

Counselor

Not as glamorous a management position, yet critical to an organization's ultimate success and team attitude, is the style known as the *counselor*. When considering the deployment of this interaction or intervention style, consult with your human resource professional or legal counsel as appropriate, as there is a heightened likelihood that people that you assess in this need-state (and the disciplinarian need-state) have the capacity to play victim and may find a sympathetic ear with fellow ignorant individuals. But do not abdicate; forward focus is necessary.

The management cliché "out of sight, out of mind" unfortunately does not apply here. While management tries to ignore a difficult and unpleasant situation or player, everyone else on that team will know exactly what is going on, and more importantly, who is getting away with what. Consequently, when management does decide it is time to deal with the negativity, there will be more than just the initial problem at hand. Additional challenges always develop as a result of management inaction.

When a problem surfaces or a difficult player is on a team (as the SA Model illustrates later in this chapter), and management has exhausted all pleasantries and niceties, only one management option is left, and that is to assume the role of counselor.

The counselor role can be unpleasant, as this is where management stands and must hold its ground. While limited give-and-take negotiation may be allowed, when a relationship has advanced this far and management has assumed the style of counselor, the worst-case scenario has already been prepared for (living beyond this person's presence on the team). Management must go one-on-one with the problem player (and/or her representative, if your environment is conditioned for such instances).

Things are serious at this point. The player with the challenging or negative behavior or attitude becomes counterproductive to the team and organization and must be dealt with.

It is in engaging an individual in this area that a detailed behavior-focused Performance Improvement Plan (PIP) should be administered with detailed KPIs for action, time dated for execution, with detailed next steps for improvement, and next-step ramifications for continued unimproved performance. As and when appropriate obviously you should consult with your organization's Human Resource (HR) leadership team for any specific guidance on how to proceed and how to administrate a PIP. If you do not have a staffed HR team check with your outside HR benefits firm or legal counsel (any human resource trade association can provide you with template PIP forms).

Chapter 9, "Nine Tactical Steps to High-Impact Leadership," provides a detailed approach to dealing with a difficult and challenging player. Should the situation dictate a one-on-one interaction or a formal counseling session, refer to the section in that chapter on counseling the player for a step-by-step approach to structuring a win/win session.

Disciplinarian

Everything detailed for consideration and delivery as the counselor would apply in this role as well.

This is the most uncomfortable of all positions. At this juncture, you have no alternatives left for engaging a person. While there has been a substantial investment in time and training, and institutional and industry acclimation with this individual, her behaviors have become so cancerous that they must be eliminated.

Meeting with this individual is now a situation of last resort, and the other person must understand the gravity of his actions. Significant documentation is provided and created here, with a clear understanding that this will be the last time it will ever be addressed by you and the organization. Having this meeting is held entirely for your benefit and that of the organization. Such encounters are damaging and not held because of any mindset that you care for them. Rally your disgust for this session, so the other person and his representation—should you be working in an arcane, union-based organization that protects pathetic, worthless individuals (as opposed to some forward-thinking unions that do hold employees accountable for their actions)—will know there is no negotiation room here on your part and no further discussion will be held; you are merely meeting with this person now after having worn the counselor hat with no success. If he wants to remain on the team, there will be significant behavior change instantly, or he will be creating his own exit.

A great opening line in this managerial leadership intervention could be, "We are here because of decisions you have made and choices you have refused to adhere to that are not acceptable to this organization...!"

Coach

The ultimate goal of management is to assist players to reach peak performance and to position themselves in the management style of *coach*—there when players need him, off to the side otherwise, navigating the team.

When management acts as coaches it can focus energies on developing the team, meeting needs, and budgeting energies for future successes. Also when management acts as coaches, it can concentrate on the responsibilities of management and not worry about what the players are doing or "how" they are doing it. Management at this level realizes that players assume accountability for their own actions. They act as if the organization is their organization, not as if they are merely a part of some sort of large machinery.

When management arrives at coaching it is actually practicing a hands-off approach to leadership. The players here realize that management has its own unique responsibilities; doing a player's job is not one of them.

The primary focus of the coach is to help players maintain mental and physical perspective and focus on goals. The coach is charged with maintaining the proper attitudes for a healthy, happy, and productive environment to develop and sustain productivity. The coach is the constant attitude adjuster, motivator, and encourager of peak performance in each individual he comes into contact with.

As management learns from the Managerial-Leadership-Coaching Engagement Model, the ultimate objective is to advance each player in his own way to the quadrant, which puts each in a mentor position for future growth and daily effectiveness. In this way the manager can assure the position of coach. He can strategically interact as needed and assist each player individually for ultimate growth and success.

Reduce your management workload by coaching the team to success and not worrying about being a hands-on manager. By being able to determine what management style (or hat) is required at any given time, you can substantially reduce your interaction time and workloads.

Recognizing what position a player, colleague, or customer is in at any given time determines which management style is required and lets you know when and how to increase your level of interaction effectiveness. One technique or model you can utilize to determine where a player is, and therefore, which management hat you need to put on, is the SA Model.

Every player is operating professionally within a need level; she is always in need of something to maximize her potential. As you review the six alternative management styles from Table 4.1 (mentally or physically), recognize that only one style should be used at a time. By identifying what need level a person has, you can more quickly identify which to use, reducing your interaction time while increasing your interaction effectiveness.

To determine the managerial leadership need level of another person, and how best to engage her to avoid micromanagement and miscommunication, consider two simple variables. First, assess the skill level (knowledge, education, training, skill set...) on the vertical axis from low (score as a zero) to high (score as a ten), with the middle area (score as a five) representing the difference between acceptable and unacceptable skill or aptitude levels. Second, assess the attitude level (desire, motivation, willingness, ownership, acceptance, demeanor, emotions, attitude...) on the horizontal axis from low (zero) to high (ten), with the middle area (five) representing the difference between acceptable and unacceptable attitude levels.

Review the Managerial-Leadership-Coaching Engagement Model illustrated in Figure 4.1 and plot a few of your present players mentally on it as to their overall skill and attitude on your team. Once you have plotted a few players (transmitters, transformers, terrorists), you will recognize the need level or managerial leadership style for them.

1. Plot high to low on the vertical axis line the skill/aptitude level of the player as associated with an issue in your mind.

2. Plot left to right on the horizontal axis line the attitude level of the player as associated with that issue and in your relationship on this specific issue. Now put her initials in the appropriate quadrant (box) where these marks intersect.

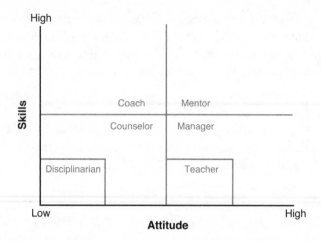

Figure 4.1 Managerial-Leadership-Coaching Engagement Model a.k.a. SA Model

Now, based upon which quadrants you have your players plotted on (and you may want to visualize or plot on the chart an additional terrorist, transmitter, and transformer from your team), you now know which management styles to assume.

Based on which quadrant you have a player in, you must take on the responsibilities of that specific management style. Remember, the management cliché "out of sight, out of mind" may make sense to you with a problem player on occasion, but once this player is identified in the counselor quadrant, you must deal with him. The longer you allow this situation to continue, the longer everyone else on the team is aware of what is going on and, more importantly, who is getting away with what on any given day.

Diagnostically, there are two powerful ways you can utilize this instrument to assist your managerial leadership engagement style. You can assess individuals for

- Immediate intervention needs based upon the situation you face
- Succession planning and succession management purposes for intermediate and long-term success

The ultimate objective of the Managerial-Leadership-Coaching Engagement Model is to recognize which players are operating in the mentor quadrant. Those players are your high, peak performers and may be viewed as your transformers. The model is also designed to assist you in determining your best course of action (BCOA) to motivate and manage every player to the mentor quadrant, eventually. And remember that you don't have to serve as the mentor. It would probably best be left to another to serve in this valuable role. Many studies indicate that you attain maximum mentor-mentored interactions when the mentor is at least two positions removed from the mentored, thus freeing up one of your hands for something else.

Based on the quadrant in which you mentally or physically plot players, colleagues, and superiors, you will gain the needed insight for successful interaction and increased persuasive ability.

For example, you have two alternatives for moving a player in the counselor quadrant toward mentor. One option is for you to move her from counselor to manager/teacher and then ultimately to mentor. The problem with that is that it becomes labor-intensive for you as a management option, as manager/teacher means hands-on. Otherwise, a second alternative would be to move that player from counselor to mentor through the coach quadrant, as coach means hands-off. Every decision brings with it another set of decisions and questions, each unique and impacting the ultimate productivity, attitude, and performance levels of you and your organization's team.

Consider the reasons a player may appear in one quadrant on one day and in a different quadrant on the next. There are a multitude of management explanations for why players appear in the various SA Model quadrants.

- A player who lacks proper knowledge or education on an issue, task, project, or subject may procrastinate. Fear factors set in and cause delays in productivity. The player becomes a transmitter, waiting for influence and direction. Your role then becomes that of manager.

- A player who has a lot of enthusiasm for issues, tasks, and projects may need a subtle push of encouragement. Your role becomes that of a coach.

- A player who appears onsite as an overeager and power-charged individual can become a loose cannon on the team. While you want to maintain that energy level, it is critical to ensure that his energies are aimed in the right direction. The role you take on, or empower someone else to assume, in relation to this player is that of mentor.

- A player who resists activities that lead to productivity, team interaction, and success, or who spreads rumors about others, serves as your terrorist behind the scenes and has to be dealt with immediately. This player typically has low levels of skill and/or asserts a low (and thus poor) attitude toward you and management in general. When you can mentally or physically plot a player into the lower-left quadrant of the SA Model, the role you must assume is that of counselor.

What are some of the variables that lead players toward or away from any specific quadrant? Consider how the following environmental stimulants impact actions, feelings, and human motivation:

- Merging organizations, business units, and teams.
- New positional requirements from a pre-existing person may put a person low on the vertical axis line yet high on the horizontal axis line.
- Merging markets and competition.
- Decreased customer demand for specific products or services.
- Management changes (personnel or styles).
- Retiring peers or superiors.
- Fired peers or superiors.
- New product or service introductions in one of your markets.
- Increased organizational profits.
- Decreased organizational profits.
- Increased onsite educational and training opportunities.
- Decreased onsite educational and training opportunities.
- New transformer introduced to the team.
- New player to the team turns out to be a terrorist.
- On-the-job traumas of some degree.
- Offsite traumas (in personal life, at home, with family members, and so on) to some degree.

Always remember that players are not static and will appear in differing SA Model management/player index quadrants.

Consider some of the explosive applications to this Managerial-Leadership-Coaching Engagement Model in your work environment today. Imagine you are sitting in a meeting and someone has said or done something to which you feel compelled to respond. Glancing down at your left hand, placed on your left kneecap, you visualize the SA Model with your finger pointing upward at a right angle to your thumb, and you score that person and situation against that gesture. Based upon the immediate situation and where that person is plotted, you now know which of the six managerial leadership engagement styles is best for deployment.

Later in the book, we explore specific tactical ways to facilitate the four primary quadrants of this model to reveal the six core managerial leadership styles. Techniques are presented that have immediate application with your organization.

A strong reason for utilizing the six management alternatives is to stimulate greater individual participation and growth, to infuse energy into a team (or department) with minimal effort on behalf of management personnel. Traditional management techniques and policy demanded close interaction with players and placed the burden of accountability on the shoulders of management, not on the players on a team—where it should be.

The new ideologies, methodologies, and doctrine of *The Managerial Leadership Bible* suggest that all players on a team equally share accountability. And for an organization to attain peak levels of performance, profitability, and productivity, management needs to empower players to a level of take charge attitude and performance not witnessed before. Therefore, management needs to pull away from traditional interactions and their "doing" behaviors and allow players themselves to explore, do, fail, and succeed for ultimate growth and prosperity. The more management is involved, the less player (team) interaction there is. The less management participates, the more the player (and team) participates and accomplishes.

View traditional management and the proposed transition to this new concept (as outlined in Chapter 1, "Ground Zero, All Factors Being Equal") in Figure 4.2. Consider where you, your supervisor, and your organization as a whole would plot on the diagonal line, as representative of your managerial leadership operational style. Traditional organizational styles tend to land to the left of the diagonal line; this management style could be labeled as bureaucratic and autocratic in nature, which builds contempt and resentment in the business environment of tomorrow. The more you land to the center or right of the diagonal line, the more empowered individuals are, the more ownership people assume, and the more management can let go and sustain innovation and success today for tomorrow.

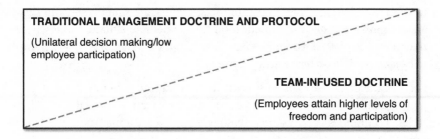

Figure 4.2 Span-of-Control Index

With a more detailed Managerial-Leadership-Coaching Engagement Model (see Figure 4.3), you can design more in-depth diagnostics if you want to determine with greater mathematics where someone may land on the vertical axis or horizontal axis at any situational micro moment in time, as well as where someone may land from a more macro overall perspective. You could also explain this to employees, members of your team, and have them self-assess from their self-awareness perspective. And then benchmark your score with theirs for managerial leadership interventions.

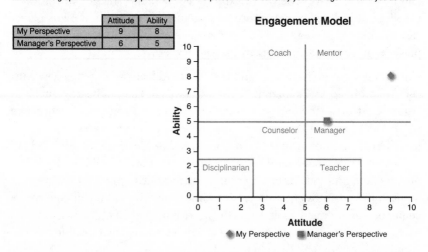

Figure 4.3 Managerial-Leadership-Coaching Engagement Model

To hold yourself or others on your management-leadership team accountable, use Figure 4.3 (request an Excel spreadsheet version through me at DrJeffSpeaks@aol.com) and date stamp it once a week or once a month and assess all your direct reports, employees, team members, and peers onto the chart from a macro perspective. Then you can track your commitment to engaging them and see how they progress throughout the Managerial-Leadership-Coaching Engagement Model from one assessment period to the next. This also holds both you and them accountable to actionable behaviors to ensure everyone is always growing, thriving, and contributing.

View the diagnostics of both the vertical and horizontal axis lines as a scorecard. Low scores from zero through 4.9 should be deemed unacceptable, and strategies and actions are necessary to engage the other person to grow them forward on both axis lines. If that movement is not possible, actions should be taken to remove them from that team for another appropriate place within your organization, as long as their Player Capability Index measurements determine that there is real value from them in the organization. If this is also low and/or a no answer, immediate removal from the organization is necessary for the health and wealth of others—and the organization!

A score hovering around the five on both axis lines reflects an individual who is showcasing a minimum level of acceptance. Engagement must take place to develop appropriate positional pathway or career pathway improvements with specific KPIs.

The real-time power of this Managerial-Leadership-Coaching Engagement Model is that it can aid you in managing a positive or critical bias of another person and objectively diagnostically measure a person's performance against this instrument to determine which engagement style and documentation approach to use. Remember a superstar may be a tenured member of the team, or it may be the newest or youngest member to the team. True performance effectiveness is not about tenure; it is solely about the value one brings to the team and himself, based upon his ability to deliver. I have met 50-plus-year-old men who came off professional and polished until I applied these models and recognized the charlatan in my presence. Likewise, I have had the opportunity to work with twenty-somethings who, while they may lack some of the polish that comes with age, are exceedingly proficient and creative members of an organization!

With a firm understanding of how to engage others and attain peak performance, now is the time to proceed forward with an understanding of how these individual interactions play a role in the overall group or team interactions you have.

Management/Team Control Model

As an overlay to the previous management engagement strategies and operational system approach to human behavior engagement (refer to Figure 4.2) this model wants us to recognize that how management sees its role and how the team wants to experience its role may be a point of contention and dissention. Aligning them appropriately allows for optimal buy-in, collaboration, synergy, and ROI.

The team approach adds increased participation, player ownership, quality, and value to efforts. It also reduces the degree of responsibility and accountability on the part of management personnel. The more opportunity that management affords players to interact with one another, the greater the management and organizational yield will be. You will notice the following:

- **Significantly increased synergy and higher quality solutions**—The ability to ask questions and interact to determine what is best—people interaction.

- **Increased player ownership**—By allowing players to interact and by reducing the volume of management hand-holding, players learn that they need one another to be successful—not only individually, but also as a team, unit, department, and/or organization.

- **Increased awareness, cooperation, cohesion, commitment, and productivity**—By empowering management to back off and let go, and thus allow the players (who constitute the team) to make educated decisions that impact their productivity by themselves, the organization benefits in two ways. (Note that this is all impacted by an understanding and participation of the players in the mission statement principles set forth in Chapter 2.) First, by placing each player in an organization at a level of optimal performance, negativity goes down. Second, management is now maximizing all resources—including the most valuable of all, its people.

The more management works to let go and the more the players on a team recognize that they are in greater control of their destiny, the greater the level of organizational accomplishment will be. As you make the transition from your present management style, start with small team interactions. Work specifically from that point to strategically assigned *self-directed work team environments*—you have to initiate one step at a time. Gain small team or unit wins, build from these smaller, more attainable victories, and work outward toward larger and more involved tasks and projects.

The ultimate management and team empowerment grid may look more like Figure 4.4 than the grid in Figure 4.2.

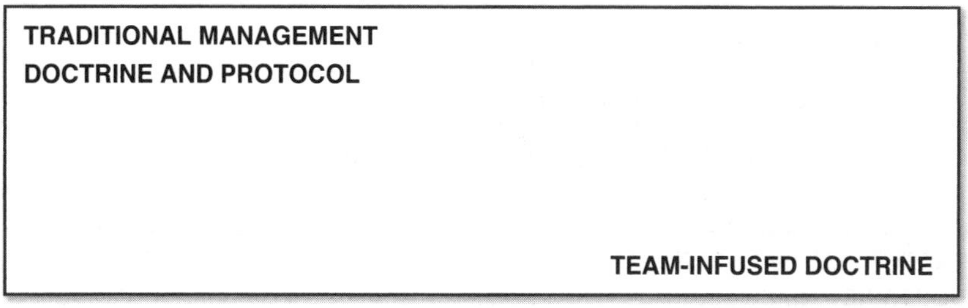

Figure 4.4 Management/team control model

The greater the team involvement becomes, the greater the team's level of participation in taking control and managing change effectively, and the higher the team's level of accountability and authority will be.

The more management releases controls, decision-making abilities, and access, the greater the need of teaming will be. Distribute the power to the individual. This leads as a progression toward greater interacting teams and unity. In reverse, the greater the management role of authority and control is, the lower the level of player participation will become. As an interaction style, consider the six management alternatives as guideposts toward interaction in future situations and work to involve others, not alienate them, from activities and productivity.

Another way to review this management model is to overlay the six management styles and determine at what level of management participation an organization experiences such-and-such levels of player participation and effectiveness. Consider what level of player participation and ownership management would receive from players with each management style and one-on-one interactions, regardless of the authority or seniority issues of the players involved. There is a parallel with these four styles and that of parenting—change your interaction style to attain differing net results.

The six specific management styles would fall into alignment with the model as shown in Figure 4.5.

The six core management styles from left to right on the diagonal line impact player and team performance in direct proportion to management's role in interactions. The styles on the model shown in Figure 4.5 are

1. **Disciplinarian** style as the management role (or hat)

2. **Counselor** style as the management role (or hat)

3. **Teacher** style as the management role (or hat)

4. **Manager** style as the management role (or hat)

5. **Mentor** style as the management role (or hat)

6. **Coach** style as the management role (or hat)

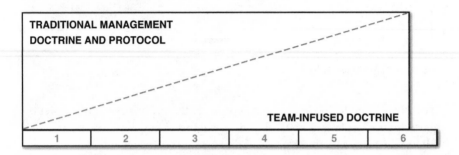

Figure 4.5 The Span-of-Control diagram also reflects traditional default management styles, based upon where one would land on the diagonal line—the more to the left one's self-management style is, the more one reflects #1 or #2 styles; the more to the center one lands, the more like #3 or #4 your interaction style may be; and the further to the right your self-management style is, the greater the likelihood is you would reflect the #5 managerial-leadership style.

With each style management utilizes, increased player participation occurs and team effectiveness develops. With each style you deploy, different new results are possible. With differing players on a team you may need to fluctuate between the six styles to effectively use the correct one, given the players and circumstances that you are faced with; always work to keep mentally focused on what the immediate management goals are and how those interface with the medium- and long-term goals.

With an understanding that there are alternative styles of interaction from which individuals can exhibit and work to attain desired results, the next management objective is to realize how the daily operations of an organization evolve, and how the management alternatives can be further utilized.

As you explore the five organizational dynamics and operational levels in Chapter 5, "Five Differing Organizational Structures and Levels," consider first how much time you currently spend as a teacher, manager, mentor, disciplinarian, counselor, and coach. When you interact with players in your organization, and in working to motivate and empower those around you to greater levels of participation and ownership (as outlined in the previous management/team control models), determine just how much time is consumed at stages one through six from the chart shown in Figure 4.5.

For most managers working in traditional management and organizational structures (refer to Chapter 1), the greatest amount of time is spent acting as a counselor and manager. This is also where the organization realizes the lowest player participation, creativity, ownership, and proactiveness. Only when management begins to let go and trust, educate, and support the players does an organization experience true successes. This transfer of responsibility typically occurs when management lets go and takes on the styles of mentor and coach (a more hands-off perspective, as outlined in Table 4.1).

You can see the problem in terms of how much time organizations and management spend when it comes to the five differing and always present organizational structures or levels (as outlined in Chapter 5). Most organizations invest significantly too much time in maintaining the status quo and dealing with challenges, problems, wildfires, conflicts, confrontations, in-fighting among players, and negativity. This can typically be traced back to the same management members not having spent adequate time in the foundational organizational levels (see levels 1 and 5 in Chapter 5).

You can apply this same model (Figure 4.5) to how traditionally different generational segmentations have been raised and conditioned to operate (there are always exceptions to any concept or rule; the following are generalizations).

1. **Centurions** tend to be more comfortable in Level One with limited degree of authority and involvement when they are the team/employee role stakeholder, and when in the leadership role prefer greater control. Conditioned to operate in more autocratic environments.

2. **Baby-Boomers** tend to be more comfortable in Level Two with increased situational degrees of authority and involvement when they are the team/employee role stakeholder, and when in the leadership role prefer again to release situational degrees of control or involvement to others. Conditioned to operate in more democratic environments.

3. **Generation X** tend to be more comfortable in Level Three with shared degrees of authority and involvement when they are the team/employee role stakeholder, and when in the leadership role prefer shared control. Conditioned to operate in more consensus environments.

4. **Generation Y** tend to be more comfortable in Level Four with limited regulation and participation of authority and involvement when they are the team/employee role stakeholder, and the same when in leadership. Conditioned to operate in more collaboration environments.

5. **Millennials or Next Generation** tend to be have qualities of both the Centurion and that of the evolving Generation Y, so they are situationally driven as both a team member and team leader.

If managers can train themselves to invest equal amounts of time in the five different levels, everyone on the team will experience greater rewards and accomplishments.

At the Regents Park Hilton Hotel in London, customers experience a finely tuned team, which emulates these ideas. While on a tour of the United Kingdom and presenting conferences on Leadership as Customer Service, one of my venues was this Hilton facility. The meeting's facility manager and his team were consistent in reaching and surpassing expectations. Nothing was beyond their capabilities. Any request made was immediately addressed, and never were customers (including me) ever made to feel as if a desire were unreasonable, undoable, or unattainable. Never did a member of the facility team have to check with someone for permission; every player was made a significant member of the team and was able to make command decisions on the spot—no matter what the question.

Beyond making independent decisions, the members of the team were vested with the power to make the difference, to give others a powerful reason to want more and want to come back to them when a need developed.

> EMPOWERMENT = *Knowledge + Ability + Authority + Attitude (willingness!) + Access*

What makes the management/team control model™ so powerful is that when you experience an encounter, such as this one, you then have a point of reference to measure future interactions by. It becomes clear when you experience both peak performing teams and teams bogged down by sabotaging, mid-management players demanding tight controls that stifle creativity and success.

Managerial Leadership Bible Lesson Four

Ascending upward to managerial leadership greatness requires a willingness and ability to fluidly assess any engagement situation on a need-be basis and assume the appropriate managerial leadership style, while at the same time looking for continual opportunities to take a hands-off approach to one's team for peak sustained performance.

Review Questions

The review questions accompanying each chapter or section are designed to assist you in achieving the learning objective stated at the beginning of each chapter. The review section is not graded; do not submit it in place of your final exam. While completing the review questions, it may be helpful to study any unfamiliar terms in the glossary in addition to course content. After completing the review questions for each chapter, proceed to the review question answers and rationales.

1. Only one style of managerial leadership intervention can be efficiently utilized at any one time.

    A. True

    B. False

2. The _____ is the person who watches out to ensure that organizational rules, policies, and guidelines are being followed and addressed.

    A. Teacher

    B. Manager

    C. Counselor

    D. Disciplinarian

3. What is the difference between the teacher and manager management styles?

    A. Managing requires more training.

    B. Teaching does not involve encouragement.

    C. Managing is a hands-off style.

    D. Teaching requires more patience.

4. Which management style should be used when all other styles have failed?

    A. Disciplinarian

    B. Coach

    C. Mentor

    D. Manager

5. Utilizing the different management styles can _____ a manager's workload.

    A. Increase

    B. Decrease

    C. Eliminate

    D. Maintain

6. For most managers working in traditional management the greatest amount of time is spent acting as a _____ and manager.

    A. Mentor

    B. Coach

    C. Teacher

    D. Counselor

Review Question Answers and Rationales

Review question answer choices are accompanied by unique, logical reasoning (rationales) as to why an answer is correct or incorrect. Evaluative feedback to incorrect responses and reinforcement feedback to correct responses are both provided.

1. Only one style of managerial leadership intervention can be efficiently utilized at any one time.

    A. Correct. It would be confusing to use different styles at one time.

    B. Incorrect. Since each intervention style is different, combining them could be counterproductive.

2. The _____ is the person who watches out to ensure that organizational rules, policies, and guidelines are being followed and addressed.

   A. Incorrect. The teacher can educate workers on these rules and policies but is not there to enforce them.

   B. Correct. The manager is essentially a watch-dog style.

   C. Incorrect. The counselor does almost the opposite. Instead of enforcing rules, the counselor helps ensure employee well-being.

   D. Incorrect. While the manager watches out for these guidelines, the disciplinarian punishes those who do not follow them.

3. What is the difference between the teacher and manager management styles?

   A. Incorrect. Teaching requires more training.

   B. Incorrect. Both styles need to use encouragement.

   C. Incorrect. Both teaching and managing are hands-on styles.

   D. Correct. According to the author, teachers "must be patient in interactions with (another) person."

4. Which management style should be used when all other styles have failed?

   A. Correct. This style is the last effort made before employee termination.

   B. Incorrect. Coaching should have come long before discipline.

   C. Incorrect. Mentoring should have come long before discipline.

   D. Incorrect. Managing should have come long before discipline.

5. Utilizing the different management styles can _____ a manager's workload.

   A. Incorrect. Utilizing different management styles will decrease a manager's workload, while stimulating greater individual participation and growth.

   B. Correct. According to the author: "A strong reason for utilizing the six management alternatives is to stimulate greater individual participation and growth, to infuse energy into a team with minimal effort on behalf of the management personnel."

C. Incorrect. Although utilizing different management styles can decrease a manager's workload, it will not eliminate it altogether.

D. Incorrect. The benefit of the different management styles is that they can decrease a manager's workload.

6. For most managers working in traditional management the greatest amount of time is spent acting as a _____ and manager.

A. Incorrect. Managers working in traditional management spend more time acting as counselor and manager than they do mentoring.

B. Incorrect. If a manager focuses on "trouble" employees, he has no time for coaching.

C. Incorrect. Because of the micromanagement involved in traditional management, little time and energy are left for teaching.

D. Correct. In traditional management, managers are too busy dealing with problems and directly supervising employees, leaving no time for other management styles.

5

Five Differing Organizational Structures and Levels

The task of the leader is to get his (her) people from where they are to where they have not been.

—**Henry Kissinger**

For it remains true that our only sure guides to the present, which so often seems so bewildering, are the lessons—the often terrible lessons—of the past.

—**Henry Cabot Lodge**

Learning Objective

After completing this section of the course, you will be able to describe and compare different organizational structures and levels.

To truly maximize your time and managerial leadership capabilities and those resources at your intellectual disposal, you must realize and accept that every organization is in a constant state of fluctuation—change is the norm. No player (including yourself) within an organization or in any layer within an organization is ever at a static position or level—or you are dying. New stimulants may cause a player or department to evolve from any specific level into another without warning.

Organizations on both a macro and micro level evolve in and out of five spheres, levels, or stages, in essence. Understanding the fundamentals of each level enables you to navigate it more efficiently and mentally empowers you to guide players and situations from one to the next for peak performance and optimum results.

True success, effectiveness, productivity, and maximum profitability arise out of facilitating or managing resources and individuals through these five levels in an effective manner, ensuring that you avoid getting bogged down in the traditional levels that lead to inefficiencies and redundancies, and that ultimately lead to an organization's death.

Management experts—from Deming, Covey, and Drucker to Peters, Senge, Garfield, Blanchard, and Maxwell—have called the five organizational transformational layers by many names for decades. We can focus our energies on the five structures as levels that we grow in and out of, depending on the circumstances about us. The five range from a startup or beginning stage/level and progress to a conclusion or ending stage/level. This chapter focuses on the five levels as a sequence of steps that players and organizations migrate from and toward on a regular basis—as if operating in autopilot mode.

Again, let's go back to some seminal management works; Tom Peters called some of these levels *chaos* in his classic work *Thriving on Chaos*. His premise is that nothing is a constant; things around us are always causing change, conflict, confrontation, and new, evolving challenges and opportunities. No matter how you view it, the premise still goes back to minds, such as W. Edwards Deming and Peter Drucker postulated.

Table 5.1 lists the five traditional organizational functionalities and the actions that could be assigned to each. As you review the table and reflect on your managerial leadership behaviors, imagine that a hidden videographer has filmed you for the past week while at work. Now as you review yourself in your own element and in your normal operational style/behavior, affix a percentage sign to each individual level that would be reflective of your standard operating procedure as measured by any day of 100 percent. What would the percentage of time consumed by each level be? Consider this same exercise for a traditional meeting that you facilitate or attend. How much time is consumed by which levels?

Table 5.1 The Five Organizational Levels

Level	Characteristics
Begin	Formation or start-up stage, expectations developed. Introduction of new policies, ground rules, procedures, memos, products, services, meetings, beginning of the day or week, etc.; 80%-10%-10% all live here. Hiring of a new player, interviews, etc. Transfer of a player and the receipt of that new person into your area, department, team, work, unit, etc. Brainstorming session, designing mission statements, setting objectives and goals into motion.

Level	Characteristics
Defend	Conflict in meeting, someone challenges a new policy, procedure, idea, rule, etc. Terrorist (10%) on the loose in your organization. Delegation disaster. Break down in interactions and communication. Tension among players calls for patience. Lack of commitment among players toward something and a feeling of forced defense of positions.
Blend	Things begin to come together and get done, norms. Players are falling into a flow, pacing. Decisions take less time to make. Your transformers are taking the lead, and the transmitters/followers are falling in behind them. Productivity is maintaining your status quo and routine expectations are met.
Transcend	Some players attain peak performance, rise above. Your results and expectations are exceedingly high. Players are interacting with low stress, little tension, and effective communication, and decisions are being made jointly among the players at this level. Commitment to decisions is attained. Players perform outside boundaries to attain results with no complaints. Players assume responsibility and accountability, and the team is moving ahead of competition and beyond status quo.
End	Analysis is allowed to take place at conclusions for better planning of future actions. You are able to monitor and modify for tomorrow. Final analysis activities, lessons learned, benchmarking.

The significance of these five operational levels is critical to your assessment needs, both in terms of which developmental level each player is in at any given time and of identifying which operational level your organization is at, with respect to a given issue, project, problem, customer or vendor relationship, or the alliances you are forging with others. Being able to mentally put your finger on the level you are in will assist in directing your future responses—from reactionary management (autopilot) to responsive and proactive (logic-driven) management.

These five core organizational structures or levels will guide your management style and assist you in putting the proper style into action. The levels also give you perspective in designing team focus and organizational mission statements, assisting in strategic planning, and enabling leaders to gain momentum.

An organization not capable of perpetuating itself has failed. An organization, therefore, has to provide today the people who can run it tomorrow. It has to review its human capital. It should steadily upgrade its human resources.

> *An organization that simply perpetuates today's level of vision, excellence, and accomplishment has lost the capacity to adapt. And since the one and only thing certain in human affairs is change, it will not be capable of survival in a changed tomorrow.*
> —**Peter Drucker,** *The Effective Executive*

You know that you're a peak-performing leader within a peak-performing organization when everyone has clarity of purpose derived from clearly defined mission statements that drive the correct descending percentage of time invested into each of the five levels. Also, the application of the Player Capability Index discussed in Chapter 6, "Analyzing Players and Prospects for Team Success," is in full 360-degree utilization. Your time should be spent first to last in the following chronological order:

1. Transcend
2. Blend
3. End
4. Begin
5. Defend

The further out of sync you are, the greater your needs will be for the strategic and tactical ideas in *The Managerial Leadership Bible.* The closer you are to its ideals, the more you need to be vigilant in your behaviors, model success for those around you, and work to not implode due to complacency and overconfidence.

As a management alternative, a successful manager has to realize there are many different styles or roles one assumes in the quest for success and in search of being the best.

Why do so many authorities on the subject of organizational management miss the core issue? Why have so many organizations that have followed these popular doctrines failed so miserably? Lack of common sense has a lot to do with it. Lack of immediate application of people-oriented skills could be another.

Ken Blanchard, author of *The One Minute Manager,* asserts a concept in management and in people development that proposes a major reason for organizations not spending adequate time in each of the five organizational levels. Being sidetracked into spending disproportionate amounts of time in only a few is a concept called the Grief Cycle™. The Grief Cycle (see Table 5.2) says that for most players (transmitters and terrorists), the reason it takes so long to get to the blend, and ultimately to some degree of a transcend, level is that many get caught up in opposing anything out of the norms of the organizational flow and society (are change-averse)—regardless of the merits.

Table 5.2   Grief Cycle

Today	Future
Denial	Commitment
Resistance	Exploration/Investigation

If management could become more efficient in its early stages or levels (begin, defend), it would actually be able to reduce everyone's grief and pain (thus reducing defend) and enable players and teams to reach operational levels and productivity faster (blend, transcend). This would also allow management more time to plan, organize, strategize, and foresee needs and market patterns (end).

The better one's understanding becomes concerning the five organizational levels and the six managerial leadership styles (discussed in Chapter 4, "Six Alternative Managerial Leadership Intervention Styles"), the faster a manager of people can move through the Grief Cycle, like a bell curve from which the following happens:

1. One starts in the face of something not desired, at the resistance stage.

2. Then he moves upward to denial, when resistance does not accomplish a desired outcome.

3. From denial, one transitions to accepting the inevitable and attainment. Acceptance, buy-in, and ownership may be embraced by all at this third level, finally.

4. Then one evolves into the exploration/investigation stage of ways to proceed and grow forward.

Most organizations, however, live in the grief area of the Grief Cycle by spending major amounts of time in denial and resistance (begin and defend)—an orientation that makes the organization look like an inverted bell curve when plotted in a Grief Cycle. In many organizations the art and science of "thinking" is not taught or demanded, so many individuals fall within the first two stages due to a heavy base of rhetoric, invalid facts, and lack of data leading to their observations and conclusions. When, as a managerial leader, you move personally and professionally to guide others through these four stages, you can see the overlay of the five levels at work as well:

1. Resistance = Begin
2. Denial = Defend
3. Commitment = Blend
4. Exploration/Investigation = Transcend and End

As a manager, how would your immediate team (department) plot on the previous chart? How would your organization as a whole plot on the chart?

Manager (Vocabulary) Style Changes

Management must also realize that a major transformation (paradigm shift) must take place mentally and verbally when management (especially managers) interacts with players. Traditional management focuses on and uses words, such as *how* when interacting with a player, especially if that player has done something either wrong or not as management wanted. When you interact with someone and use a word, such as *how* (for example, "That is not how I want it done"; "That's not how we do it"; "Let me explain how I want this done"), you are directly challenging his intellectual capacity in today's workplace. This can lead to tension, and with a terrorist it can lead to a conflict and confrontation.

The management mindset and vocabulary should be to move from the use of words such as *how* toward the *whats* and *whys* (see Chapter 10, "Improving Interactive Communication," for more communication ideas).

To determine how best to merge the six management styles of the Managerial-Leadership-Coaching Engagement Model a.k.a. the SA Model into the five organizational levels, first analyze your team.

To gain a better objective insight into each player on your team (as a direct report or an indirect report), you should consider Chapter 6. With a better idea of each player's strengths and weaknesses, a better perspective on a player's attributes and detriments, managers can determine a player's capabilities and thus what level of results can be expected from each player. This analysis of each player gives a valuable and powerful position to the organization or team overall.

With a better fluid understanding of the five organizational levels and the four stages of the Grief Cycle, you, as the managerial leader of tomorrow, begin to acquire a new vocabulary to monitor business trends and growth opportunities—for yourself, your team, and the strategic business units that constitute your organization.

Managerial Leadership Bible Lesson Five

Micromanaging a situation or person does not lead to self-confidence on the part of others whom a managerial leader serves. Being able to continually recognize the five-level table (like a child's hopscotch game) serves as a guidepost to recognize where one is with every endeavor. By recognizing what activity you are engaged in at any time, you can determine where you are in the table and whether that is the best use of your time or whether you need to make immediate tactical adjustments to get yourself into the appropriate area of the table as an effective managerial leader. Gauge yourself according to the grid to get to and maintain peak performance from the Transcend level to the End level, noting lessons learned and benchmarking activities.

Your ability to do this will limit the amount of time consumed by the Grief Cycle and counterproductive activities.

Review Questions

The review questions accompanying each chapter or section are designed to assist you in achieving the learning objectives stated at the beginning of each chapter. The review section is not graded; do not submit it in place of your final exam. While completing the review questions, it may be helpful to study any unfamiliar terms in the glossary in addition to course content. After completing the review questions for each chapter, proceed to the review question answers and rationales.

1. Defend is the level in which new employees are hired or existing employees are transferred to new positions.

    A. True

    B. False

2. In which stage do employees assume responsibility and accountability?

    A. Blend

    B. Transcend

    C. End

    D. Begin

3. _____ managers get caught up in opposing anything out of the norms of the organizational flow and society—regardless of the merits.

    A. Terrorist

    B. Coaching

    C. Adaptable

    D. Change-averse

4. Most organizations live in the grief area of the Grief Cycle by spending major amounts of time in _____.

    A. Denial and Resistance

    B. Commitment

    C. Exploration/Investigation

    D. Commitment and Resistance

Review Question Answers and Rationales

Review question answer choices are accompanied by unique, logical reasoning (rationales) as to why an answer is correct or incorrect. Evaluative feedback to incorrect responses and reinforcement feedback to correct responses are both provided.

1. Defend is the level in which new employees are hired or existing employees are transferred to new positions.

    A. Incorrect. The defend level is about resolving conflicts within a team to defend the already existing staff.

    B. Correct. Begin is the level where employees change.

2. In which stage do employees assume responsibility and accountability?

    A. Incorrect. Blending must occur before transcending.

    B. Correct. At this level, employees have transcended conflicts to become more productive.

    C. Incorrect. At the end level, employees have already assumed responsibility.

    D. Incorrect. Employees cannot transcend when they are just learning how to work together.

3. _____ managers get caught up in opposing anything out of the norms of the organizational flow and society—regardless of the merits.

    A. Incorrect. This term is usually applied to employees who are constantly complaining about or changing the norms.

    B. Incorrect. A coaching manager reinforces the productive norms that are already in place.

    C. Incorrect. An adaptable manager is willing to analyze and change norms at any time.

    D. Correct. Typically these types of managers are thought of as "old school" and are counterproductive to organizational growth.

4. Most organizations live in the grief area of the Grief Cycle by spending major amounts of time in _____.

    A. Correct. This leads to the inability to finish the Grief Cycle and improve your organization.

    B. Incorrect. Commitment is the resolve to change what needs changing to end the Grief Cycle.

    C. Incorrect. This level is about exploring options, not denying problems exist.

    D. Incorrect. These two stages contradict each other.

6

Analyzing Players and Prospects for Team Success

Don't tell people how to do things, tell them what you want and expect. Then let them surprise you with their abilities and ingenuity!
—**General George Patton**

Learning Objective

After completing this section of the course, you will be able to gain a better objective insight into each player on your team.

The most overlooked component of people management today, in the academic halls of America's colleges and universities, in the classrooms of today's managerial leadership training programs, and at executive retreats, is the element of "how-to": how to objectively, thoroughly, and analytically assess the abilities and capabilities of yourself and of the players on a team.

If organizations and societies were capable of delivering this essential task, would we have such staggering figures for high employee turnover within certain industries? Consider that in 1993, U.S. Department of Labor statistics associated the highest level of job displacements (after downsizing, mergers, and bankruptcies) with people interaction problems. In March 1996, then-Labor Secretary Robert Reich attributed the highest number of such job displacements and lower-income-receiving positions to those individuals with the least amount of education.

Today, fascinatingly, two decades later a review of Department of Labor statistics and surveys by the leading executive and staff level employment search firms reveals practically zero movement on these statistics. Worse yet are estimates by organizations celebrated by *Training* magazine as being the best in the nation for developing their personnel assets. Yet their very employees report limited to no soft-skill training among the hours spent in skill development classes with managerial leadership content and disproportionate time invested in institutional education and information dissemination.

Imagine an athletic team where the coach is given players to perform results but also has an empty employee personnel performance file. And the coach is not allowed to observe the players in pregame warm-ups or during weekly practices. Imagine a baseball season where coaches are unable to have any spring season workouts, games, skill assessment, or development time, yet are expected to produce a winning team come game time in the active season!

Now let's add the dimension that a coach could not provide real-time assessment or performance feedback until the season is over.

A winning coach would surely understand who his best players are, and in which positions those players would excel. This coach would surely know if his best player for a task/position were unable to perform and who would be the second most proficient. And if that player were deployed strategically into another needed position, would this coach know who to get, to go three or four levels down and thus into his bench?

Unfortunately, this comparison is not reflective of how most managers operate or have been trained in the workplace today. In many cases, most managers have limited real-time knowledge of who is their best player. For any position, it is merely the evolution of tasks assigned to players that most managers perpetuate daily. And if a manager knows who his best player is for any given need, then let's drill downward and ask if he knows definitively who the second- and third-best "go-to" players are.

Better questions should be how do I objectively assess individuals and benchmark that against needed performance by job expectations or job description and calibrate that in terms of succession development, succession management, and succession planning?

To maximize your time and strategically use the resources at your disposal, consider a few basic objective analysis optics/metrics/diagnostic concepts for identifying and more thoroughly profiling the players on the teams you interact with. To analyze those around you, let's start with some self-analysis and see how objectively you can analyze yourself,

Participate in the following self-profiling exercise. Mentally, if not physically, fill out this inventory. Time yourself for 60 seconds. Focus your attention on the right column and fill in any responses that come to you in connection with the question posed. After the 60 seconds are up, stop writing in the right column and do the same drill for the left column. Don't read the next paragraph until this exercise has been completed.

Consider this same self-awareness drill to be facilitated by each of your direct reports and by every member of your organization, management team, executive ranks, board, and candidates being interviewed for consideration to your organization in the future.

Instrument One: The Self-Analysis Inventory (A.K.A. Ben Franklin Decision-Making Model)

2-Minute Self-Analysis Inventory	
List your attributes/strengths/positive traits:	List your detriments/weaknesses/negative traits:
SCORE:	SCORE:

Go back to the preceding inventory and add up the number of entries for each column. Write that total score at the bottom of the appropriate column. As you look at your total score, which column has more entries? Most people find it easier to respond to the negative or critical analysis side (the right column) and there will be fewer entries for the positive (left) side.

Where did you find yourself? Ultimately, there should be three to five times the number of positive entries as there are negatives. Are you there, or is there some homework ahead for you?

Successful individuals can innately recognize the depth of their strength indexes, and thus draw upon those attributes, skills, abilities, and experiences at the right time for greatest impact. Great leaders can innately do this same drill for those whom they lead, grow, empower, and serve.

Take this same concept one step further. You should conduct a profiling page, such as this one on every direct report or player within your sphere of responsibility. The responses to the questions will give you insight as to what you know and what you don't know professionally about those around you. If you expect to motivate and manage others to greatness, you must first know who they are—inner mettle—and what is important to them—core values and beliefs.

Some valuable insights come from this first analyzing technique. How you see yourself, for example, on the Self Analysis Inventory gives you a better introspective as to how others see you and treat you. Having more initial negative entries than positive entries may be an indicator of low personal self-esteem, self-worth, and self-confidence, and an overall low self-image. This impacts your inner motivation and outward interactions with others. Imagine a coach with a low self-image trying to manage a World Series baseball team.

There are studies that connect personal performance to one's self-image. Judge how you fare against these studies and let that be an indicator as to why we observe player performance to the degree or lack of degree that we do. Consider the following: Robert Schuller in the 1990s commissioned a survey through the Gallup Organization that found that 80 percent of adult Americans view themselves as having low self-esteem. Stanford University polled incoming freshmen and found that those students, among the top in the world, could identify six negatives within themselves for every positive.

Now, 25 years later, all data points show very little forward movement.

In this chapter, there are five objective ways to assess your human capital, so you can manage individuals as talent assets more effectively. Whatever you call these ultimate optics/metrics/diagnostics, they can serve as practitioner-based instruments or models that you can use for better understanding those on your team presently and those you may consider adding to your team in the future. These models allow you to objectively assess the players' potentials and abilities, as well as consider the talent required for any need. Consider each model independently of one another. They are

- **Instrument One**—The Self-Analysis Inventory
- **Instrument Two**—The Player Capability Index
- **Instrument Three**—The TE (team expectations) Factor
- **Instrument Four**—Player-Task Function-Trait Comparison Index
- **Instrument Five**—The All-Star Player Matrix

These models can be used to

- Assess immediate, intermediate, and long-term growth needs for a project, department, business unit, or organization.
- Look at market trends and customer needs as a reference instrument to determine whether, when the future arrives, you and your team will be ready to fulfill those needs.

- Scope a job description.

- Promote and advertise position opportunities.

- Interview, promote, and hire as a template to ensure non-emotionally based decisions.

- Assess transfers, promotions, and assignment dissemination.

- Determine layoffs, downsizing, and elimination matters with staff.

- Assess mergers of talent pools: Who should be in a lead position, and who should be in a facilitator position?

- Facilitate Performance Development Plans (PDPs).

- Facilitate career pathway trajectory, Key Performance Indicators (KPIs), and growth plans.

- Facilitate succession development, management, and planning endeavors.

- Manage your own self-awareness and developmental needs.

As a managerial leader, you need to efficiently analyze the players around you so you can reduce your interaction times (micromanagement avoidance tactic) and more effectively place players in positions that draw upon their strengths, not positions that play upon their weaknesses (mentally or physically).

Instrument Two: The Player Capability Index™

Imagine being able to scope a project, tasked assignment, or craft a thorough real-time based job description. Or imagine a methodical formula for scoping a job opening to find a better pool of prospective candidates for your cause or organization. Maybe your real need is in a better on-boarding process of new talent, to be able to manage that talent acquisition more effectively, generate a better career pathway trajectory, and address succession planning at all levels and with every position, next level leader candidate, and your present managerial-leadership-executive team.

I have learned that understanding the human capital talent whether within an entrepreneur or institutional employee comes down to a simple matrix I have designed and call the *Player Capability Index.*

Your ability to understand objectively within yourself and others the depth of what each letter represents in the Player Capability Index formula will allow you to directly connect to the entrepreneurial energy, capability, and capacity of a person. The letters reveal what contributions may need to be calibrated into a person to enable him to function ahead of market needs tomorrow. The formula:

$$C = (T2+A+P+E+C)\ E2 \times R2 = R$$

- **R=Results.** R appears on the far right side of the equation, the last letter in the formula. Any output or ROI desired is the R. So a delegated assignment, a job description, goals, expectations, work product, and so on are all represented as the R. So how do you get to that R? You must objectively and thoroughly understand the chemistry of the C at the opposite left side of the equation.

- **C = Capability.** This is the driver that enables significant results to be continuously generated or not. The greater the depth of any and every subsequent letter within the parentheses enables the results to actualize. Conversely for the complacent among us, it is the diminished desire to not draw upon any lettered capability driver nor the desire to add any real-time relevant depth to any lettered category that serves as the cancer to entrepreneurialism. So the letters within the parentheses drive the capability level. Knowing what each subsequent letter in the formula represents empowers you to excel or recognize a self-imposed weakness to be addressed or compensated for, and thus a reduction in failure will occur. The formula empowers individuals to assume control of their future by ensuring they are always growing in the present tense to be relevant contributors to society tomorrow. This formula guides thought-based, fact-driven decisions en route to avoiding rhetoric and emotions to cloud one's logical judgment.

- **T2 = Training.** This refers to training as represented by any deliverable of knowledge, whether formal or informal education, technical or nontechnical education, certification driven or simply on-the-job (OTJ) knowledge acquisition. So the letter T in this formula and context represents knowledge acquisition. And knowledge is never ending, continuously evolving to remain relevant and forward prepared.

  The number 2 adjacent to the T simply reminds you of two applications of the T to be considered individually and in growing, developing, and leading others. The first interpretation of the letter T is for past tense context, the total T gained from birth to present tense—so T-1 is past tense training. If you have answers to this first letter, you start to recognize the depth of T that can guide your C (capability) that determines your R (results). If you lack the T to be able to possess the C to deliver on an R or be market relevant in a changing world, then the second T-2 is simply your trajectory indicator of future tense T (training) that you need to seek, engage in, understand, and possess to be an MVP within your organization or for yourself in tomorrow's marketplace.

If an individual or organization possesses a learning culture, mantra, or structure, then T is embraced in real-time, formal, informal, and sequential ways to ensure an educated talent force.

- **A = Attitude.** Attitude is reflected in that which is projected in a sense of confidence or being a winner and not a whiner. The A serves as a driver of passion, desire, commitment, and a sense of belonging to be one's willingness to contribute. A person's willingness to contribute meaningfully to others and an organization is driven by attitude. A presence of servantship and collaboration and execution of the mission statement is A just as a narcissist self-absorbed A detracts. A person radiates her A, and it comes across as either an attractor or a deflector to others.

- **P = Performance.** Performance is reflective in the totality of past accomplishments, records, participations, titles, certifications, leadership, and follower positions that would serve as a mental imprint of self-belief and awareness of what can be done. You can harvest guidance to assist in elevating your C to attain greater R by recognizing your P from immediate past life, the more intermediate past, and even digging deeply into the long-term past for guidance and self-confidence.

As an example, as indicated with T, knowledge is never ending and continuously evolving to remain relevant and forward prepared. Rejecting continued knowledge attainment would be an example of a potentially cancerous negative attitude.

- **E = Experiences.** Experiences from birth to present tense are enormous windows through which individuals see themselves and from which one can draw strategically for entrepreneur Results to attain greater R by recognizing your E from immediate past life, the more intermediate past, and even digging deeply into the long-term past for guidance and self-confidence. Many times your gut instinct from your E sends you soft clues. By sharing the E or in evaluating another person's and recognizing his E, you can use that information (just as from the other letters) to forecast both potential success and possible detriments. Now you can plan more effectively and accordingly.

- **C = Culture.** Awareness from many indicators also calibrates performance and self-worth, what you know you can draw upon, and what you know you can manage. But what you fail to recognize may be the driver of results or implosion. This letter (as with all the letters) is not designed to put the observer into a position of judgment of right versus wrong. This letter and the formula are designed to empower and embolden you to be more objective and provide you with an analytic to be radically more successful. So understanding C allows you to be more informed, and culture can be the imprints upon a person that influence the other letters in the formula and the overall final R of the formula. Cultural drivers are varied, and some may be professional backgrounds, family, community, financial/economic, inspirational, social, health, knowledge/education, spiritual/religion, generational, gender, lifestyle, ethnicity, politics, and many more.

- **E2 = Expectations.** This calibrates what really shows up within a true contributor or the complacent individual. The number 2 reflects the two applications of E. The first interpretation of E-1 is yours. How you see yourself calibrates whether you bring your first-rate game or your second-rate game to the show. In the professional place of application for this formula as an example, there are three applications of E as a minimum that you may allow to influence how you see yourself and thus how you will draw upon your E:

  - **Positional**—The position or role that you expect the other person to participate in will influence how you see the other person and how you will or will not draw upon the depth of each letter within the parentheses as it relates to the other person. Make sure you convey to the other person what your expectations are of him in the position he occupies or is expected to perform.

  - **Organizational**—Beyond the actual "position" one operates from, also ensure you have communicated any additional expectations the organization has of a person and recognize how one is expected to participate and how this will influence how you see the other person and how you will or will not draw upon the depth of each letter within the parentheses.

  - **Personal**—And sometimes you may have additional "personal" expectations of another person above and beyond that spelled out in the "positional" and "organizational" expectations; make sure these are conveyed as well.

The second E-2 is the other person's E. This is critically important because it helps you work with another person. Recognize that you and the other person can attain peak performance when your E is in sync with the other person's E. When they are not in sync, one of the two of you will be disappointed, and a potential conflict may arise. This can even become further compounded if there is a disconnect of any one or a combination of the three interpretations of E, and management misreads a lack of performance for a need to create a Performance Improvement Plan (PIP). So always check to make sure that the meeting of the minds allows for a fluid conversation among participants where everyone's E is calibrated and in sync before results are expected.

Make sure that the other person's three Es are congruent with yours (see the previous "Positional," "Organizational," and "Personal" bullets).

Knowing your expectations and the other person's and calibrating them together allows for entrepreneurial effectiveness.

- **R2 = Relationships.** The final letter in the formula before the equal sign and Results is a force multiplier or accelerator to the depth and meaning of each individual letter that one has. A person can serve as the multiplier to the entire formula, and that is how achievers leverage everything. Or sadly for far too many today their entrepreneurial energy is snuffed out because of the ever-increasing circle of negative influencers and stimulants around them. Recognize the immediate ring of Rs that you or others may have and how those individuals influence your Player Capability Index, how they influence how you see yourself, and how they may be accessed and leveraged for increased impact and ultimate Results.

The number 2 adjacent to the R simply reminds you of two applications of the R to be considered individually and in growing, developing, and leading others. The first interpretation of the letter R is for past tense context, the total R gained from birth to present tense, so R-1 is past tense relationships. So if you have answers to this first letter, you start to recognize the depth of R that can guide your C (capability) that determines your R (results). If you lack healthy or appropriate R to be able to possess the C to deliver on an R or be market relevant in a changing world, the second R-2 is simple as your trajectory indicator of future tense R (relationships) that you need to seek, engage in, understand, and possess to be an MVP within your organization or for yourself in tomorrow's marketplace.

For self-application, consider if you set a goal only to find that you can easily exceed it; was it really a goal at all? Understanding the *solo achiever mind* and how to singularly take control of your destiny by inventing an ever-growing Player Capability Index is the DNA of an individual.

The *Player Capability Index* affords you valuable insight into an individual's strategic and operational DNA, in terms of knowledge, training, and abilities, via her performance history from birth to date. Using this formula as an overlay you can evaluate objectively for insights, facts, and data for greater understanding from sources such as the employee personnel file, accomplishments, awards, degrees, certifications, accolades, press releases, publicities, intellectual property, body-of-work products, patents, trademarks, copyrights, and the performance that you immediately observe. This is enhanced further by what attributions may be made and posted on professional social media sites and walls (that is, LinkedIn, Facebook) as well as personal expectations of the position, the colleagues, supervisors, the organization, and in general terms her overall expectations. When you merge the finding of each variable from the preceding analysis chart, you gain a valuable and powerful picture to tap into of the player on the team.

At the point of any variable in this formula, you can analyze which management style you need to assume to interact with the player, to help her grow and to move toward your management goals and objectives, so as to produce the results required. Another reason for this analysis is that most human problems and errors occur due to a breakdown in one of the variables presented—for example, the ability becomes overshadowed due to a problem or an overburdened P or T or E.

Consider the applications of this index. You can use it to objectively assess:

- Yourself and hold yourself accountable to real-time showcasing of the best of the best of you
- The people on your team you know or don't know
- Prospects that may come onto a team
- A job opening and job description (Remember every letter in the formula should be addressed in a job description.)
- Announcements for new opportunities (Remember every letter in the formula should be addressed in a job posting, and not to just reference the job tasks Results Expected for a candidate, but more importantly the training and real-world applicable performance necessary to be considered. If relevant and applied across all business units,

speak to the capability as well to avoid labor dispute challenges after you hire someone who turns out to be a whiner.)

- People in the interview process, internally or externally applicable (Remember every letter in the formula should be used as past tense and future tense-oriented questions.)
- Performance of individuals for performance reviews
- Performance of individuals for Performance Development Plans
- Performance of individuals for Performance Improvement Plans
- Performance of individuals for positional and career pathway management
- Performance of individuals for positional and organizational succession planning
- The next evolution of thought leaders in your organization, staff to board alignments
- Future market needs and how you will need to manage the human capital talent you need and will lose

And more....

Instrument Three: TE Factor

By understanding the expectation level of each player individually whom you work with, work for, interact and engage with, or lead, you can determine ways to draw upon that individual's energies as one common synergy.

The *Team Expectation* (TE Factor) represents to a managerial leader a way to identify that common thread that holds the team together. Once you have identified the commonalities among the individual players on your team, you can draw upon them, thereby pulling the players collectively together as a cohesive team. Synergy develops!

$$TE \text{ FACTOR Team Expectation} = A+B+C...$$

Team expectations are arrived at by learning more about the people around you, and in that pursuit you may happen upon identifiers for each individual, which may lead to group commonality. Then by taking the common expectation trait from the group you are leading, you can use that variable to bring the players together to create a cohesive unit. These commonalities may come along irregularly, so as a leader, knowing when you have one of them is critical.

When history presents itself as a TE Factor, that is when you launch major initiatives and labor-intense activities. In recent times (go back nearly two decades for an imprint on most workers' psychology), the best example of a TE Factor was after the 9/11 terrorist attacks on America. A classic public service commercial that played on television for years afterward powerfully depicted this. The commercial showed pictures of the horror and damage of the attacks on the World Trade Center, the Pentagon, and the downed plane in Pennsylvania, with a voiceover saying, "They came to change America...." Then, as the picture faded out with those images, another faded in—a row of houses with the American flag waving in front of each. The voiceover came back to say, "And they did!"

For months immediately afterward, if the managerial leader (President Bush) of the organization (the United States of America), with this explosive window of opportunity as the common thread among the majority of Americans, were to say that we were going to attack the planet, everyone would have said, "Let's go!" As it was, cooler heads prevailed at that immediate moment. With that unbridled common energy, it was crucial not to react emotionally but to respond logically. Unfortunately, by the time a game plan was prepared, that common thread or window of opportunity had faded and the TE Factor had diminished greatly. A powerful lesson here: Always remember that the TE Factor comes upon you as a managerial leader quickly and leaves just as fast!

As a managerial leader, you don't want to invest the TE Factor energy in low-level activities; you always want to launch high-yield endeavors when you have those common energies in your presence.

Instrument Four: Player-Task Function-Trait Comparison Index™

Let's go old school for this model; it is a powerful way to slow down and recognize what your organization and you are really doing. You can apply a level of technology to this later.

In many organizations today, the tasks assigned or being addressed by individuals in many cases are not being done by the most qualified or appropriate persons.

Many businesses actually mirror the military and, while the system used for administering functionality within the military for the past 200 years works, the world has changed and a new model is a reality. For example, in the military, for an individual to ascend and be promoted, she is in many cases taken directly out of her center of knowledge, experience, and proficiency. To get promoted, the person often is transferred to wherever that higher rank and position are open. I once had a client who had been trained for his entire tour in the military in the medical corps. Yet to be promoted into a senior officer position (white-collar position), he was promoted and transferred into a recruiting command position (that is, selling and marketing). This begs the question, "Who is working in the hospital—the motor pool?"

Because of this standard operating procedure (SOP) and tradition within the military, the largest business employer in America, these norms, policies, habits, and models have been replicated in far too many instances within the commercial world. Then these habit-bearing approaches have in many instances manifested into the Peter Principle: Eventually, good, competent people will be promoted up and out of their realm of ability and into places of complete incompetence!

To address this issue on a logical level, there needs to be a computerized or even an old pencil-and-paper approach to gaining a better understanding of the actual requirements for the core functionalities of an organization or a business unit. Then the results could be used as a cross reference for the actual talent pool you possess, versus that which you may need to acquire (whether for short-term use or long-term acquisition).

The Player-Task Function-Trait Comparison Index serves as a powerful and fast model for evaluating individuals, tasks, and essential traits necessary for success. An objective eye can then see who should really be doing what, where, and when. To administer this approach, start by doing the following:

1. List all the primary functions, roles, and responsibilities required in facilitating your organization's business—a list of job functions, in essence, without identifying anyone's name on the team. List those job functions, duties, responsibilities, skills, and so on on an electronic spreadsheet, a piece of paper, or one entry per index card. When you have identified all the preceding entries, place that list or stack to the side.

2. Write the name of every player on your team or in your organization on a separate piece of paper or on individual index cards as well. Then default to Instrument One: The Self-Analysis Inventory detailed previously in this chapter. Run that model for each player in question and detail the quantity and quality of data appropriate to that person.

3. When you have completed these two steps, you will have two stacks or piles. The third step is to set out all the cards or papers side-by-side. Take the list of organizational duties and place one at a time on the

paper with the person's name who is realistically most qualified to deal with it—regardless of whether he is the player currently taking care of it.

Player "A"	Player "B"	Unmatched Tasks/etc.

4. Once this is completed, you can move forward by realizing that to truly lead a peak-performing team, you must recognize whether you or your organization has been inadvertently working against yourselves by tasking ineffective people. This also gives you perspective as to which of the six managerial leadership styles need to be assumed.

The default outcome from this analysis is to recognize that for every task item left over in the unmatched stack, you have to assume the position of manager or teacher and train someone, hire someone, outsource to facilitate that item, or possibly eliminate the task if in your new reality it no longer serves a purpose.

Now with any items that have been attributed to nontraditional players, you can decide if that is where they really should be (delegated, tasked, assigned, flowed, and so on), or whether you need to entrust the players to train and motivate other players to rise to new levels of organizational ability and to enable others to perform at the level of expectation at which you want them to.

Other items will fall to players you had not thought of assigning to the tasks before. This helps you realize that many times managers become habit-bound and assign items to players out of habit with little regard to whether they are the most qualified to do the jobs.

Finally, you will have items left over that don't make sense for this team to address. Or, you'll have players left over with no items on their names. In this case, either training needs to take place with a player to get him up to speed for facilitating those leftover items, or horizontal or vertical movement of that player needs to take place.

This last technique is perhaps the most powerful, objective way to go about shaking up an entire organization (including you) to arrive at a new one that is realigned for greater success, centers of greater efficiency, increased productivity, and enhanced profitability for the future.

Think of it this way: It is like taking the names of all the players in your organization and putting them on the reverse sides of jigsaw puzzle pieces. Then you put each individual piece in a paper sack. You shake that sack up and let all the names fall out. Now put the puzzle back together the right way, with only the appropriate positions and functionality of what your organization would look like if you were to create it today instead of how it was thrown together initially.

If you have the luxury of responsibility and the power or flexibility to utilize a technique, such as this last one (after you have determined each player's strengths, weaknesses, abilities, and expectations), you will find that significant organizational growth, productivity, and team spirit develops.

Looking from within also helps answer what you need to look at from the outside to complement your team for future growth and success. Consider the number of personal experiences you've had in your professional career: Interviewing a prospect for your team (or interviewing by team approach a candidate for a team you are a part of), extending an offer to the prospect, and then having him turn out to be a terrorist, after you have hired and placed the new employee on the team. It seems that while we work hard to develop current players in an organization, management keeps hiring more nightmares for the team—terrorists and transmitters.

Many of the same organizations that experience the pain of misguided interviews, as seen in high turnover statistics nationally, actually have scripted interviews. The players who conduct the interviews are not even trusted by the organizations to do fact-finding and are relegated to asking a series of predesigned questions. The prospect's responses are then graded against a score sheet. Prospects who reach certain numerical levels are taken to another level in the interview, while those who score below those levels are declined further interviews. In the attempt to find the right candidate who fits an organization's needs (technically, intellectually, academically, skill-wise, and so on), many of these "right" players are hired, but they are the very ones who actually hold an organization back from actualizing true success.

Organizations and managers have been conditioned through years of wanna-be managers and consultants (people who want to be professionals, yet their resumes can be written without using an entire sticky note) to look for candidates and prospects who fit a certain organizational profile—and are technically qualified for the organization's needs.

In fact, what organizations are really looking for in a potentially successful prospect has little to do with what you might initially feel organizations are looking for. So how do we make sense out of this last statement? Consider the following instrument as an exercise and you will see the answer.

Instrument Five: All-Star Player

This instrument is a way to identify what you are really looking for in an ideal new player for an organization. You can perform this drill by yourself. Have colleagues and coworkers participate as well.

Start by identifying whether you are analyzing a specific position in need or merely looking at an overview of an individual to integrate to your team overall. On the following chart, write in any response to the question given. There are no right or wrong responses—merely responses. Once you have an exhaustive list of several All-Star Traits, proceed to the next paragraph.

All-Star Player Winning Traits
If you were interviewing a player for consideration on your team, what are the traits that you would be looking for, and if she possessed these traits or characteristics, would you feel you had found a winning player for your organization?
MEASURING KEY: A =   **S =**

With those responses filled in on the chart, go back and qualify each entry individually with the following measuring key. Place an A or an S adjacent to each entry. Then do the math and place your score in these two categories at the bottom of the score grid: "A" for Attitude and "S" for Skill.

Notice from your entries what makes for a winning player in your organization. Which letter comes up the most?

What you will find as you do this exercise, individually or as a team effort with your colleagues, is that the dominant response—what you and everyone are really looking for—is a winning attitude. With a positive attitude, practically all training and education of a player can occur; with a negative or bad attitude, training and education are an uphill challenge.

In conducting this exercise with managers (a manager is defined here as anyone in any position with responsibility for other players and/or who has other players reporting to him) across the world, the collective responses always take them back to the bottom line, measuring key response. What people are really looking for are attitude traits and not skill/knowledge traits if a choice has to be made between the two.

So how do you find these attitude traits in candidates? That answer is really easier than you might expect. First, recognize the nuances of your organization, industry, and geography, as in many places there are rules, regulations, and even laws that prohibit you in the interview stage from asking the legitimate questions a business owner or leader should be able to ask to develop a truly cohesive, winning team. In spite of the mediocre individuals (terrorists to capitalism) who legislate what can be asked, you can still be successful.

The bottom line to both every position for business today and any interview situation for management is to determine two answers. Every person must answer these two items, or the consideration of why he or she is on your team should be discussed. The two critical core questions today are

- How can this player help the organization make or save money?
- How can this player help the organization increase productivity and efficiency?

Every position in an organization ultimately comes down to these two variables. If a player does neither, then what purpose does the player serve?

And in tight economic situations, with the necessity for lean organizations, the players management must keep first are those who answer the question(s) correctly. To remain economically viable as a business and thus a contributor to one's community, this exercise must be done regardless of past efficiencies, redundancies, union beliefs, EEOC mandates, or other legislative edicts.

In your attempt to find candidates who answer those two questions most effectively, remember what you identified earlier as desired traits for a winning player. In every interview situation, along with the other questions you pose to the player in front of you, listen to the responses as you search for answers to the preceding two questions, and identify two answers that come from every question in life anyway!

Every question you pose to players already on your team, and to those individuals you consider adding to your team, affords you two insights.

Ask them to tell you their qualities.

- **The *Skill* aspect**—The technical answers you seek are in the actual words out of their mouths.

- The *Attitude* aspect—Listen to the tone of their voices in the responses they give you, and watch their body language. This gives you an insight into their attitudes, and thus the attitudes they may have if made active players on your team.

Identifying the attitude level of a player is critical to effective management—both in the players on your team now and in those individuals you may consider adding to your team in the future.

With the proper and thorough analysis of the players who constitute your team comes the aggressive development of those players. When organizations invest in their players to develop them, the return on that investment is almost always greater than any losses.

Player development is critical to organizational success and to the overall effectiveness and success of the winning coach today. By using all these instruments as objective templates for analysis, you can benchmark your status quo and gauge your forward movement toward continual success.

Being committed to the development of all the players on your team(s) is what differentiates the managerial leader greatness within you from that of a mere administrator or bureaucrat in an organization striving to just get by daily.

Managerial Leadership Bible Lesson Six

Optimal performances by managerial leaders and from the members of the team are continuously appraised, developed, held accountable, and grown for future needs and successes. Managerial leaders have multiple instruments that can be used mentally and physically, to determine how best to assess the individuals they are responsible for, so as to always remain objective in this thorough analysis.

With these instruments managerial leaders can deploy individuals as personnel assets and task projects to them accordingly.

Review Questions

The review questions accompanying each chapter or section are designed to assist you in achieving the learning objectives stated at the beginning of each chapter. The review section is not graded; do not submit it in place of your final exam. While completing the review questions, it may be helpful to study any unfamiliar terms in the glossary in addition to course content. After completing the review questions for each chapter, proceed to the review question answers and rationales.

1. In his discussion of analyzing player performance, the author cites studies that connect personal performance to one's _____.

   A. Education

   B. Self-image

   C. Organizational skills

   D. Age

2. _____ is projected by tone of voice, body language, posture, motivation, assertiveness, desire, and so on.

   A. Training

   B. Performance

   C. Expectations

   D. Attitude

3. Which profiling formula helps to create synergy?

   A. The Player Capability Index

   B. Player-Task Function-Trait Comparison Index

   C. The All-Star Player

   D. The TE Factor

4. In many organizations today, the tasks assigned to or being addressed by individuals in many cases are not being done by the most qualified or appropriate persons.

   A. True

   B. False

5. Player _____ is critical to organizational success and to the overall effectiveness and success of the winning coach today.

   A. Education

   B. Attitude

   C. Development

   D. Likeability

Review Question Answers and Rationales

Review question answer choices are accompanied by unique, logical reasoning (rationales) as to why an answer is correct or incorrect. Evaluative feedback to incorrect responses and reinforcement feedback to correct responses are both provided.

1. In his discussion of analyzing player performance, the author cites studies that connect personal performance to one's _____.

   A. Incorrect. Education may have little or no impact on one's self-image.

   B. Correct. No matter your other abilities, a poor self-image undermines them all.

   C. Incorrect. While they are important, you can organize a lot of things, but with a negative self-image you may feel your work is unimportant or insufficient.

   D. Incorrect. Age has negligible impact on self-image.

2. _____ is projected by tone of voice, body language, posture, motivation, assertiveness, desire, and so on.

   A. Incorrect. Training is displayed by degrees, certificates, and education.

   B. Incorrect. While performance may affect attitude, performance is projected by projects completed.

   C. Incorrect. A manager has many ways to explain expectations besides attitude.

   D. Correct. Attitude is an excellent way to assess an employee's willingness to draw upon his training.

3. Which profiling formula helps to create synergy?

   A. Incorrect. Synergy cannot be established by analyzing one specific player.

   B. Incorrect. Synergy cannot be established by analyzing one specific player.

   C. Incorrect. Synergy cannot be established by analyzing one specific player.

   D. Correct. By finding commonalities between employees, a manager can utilize the commonalities to help employees work together.

4. In many organizations today, the tasks assigned to or being addressed by individuals in many cases are not being done by the most qualified or appropriate persons.

   A. **Correct. Due to ineffective interviewing and inattention to employees' skills, tasks are assigned randomly instead of effectively.**

   B. Incorrect. The high turnover rate in businesses today is a result of poor employee placement.

5. Player _____ is critical to organizational success and to the overall effectiveness and success of the winning coach today.

   A. Incorrect. Education is only the beginning for employee development.

   B. Incorrect. By following the profiles discussed in this chapter, attitude can change drastically and is part of employee development.

   C. **Correct. Being committed to the development of all the players on your team(s) is what differentiates the managerial leader greatness within you from that of a mere administrator or bureaucrat.**

   D. Incorrect. Whether a player is liked by other employees can be changed through development.

7

Sustaining Your Professional Success Quotient

Always bear in mind that your own resolution to succeed is more important than any one thing.

—**Abraham Lincoln**

Learning Objective

After completing this section of the course, you will be able to describe personal and organizational systems to promote success.

s a managerial leader, your ability to maintain personal balance; stay focused on productivity endeavors; and avoid time wasters, situations, and people that zap you is critical to leading a winning team.

To maintain perspective and keep the professional flame within you burning hot, you must sustain your success levels through a definite mental perspective that allows you to focus, focus, focus.

There are several ways you can go about maintaining a focus and sustaining both the personal and professional success levels you desire. You can maintain your professional quotient in several ways:

- By developing your own professional mission statement and referencing it regularly to ensure that you are on track with whom you associate and in what you indulge yourself (as developed in Chapter 2, "Five Mission Statements for Ultimate 'New View' Success").

- By developing and associating with powerful positive centers of influence (COIs), such as colleagues, mentors, advisers, associations, networks, and the FIST FACTOR® (presented in Chapter 3, "The FIST FACTOR®, Your Mental Board of Directors").

- By focusing your energies and efforts around those strengths you possess (training, attitudes, and professional experiences, as presented in Chapter 6, "Analyzing Players and Prospects for Team Success").

- By designing downtime or recharging time for you and your fellow managers.

- And, through the use of organizational management systems, you can maintain a balance among all these elements.

On a daily operational basis as a managerial leader and stakeholder within your organization, you need some sort of a system to manage yourself, your workload, and the demands that others around you place upon you. To sustain your focus in the face of daily demands, unexpected issues, urgencies, emergencies, and unplanned interruptions, recognize that all organization workflow can be attributed to one of four specific acts that consume our time—they are activities *to do*, people we need *to see*, individuals we need *to call*, or activities that require us *to write*.

High-impact leaders innately accomplish those items that yield the greatest bottom-line output, and in doing so they seem to continually elevate themselves and the organizations they lead. Regardless of what system or instrument you or your organization uses, the choice you make should allow you to monitor workflow and sort it into four core categories: do, see, call, and write.

One technique that affords you the objective ability to prioritize your workflow by important or urgent work items and gives you daily professional control is a time management tool called the Quadrant Manager™. This tool can be done on a blank piece of scrap paper, on a note card system, directly in a day-planner device, and on electronic systems as well. The system must be easy to use, monitor, and deploy, or you will not be able to sustain it, a catalyst to both individual and organizational dysfunction.

Let's develop the Quadrant Manager tool for your immediate use and design ways by which you can implement it today.

As professionals and especially from the level of managerial leaders, the four core areas in which we concentrate our working time daily, into which all work-related items can be categorized, are to do, to see, to call, to write (see Figure 7.1).

DAILY PRIORITIES!
Create three entries for each quadrant; then prioritize.

_____	_____
_____	_____
TO DO	**TO SEE**
TO CALL	**TO WRITE**
_____	_____
_____	_____
_____	_____

Figure 7.1 Quadrant Manager tool

In other words, every day we have items that we have to do. Every day we have items that dictate we see other individuals. Every day we have people we have to contact/call to facilitate work. And every day we also have things we need to write, finish, draft, authorize, and review. The Quadrant Manager system may look as simple as the diagram shown in Figure 7.1. You can convert this to a sticky note pad or add it to your technology suite.

To maximize the use of a Quadrant Manager system, follow these four steps for peak performance:

1. Mentally or physically identify the four categories that comprise the system: do, see, call, and write.

2. Enter items into each category in multiples of three as they come to you without numbering the entries. Merely log in the appropriate entries via dash, dot, line, star, and so on—no numbers.

How do you arrive at what should be entered into this system? Weigh any potential entry against the question, "What is most important: If I could work on three, complete three, or address three, which three items would I select from the total items that could be listed?"

3. Once you have your items listed in the appropriate categories, go back and look at each entry. Number them in order of importance, with a number 1, 2, and 3 only (an entry that is written first in a category may not end up with the number 1 next to it).

   If you have more than three entries in any one category, leave entries number 4 onward unnumbered. Place a number 1 next to the entry that is the most critical and important one in that respective category, to be taken care of either today or in preparing for tomorrow's work, thus becoming the number 1 for tomorrow. In essence, you will have four number 1s on this chart, one for each category—Do, See, Call, Write.

4. Start on your number 1s. Don't allow yourself or anyone else to side-track you to any other item until you have completed your four number 1s—or have progressed as far as you can on any specific number 1. As long as you are working the number 1s, and then on your number 2s, you are working on the most important items. Maintain your success quotient by maintaining focus.

Another way you can use the Quadrant Manager system is to enter your items into the four categories. Then go to each of the four, realizing that sometimes one category of work may take priority over another; in those situations you may also want to prioritize the categories themselves by entering 1, 2, 3, 4 in the center shaded zone. This directs you to focus on the entries in category 1 before proceeding on to the next three.

This is truly the most powerful day-planner and day-organizer system you can utilize, as this is how your brain categorizes your daily work anyway—do, see, call, write.

Keeping your own professional flame burning has a lot to do with sustaining your success quotient. Consider your management behavior patter, for example, in terms of how you typically start your day. For many managers, a day starts off by your immediately being cornered by a terrorist when you walk in the office door in the morning. Or the first items on your daily "to do" list are the problem issues or problem players. If this sounds familiar, ask yourself this question: If you are immediately interacting with these people and situations at the beginning of your workday, what does this interaction and person do to your attitude? High attitude equals high productivity; low attitude equals low productivity, for us and the players we interact with.

Sustain your daily success quotient by changing this behavior pattern. Make a behavior paradigm shift toward a different standard morning pattern. Unless a life is critically attached to your immediate action, you should never walk in the door in the morning and interact with a problem, a challenge, or especially with a terrorist.

To sustain success and model success for others around you to replicate, the first people for you to interact with each day (whether for ten seconds, ten minutes or one hour, it doesn't matter) are your transformers. Then interact with the transmitters on your team, as they are waiting for someone to influence their daily actions. This better be you or a fellow transformer, and not left up to the terrorists! Then when you have a controlled positive interaction, thus reinforcing your positive attitude and behavior, go and interact with challenges, problems, and terrorists.

By seeing a transformer first every day, you are given a mental and physical tune-up for that day. As management, it is critical to remember that our players look to us for a hint as to what attitude and performance to have each day. If we are down, they are down; if we are up, they are typically up. Surround yourself with other positive influences, and they will consciously and subconsciously help you sustain your success quotients.

Another paradigm shift that management needs to experience to sustain personal and professional success is in one's belief system.

For decades, psychology modeled a path of human behavior pattern changes via the focus on one's own behavior. That behavior is what others are responding to, whether it is either creating a positive or negative atmosphere. In management, then, managers were taught that to stimulate a change in a player's behavior, first change your own. While this variable is factual, another perspective should be added to the ABC Model of Human Behavior, designed in 1943 by psychologist Albert Ellis. We show another application to this in Chapter 19, "The Trajectory Code Model."

The ABC Model offers an explanation for human behavior and suggests how to best influence and interact with another person by asserting that each letter of the model represents the following:

A	B	C
A +	B =	C
ACTIVATING EVENT(S) BEHAVIOR CONSEQUENCE(S)		

The point of the model is that in life, there are and will be activating events that you have no control over. All the energy expended in the world won't change what has happened. Yet many people (managers) spend time trying to redo and undo what has been done, with total failure. In life, there are be consequences and those also cannot be changed. However, it is your own behavior in response to those activating events that causes the consequences. Address and change your own behavior first (which is the only factor you truly have 100 percent control over in life) and the consequences will begin to change as well.

An application of this ABC Model would be in managing or stimulating change. As presented previously, to facilitate the change process, it starts with *awareness* of a need to change. When that is attained people progress to the level of *interaction/intervention* on how to change. When that makes sense, people *commit* to the change. In applying the ABC model, it is all about your behavior and what you do to constructively encourage, motivate, and sustain forward progressive change as the managerial leader.

Behavior is influenced by one's beliefs and belief system. By understanding what your true beliefs are and what shapes them, you gain a better understanding of your behaviors and why they come about. It is your beliefs about circumstances and people, and your expectations that trigger your behaviors.

By becoming more aware of what your beliefs are and how they trigger certain behavioral responses, as a manager you can identify which beliefs are accurate and which are erroneous—thus enabling you to modify behaviors for differing consequences (outcomes) in life.

By helping you understand the link between beliefs and behaviors and their respective impact, the ABC Model of Human Behavior allows you to maintain and sustain your success quotient and to stimulate energy in the ways you interact in life.

As the leader of systems and people, maintaining focus and peak performance levels also has to do with self "quiet" time. Many times management personnel find themselves mentally zapped of energy and motivation, when anger, hostility, conflict, stress, and confrontations take place within the professional workplace. The ability to maintain personal control over these situations also greatly impacts your success ratios and your ability to sustain lasting personal and professional success.

Several techniques can be instantly utilized to gain or regain control over your emotions and challenged behavior patterns to allow your logic to reign superior. Management, of all organizational players, has to be able to maintain a public face of focus, stability, and concentration, if its expectation of its players is to do the same. Remember that players typically reflect the actions and attitudes around them.

To energize your cells and maintain management control in challenging situations, consider the following techniques for powering down for a more efficient startup. When faced with a computer problem, you power it down and start back up anew. The same paradigm applies to managing people and organizations. Sometimes what serves an individual and organization best is to focus energies away from what may have a person challenged and stressed for a period of time and toward something different. Readdressing the stimulant with a new view and approach results in greater successes. The following techniques for powering down refocus mental energies for a greater end result:

- **Breathing pattern adjustments**—Take a period of time (60 seconds or more) and adjust your breathing pattern sequences. Typically, when one becomes threatened or stressed, the breathing pattern becomes hurried and draws upon one of the two breathing passages (in and out through only one's mouth or nose). With such adjustments, you are going to force yourself to consciously inhale each breath (slowly/gradually) through your nose, hold it for a few seconds, and then gradually exhale through your mouth. Repeat this gradual pattern for 60 seconds or more. By changing the breathing pattern, this inhale-and-exhale sequence slows down your heart rate and mental rate. Thus, physiologically, your metabolism slows down and the new state of calm affords you clearer thinking abilities.

- **Mental imagery**—Take an extended period of time (two, three, or even five minutes) and close your eyes in a quiet place. Reflect upon a different environment that reminds you of a more pleasing experience. For example, if you have recently been on a vacation, remind yourself of it through your mental imagery of those experiences (turn your mental VCR to *play*). Get vivid; remind yourself of the sights you saw, the smells you smelled, the sounds you heard, the tastes you tasted, and the things you felt. By conscious stimulation of the five core body sensors, you can stimulate self-relaxation.

- **Countdown**—To gain control over emotionally piqued anger, pick a number (try 100) and begin counting down toward zero. By immediately and consciously focusing your mind off a challenged stimulant and toward something else, by the time you reach zero, you will more often than not have calmed yourself down and gained needed self-control and management control for a more efficient interaction with others.

- **60-second power vacation**—Try this powerful technique and form of self-meditation. You are and will be in complete control of yourself throughout the duration of this exercise. This is one of the most powerful ways to refocus your mind and body for greater energy and sustained success in professional (and personal) environments. To imitate this technique, there are only five requirements. You can also expand the concept and the manner in which you use this technique to gain greater self-rewards through meditation.

To evoke this technique, consider these steps for implementation success: First, secure an environment where you will not be disturbed and it is as quiet as you can possibly get it, for a few minutes. Second, give yourself a period of 60 seconds or so on a clock (or a timer/buzzer). Third, close your eyes and recall the mental imagery of a great vacation or experience in your past. Put yourself back into the imagery that you are recalling and experience the entire positive, pleasurable experiences that you did earlier. This will begin psychologically to calm and relax you. Fourth, adjust your breathing pattern sequence for the duration of this exercise. This will begin to relax you physically. Fifth, establish a slow return from this vacation, back to your immediate environment, where you must return to interaction with others for success.

This is also a relaxing soother as you soak in a hot bath at the end of the day, prior to going to sleep. Put your mind and body into a state conducive for relaxation and sleep, and you will experience a more restful night, which in turn gives you greater energy.

- **Diet and meals**—In the workplace, especially, maintain awareness of what you eat and drink, as much of the intake during the day directly relates to how one acts and reacts. For example, to maintain control in high-stress environments, minimize stimulants, such as caffeine, nicotine, and sugars.

  Common sense needs to reign here, so watch your habit patterns. You can fall victim to adding additional stress and inner stress through what you eat and drink during the day.

- **Forced tensors**—Another powerful physical technique for realigning your energies away from stress and toward success, away from anger and exhaustion and toward control and vigor, is the use of forced tensors. This is a refreshing technique that can be utilized during the day anywhere one might be (sitting at a desk, sitting in a meeting, standing in a hallway, riding in an elevator, waiting in a line, sitting in traffic in a car, and so on).

The purpose of this technique is to stimulate maximum energy toward one physical activity. Through a repetitive sequence, you conclude the activity with a new mental and physical view. This allows you to draw upon the energy of the body's muscles and at the same time serves as a pseudo-exercise workout.

Start by adjusting your breathing pattern to a count of ten. As you mentally count to five, inhale and at the same time tense up your body and every muscle within it (tighten your legs, arms, and make a fist). At the count of five, hold your breath and the tense-muscle state you have attained, then resume the count toward ten and start to relax gradually, as you exhale from the hold. Repeat this pattern for a minimum of ten times. At the conclusion, you will feel a different kind of tiredness and, at the same time, a different kind of energy level.

- **Private isolation time**— Every key manager knows the value of isolation time. Whether this time is used for work, brainstorming, and reflection or merely self-time, insist upon regular isolation time for yourself each day to enable you to maintain control and focus.

Management needs to ensure that it allows self-time for focusing and regaining self-control when pressed into challenging situations. When balancing the six primary management styles with the five organizational levels (see Chapter 8, "Your Five Organizational Levels of Operation"), these techniques will help.

As a managerial leader, your worth to your team is limited if you are mentally and physically exhausted, so ensure that you maintain professional focus for sustained success.

Managerial Leadership Bible Lesson Seven

The sound, balanced, effective managerial leader today and tomorrow is able to remain focused on what really matters and avoids the little stuff. Individuals charged with leading others to greatness continually reflect upon what they have influence and control over—themselves—and work to remain energized at all times.

Review Questions

The review questions accompanying each chapter or section are designed to assist you in achieving the learning objective stated at the beginning of each chapter. The review section is not graded; do not submit it in place of your final exam. While completing the review questions, it may be helpful to study any unfamiliar terms in the glossary in addition to course content. After completing the review questions for each chapter, proceed to the review question answers and rationales.

1. Which is one of the categories of the Quadrant Manager system?

    A. Who

    B. What

    C. Where

    D. Write

2. To sustain and model success, the first people to interact with each day are your _____.

    A. Terrorists

    B. Transformers

    C. Star players

    D. Transmitters

3. The _____ system offers an explanation for human behavior and suggests how to best influence and interact with another person.

    A. ABC Model of Human Behavior

    B. Powering down

    C. Quadrant Manager™

    D. 60-second power vacation™

4. Which system is used to readdress challenges and problems with a new view?

    A. ABC Model of Human Behavior

    B. Powering down

    C. Quadrant Manager

    D. 60-second power vacation

5. Which of these is a requirement for the 60-second power vacation?

    A. Look at a photo.

    B. Use an alarm clock

    C. Secure an environment

    D. Take a day off

6. Your diet can affect your managerial abilities.

    A. True

    B. False

Review Question Answers and Rationales

Review question answer choices are accompanied by unique, logical reasoning (rationales) as to why an answer is correct or incorrect. Evaluative feedback to incorrect responses and reinforcement feedback to correct responses are both provided.

1. Which is one of the categories of the Quadrant Manager system?

    A. Incorrect. This is part of the W, W, W, W, W, H system.

    B. Incorrect. This is part of the W, W, W, W, W, H system.

    C. Incorrect. This is part of the W, W, W, W, W, H system.

    D. Correct. The other three are Call, Do, and See.

2. To sustain and model success, the first people to interact with each day are your _____.

    A. Incorrect. These are the people you want to meet with last or you will start your day ineffectively.

    B. Correct. By meeting with transformers, you can have a "mental tune-up."

    C. Incorrect. This term is used for creating the best potential candidate during interviews.

    D. Incorrect. Transmitters are below transformers, but are equally helpful.

3. The _____ system offers an explanation for human behavior and suggests how to best influence and interact with another person.

    A. Correct. This system was designed in 1943 by psychologist Albert Ellis.

    B. Incorrect. This is a system for relaxation.

    C. Incorrect. This system is for making better to-do lists.

    D. Incorrect. This is a system for relaxation.

4. Which system is used to readdress challenges and problems with a new view?

    A. Incorrect. This system allows you to understand why you and others behave under different circumstances.

    B. Correct. This system "reboots" the mind to allow a manager to start over in his or her thought process.

    C. Incorrect. This system shows you how to make the best to-do list.

    D. Incorrect. This system is only one part of powering down; there are many other subgroups.

5. Which of these is a requirement for the 60-second power vacation?

    A. Incorrect. You use a mental image, not a physical one.

    B. Incorrect. This exercise is for relaxation, not sleeping.

    C. Correct. To properly relax, you need an environment free from distraction.

    D. Incorrect. Since this process should take about a minute it is for refreshing you at work.

6. Your diet can affect your managerial abilities.

    A. Correct. Maintaining a proper diet can help maintain your awareness.

    B. Incorrect. Stimulants such as coffee or sugar can diminish your management capabilities.

8

Your Five Organizational Levels of Operation

The difference between success and failure is the amount of energy. You decide whether to channel that energy toward a positive or negative point.

Managerial leadership is one of the easiest positions to which an individual can ascend, if an individual will recognize that the ability to ask questions to determine answers is paramount to success, and as an individual, having the answer at the outset is not always necessary.

—Jeff Magee

Learning Objective

After completing this section of the course, you will be able to integrate previous chapters into practical application.

With the tenets, presented in Chapter 5, "Five Differing Organizational Structures and Levels," and Chapter 6, "Analyzing Players and Prospects for Team Success," detailing effective managerial leadership behaviors and actions, your ability to recognize in any given situation which management style (or hat) to use, given the organizational structure or operational need, will lead to greater levels of leadership success.

As a leader, the ability to have a heightened strategic awareness of both internal and external happenings will greatly assist in your ability to design, implement, and facilitate success. Earlier chapters of *The Managerial Leadership Bible* presented a multitude of strategic planning ideas and instruments. These have been time-tested with the leading Fortune 100 firms and the Department of Defense over the past decade and have withstood times of change and resistance to deliver lasting results.

In this chapter, we blend the five organizational operational levels with the six managerial leadership engagement styles for maximum efficiencies within your immediate business unit and in an overall business operation. This area of the book focuses efforts on actual tactical application techniques for maximizing interactions among players (colleague-to-colleague) and within structures (player-to-superior). Depending upon which of the following levels you find yourself in at any given time, you are limited by what you have control over and what you merely have influence over.

Understanding these five levels and your ability to mentally forecast what may draw you in and ways to progress beyond each level is critical to effective managerial-leadership effectiveness. If you are not able to maintain a 30,000 foot macro perspective, you can get drawn into any one of these levels, and far too often the incorrect level, and your time will be consumed. The collateral damage associated with the misspent time can have far-reaching impact on systems, operations, and people.

Let's take each level, described in Table 8.1, one at a time and explain what takes place within each, and how you can manage it, or it will manage you.

Start with Level One—Begin (manager, teacher).

Table 8.1   The Five Organizational Operational Levels

Level	Characteristics
Begin	Formation or startup stage, expectations developed.
	Introduction of new policies, ground rules, procedures, memos, products, services, meetings, beginning of the day or week, etc. 80%-10%-10% all live here.
	Hiring of a new player, interviews, etc.
	Transfer of a player and the receipt of that new person into your area, department, team, work, unit, etc.
	Brainstorming session, designing mission statements, setting objectives and goals into motion.
Defend	Conflict in meeting, someone challenges a new policy, procedure, idea, rule, etc.
	Terrorist (10%) on the loose in your organization.
	Delegation disaster.
	Breakdown in interactions and communication.
	Tension among players calls for patience.
	Lack of commitment among players toward something and a feeling of forced defense of positions.

Level	Characteristics
Blend	Things begin to come together and get done, norms. Players are falling into a flow, pacing. Decisions take less time to make. Your transformers are taking the lead and the transmitters/followers are falling in behind them. Productivity is maintaining your status quo, and routine expectations are met.
Transcend	Some players attain peak performance, rise above the rest. Your results and expectations are exceedingly high. Players are interacting with low stress, little tension, and effective communication, and decisions are being made jointly among the players at this level. Commitment to decisions is attained. Players perform outside boundaries to attain results with no complaints. Players assume responsibility and accountability, and the team is moving ahead of competition and beyond status quo.
End	Analysis is allowed to take place at conclusions for better planning of future actions. You are able to monitor and modify for tomorrow. Final analysis activities, lessons learned, benchmarking.

Begin Stage Managerial Leadership Hints

Remember, the more involvement you have with your team, the more you increase the likelihood you are maintaining too much control (remember the Management/Team Control Model or Span-of-Control Index®) and that you are participating significantly more in the actual work processes than you need to or should be. The more you release controls to the players on the team, the more ownership players assume in their work and the overall organization.

The more ownership players assume, the greater player participation becomes, the greater results are attained, and the more a team develops from the traditional work organization. The more a team develops, the more interaction and synergy takes place, leading ultimately to greater efficiency and effectiveness—increased profitability, increased growth, and decreased downtime.

As you flex your management styles within the five organizational levels, always keep an eye open to your three subgroups of people (transmitters/transformers/terrorists) that you will find in the Begin stage environment. To maximize your time and the efficient use of your players, especially in Level One, interact accordingly with your three subgroups. Get buy-in or alliances with transformers ahead of time, so as to establish the pregroup dynamics you need to manage or eliminate any opportunity to undermine your starting efforts in the Begin stage.

You can evaluate the five organizational levels. Match each level where the four quadrants of the Grief Cycle align. This gives you an indicator as to which players you can cultivate (transmitters), which to empower and have lead the team (transformers), and which (terrorists) to isolate, eliminate, terminate, or interact with (as a counselor) for behavior and team dynamic changes.

Typically, the 80 percent subgroup—transmitters—fall within the first three levels of Table 8.1. They never really get up to the complete, independent speed of the Transcend level. The 10 percent subgroup, which challenges and slows down the processes—terrorists—typically get tied down in Levels Two and Three, Defend and Blend. The remaining 10 percent subgroup—your transformers—typically become irritated when tied down in Levels Two and Three, and typically operate at Levels Four and Five.

Typically, no one really likes Level One, Begin. This level usually means the beginning and that implies something new. When you bring a team or players together for a meeting or briefing to present new policies/procedures/forms and paper workflows, and so on or send out a memo, it means a change from the status quo. Most players don't have the capacity to independently determine whether that change is going to be pleasure or pain. In Level One, the terrorists become energized and are management's biggest challenge when confronted. Terrorist interaction then immediately leads you into Level Two, Defend.

To avoid this negativity and defensive interaction and meltdown, focus your energies on designing a winning structure for the interactions within Level One. Continue your planning processes in each organizational level to ensure peak performance within each. Most managers typically rush into beginning activities. This instant interaction, due to pressing deadlines and heavy workloads, is exactly what contributes to a less than 100 percent success attainment on the activities and projects that grow out of the startup stage.

View the beginning stage as the foundation upon which you plan to erect a skyscraper. With the proper foundation you can build to the stars; with a poor one the smallest factor can cause the structure to tumble downward.

To start off any organization, there are times when the management hat you must wear is that of manager or teacher. Some examples of Level One activities requiring the management style of a manager or teacher are the following:

- The beginning of a day, week, or meeting
- A new player on a team (hiring, transfer, promotion)
- A new client/customer/vendor relationship
- A new project or work assignment

In essence, when you have your first interaction or relationship with someone or something, you find yourself at Level One, Begin. The need for more structure, discipline, and formality aids in getting off to a great beginning.

Defend Stage Managerial Leadership Hints

Level Two is the Defend stage that typically sets in when the beginning is hurriedly attempted and no solid structure established. Terrorists quickly assess when they have a fighting chance at derailing a manager or teacher, and when their agendas can be presented to an entire group (transmitters/transformers/fellow terrorists) at management's expense. They take any opportunity to do so—until someone makes them accountable for their challenges in a nonconfrontational and nonpersonal manner.

Many times this stage consumes more time and energy from individuals than it should ever be allowed to. This stage becomes a breeding opportunity for terrorists and is where they come alive. With a more structured facilitation of this stage, individuals can work through it more effectively with greater professionalism and less personalization of subject matter. Manager and teacher leadership styles need to be firm in their handling of this stage to keep the terrorist from undermining objectives and organizational needs.

In Level Two, Defend management, focus efforts on limiting the confrontations (especially public ones with a colleague where there may be witnesses to the feud) and shortening the typical Grief Cycles, so as to move interactions on to productivity modes, which means Levels Three and Four of the organizational management and operational levels.

In Level Two, the management styles that afford the maximum control and leverage over and with players would be manager and teacher. If the individuals involved in this stage lack appreciation and respect for others, you must elevate your managerial leadership engagement style to that of counselor or disciplinarian.

Unfortunately, in Level Two, signs of implosion, dysfunction, tension, conflicts, and confrontations may arise. When a conflict or breakdown does develop, you can't afford to be passive and believe that you can outwait the defending posture. This does not happen!

The longer a defending process takes place, the more players become emotionally involved, the greater the problems may be in the long term, and the deeper the scars become. The more time spent here, the more individuals become frustrated and disengage from others, and thus the organization. This may create cancerous situations with lasting implications.

For the counselor or disciplinarian, additional tactical engagement ideas are presented in how to facilitate this managerial leadership role.

Blend Stage Managerial Leadership Hints

Level Three, Blend, is where most players (transmitters) live and where you need to move your challenging players (terrorists). This is the level where most organizations are, as with every position and every organization there is a high level of normalcy that constitutes the jobs, tasks, and deliverables. Blend becomes the stage where the positions populated with personnel are facilitated. No way around it—there are routines, traditions, and normal work activities, and this is the stage in which they live.

In Level Three, Blend, your management style (the hat you wear) is primarily that of limited manager, and more often mentor and coach. Through these two styles you can motivate, lead, educate, and inspire others to productivity and result attainment. You, as manager, have already (and will continue to) evaluate the players who are on your team and with whom you interact to identify whether you have the right players on the right tasks—player analysis, as developed in Chapter 6.

To ensure productivity from the team, use mentors while you are present and when you are absent. You want to cultivate others to become mentors for possible transmitters and transformers, so they have a point of contact professionally to confide in and look to. This allows them to attain higher levels of success without your direct interaction.

Creating work teams and designing decision teams allow for greater levels of productivity and growth. Strategies for maintaining operational flow are discussed as well in Chapter 9, "Nine Tactical Steps to High-Impact Leadership."

The ultimate goal of management is to grow players and teams to the level where they understand what needs to be done, take the initiative to do it, and are entrusted with the tools, knowledge, and authority to do it. This fourth level of organizational structure is uncomfortable for many traditional managers and is a primary reason why many organizations stay in Level Three. Many organizations ultimately either remain at lower levels of capacity and success, or those that start off with successes burn out from within.

> *One in every ten organizations that undertake the management changes and growth of Total Quality Management (TQM), or any variation thereof, to compete in the coming of the Global Economy, will actually succeed!*
> —**Tom Peters**

Transcend Stage Managerial Leadership Hints

In this fourth level, the management style necessary for growth and success is that of coach and mentor (whether you or someone else serves as the mentor doesn't matter).

In the fourth level, the primary function of management is to ensure that all players have the resources, support, and encouragement they need to interact and function at peak performance. Peak performance means that players are operating up to or exceeding their potential, and therefore they, the team, and the overall organization all win.

It is critical that management maintains distance between the terrorists and the transformers who live at this level.

To attain Transcend level, players are treated with respect, expected to perform up to individual potential (and not to someone else's potential), and entrusted with resources, knowledge, and access to whatever they need to function. Players, within reason, should not become bogged down in attaining signatures and authorization for every move they make.

In Level Four, players need to have properly assigned tasks and be placed in positions that allow them to draw upon their strengths (refer to Chapter 6). They should not be challenged with activities that play upon their weaknesses and place them outside their comfort zones. When players have properly assigned work and responsibilities, their attitudes improve, and so does performance.

Typically, in most organizations, the only time players attain this level of proficiency and focus is when they, as transformers, come in early, work through lunch, and stay late. This is due in large part to these being three specific time windows when terrorists are not present in the workplace.

Systems of efficiency are critical. Redundancies need to be aggressively sought out and eliminated at this stage, so players can contribute substantially to the bottom line. This is not the stage where individuals immerse themselves in mere busy work, but rather in substantial work for their cause. At Transcend, individuals accept responsibility for their positions, take ownership of the organization, and are mentally and physically attuned to mission statements, by way of action during every second of operation.

Innovation, entrepreneurialism, commitment, self-responsibility, and a sense of self are modeled by all players at this level, and others benchmark excellence off you.

Senior-level executives and team leaders are at peak performance when they can operate from this need state or level most of the time.

End Stage Managerial Leadership Hints

The final level of organizational management and the level at which most players and management spend the least amount of time is the **End**, or analysis and conclusion, stage. It is amazing how many cases of hindsight there are on this business level—for repetitive, costly mistakes by employees/players, management, and organizations operating themselves directly out of business.

The management style to be assumed here is that of mentor, and the style needed for someone else is that of mentor and coach. Here is the stage where true managerial leadership greatness can be fine-tuned. By allowing for the investment of time afterward to reflect on what was done, by whom, and in what manner, lessons learned can be gleaned for future investments in human capital and resources by both an organization and a leader in significantly greater ways.

At this End level, analysis, benchmarking, review, comparison, learning, decompression, retreats, skull sessions, and so on should take place.

Here players and management have ample time to reflect on past actions and activities, to analyze the positives and successes for future similar courses of action. Likewise, analysis takes place so improvements can be made for future actions and to identify any specific actions that could be eliminated in the future to avoid difficulties that may have been experienced in an activity or project.

Many times redundancies occur due to ineffective or no investment of time in the End stage.

Journal or track digitally your efforts, labor, projects, work products, human capital deployment, and expenses to provide sound analytics to establish better best practices for your continued endeavors.

It is interesting to analyze these five organizational levels of operation and especially to reflect upon this last level. In the daily professional environment, players tend to spend the least amount of time here, yet when adults were younger they had perfected this level and the "why" of it. When you were a child, if you had older brothers or sisters, you were always monitoring what they were doing, and whether or not they were getting away with something. If you observed and analyzed how they did that, you emulated that behavior. If that sibling got caught, your analysis told you what modifications to make for a more efficient use of your time, and thus, how to avoid a similar disaster.

Therefore, the fifth level can be considered the level at which you monitor what happened and make any necessary modifications for the future to ensure equal or greater levels of productivity, efficiency, profitability, and growth.

Chapter 12, "Developing a Winning Habit Paradigm," presents techniques and strategies for an effective ending process.

Now, with a better understanding of the five organizational levels and which managerial leadership style to assume in relationship to these levels, the following chapters arm you with immediate interaction application techniques for success at each level and with each management style you assume.

Remember: In studies of high-growth organizations with ownership-assumed traits among employees and management out of direct control (hence a wider span of control as noted in Chapter 4, "Six Alternative Managerial Leadership Intervention Styles"), effective leaders within management invest more of their direct time at organizational operating Levels One, Four, and Five. Within peak-performing environments (teams, work groups, self-directed work groups, and so on), these leaders have opportunities to invest mental and physical time at Level Five, thus reviewing all aspects after the fact and planning better for next time.

Weigh these findings against where you and members of your team spend significant amounts of actual daily time.

Managerial Leadership Bible Lesson Eight

Presence of mind and managerial leadership control of oneself allow for effective facilitation of individuals, business transactions, and an organization overall, through the five fluid organizational operational levels.

Maintaining balance within these levels and a vigilant mindset of forward thinking—to increase the percentage of time one spends in the Blend, Transcend, and End stages—leads to significantly greater productivity, efficiency, and profitability for an organization.

This increases the value of your organization to the customers it serves and the shareholders or stakeholders who empower you to deliver your goods daily.

Review Questions

The review questions accompanying each chapter or section are designed to assist you in achieving the learning objectives stated at the beginning of each chapter. The review section is not graded; do not submit it in place of your final exam. While completing the review questions, it may be helpful to study any unfamiliar terms in the glossary in addition to course content. After completing the review questions for each chapter, proceed to the review question answers and rationales.

1. In essence, when you have your first interaction or relationship with someone or something, you will find yourself at Level _____.

   A. One, Begin

   B. Two, Defend

   C. Three, Blend

   D. Four, Transcend

2. Terrorists quickly assess when they have a fighting chance at derailing a manager or teacher in the Defend stage.

   A. True

   B. False

3. Your transformers are taking the lead and the transmitters/followers are falling in behind them in the _____ stage.

    A. End

    B. Blend

    C. Transcend

    D. Begin

4. In the fourth level, the primary function of management is to ensure that all players are adhering to the rules set forth in Level One.

    A. True

    B. False

Review Question Answers and Rationales

Review question answer choices are accompanied by unique, logical reasoning (rationales) as to why an answer is correct or incorrect. Evaluative feedback to incorrect responses and reinforcement feedback to correct responses are both provided.

1. In essence, when you have your first interaction or relationship with someone or something, you will find yourself at Level _____.

    A. Correct. Any change requires a new start in the organizational process.

    B. Incorrect. This level is for initial difficulties after beginning.

    C. Incorrect. This level is for ironing out wrinkles in the process.

    D. Incorrect. This level is for achieving maximum performance.

2. Terrorists quickly assess when they have a fighting chance at derailing a manager or teacher in the Defend stage.

    A. Correct. This is who you are defending yourself from.

    B. Incorrect. Defending a project is often needed immediately after starting it.

3. Your transformers are taking the lead and the transmitters/followers are falling in behind them in the _____ stage.

    A. Incorrect. Although this may seem to be the goal, the end stage is for analyzing the process.

    B. Correct. Your employees are "blending" and working together.

C. Incorrect. In the transcend stage, employees are finished blending and can exceed performance expectations.

D. Incorrect. The Blend stage comes several stages after the beginning.

4. In the fourth level, the primary function of management is to ensure that all players are adhering to the rules set forth in Level One.

A. Incorrect. In this level a manager should ensure that all players have the resources, support, and encouragement they need to interact and function at peak performance.

B. **Correct. This type of management is referred to as micro-management and should only be used sparingly.**

9

Nine Tactical Steps
to High-Impact Leadership

*Freedom is man's capacity to take a hand in his own development.
It is our capacity to mold ourselves and empower others.*
—**Rollo May**

A basic definition of Empowerment: Knowledge + Ability + Willingness + Positive Attitude + Authority + Access
—**Jeff Magee**

Learning Objective

After completing this section of the course, you will gain immediate application skills for emerging leaders and be empowered with the tools for increased interaction with the team for increased effectiveness.

Regardless of your industry or vocation, when you assume the position as a managerial leader within an organization, there are nine commonalities that research has shown everyone in such a position must be versed in to be successful. The greater your skill level and savvy within these commonalities, the more effective you will be at fulfilling your obligations within an organization.

Every managerial leader must be good at a minimum of nine organizational activities to lead others to greatness. It's the operational reality that we live and operate from within in business, whether a virtual business or a traditional brick-and-mortar. And with the human capital diversity advantages today of 24/7 energy application (generational segmentation diversity approaches), these nine are critical to keeping everyone on the same trajectory.

The role of a manager is to provide structure and direction for those within the organization. The role of a leader is to provide belief, value, mission, ambition—and to nurture the spirits of individuals to exhibit greatness each day.

Management need not "hold hands" with the players; rather, it should "unleash" the power and capabilities that lie within the individuals in the organization. Management needs to facilitate the growth of each player independently within the organization. Over the decades, management has taken on a lot of characteristics similar to parenting. Unfortunately for most managers, they have not realized the parallel, and thus have not realized that many of the organization's players have learned how to manipulate organizational structures, resources, and people to fulfill their agendas (just as children learn how to manipulate parents). Many times, these agendas are contrary to what the organization was created to deliver.

Consider the parallel that most adults learned and perfected their behavior patterns in childhood. If a baby learns that by crying, parents give her attention, the baby continues to cry. As she grows older and yells and screams, it becomes more difficult to gain attention. If this is so, the negative behavior continues, and the child grows into a rebellious adolescent. Then this problem teenager becomes the difficult colleague on your team whom you encounter in passive-aggressive behavior, or as a terrorist to others.

To change someone else's behavior, start with appropriate tactical engagement behaviors.

This chapter is designed to give you immediate application skills for emerging leaders, by empowering them with the tools for increased interaction with the team for increased effectiveness.

Serving as a handbook for daily managerial leadership performance, the following section is broken down into the nine management activities that every managerial leader today must execute, be proficient in delivering, and be prepared to administer. In this next section of *The Managerial Leadership Bible*, each of the nine specific actions is designed with a two-part approach. Each action, concept, or "how-to" is presented and laid out as follows: action step information and premise detailed, and a detailed list of tactical ways to administer that action.

In the course of your lifetime as a managerial leader, there are a minimum of nine specific actions you must continuously engage in, manage, participate in, and lead. They are

1. Managing attitude, self-awareness, mindset, and ego

2. Motivating groups and individuals

3. Managing meetings and huddles

4. Delegation and managing ownership dynamics

5. Designing decision-capable individuals and groups

6. Engaging difficult and challenging personalities

7. Counseling the difficult player (terrorist)

8. Dealing with procrastination, disengagement, and burnout

9. Managing time, time wasters, and paper/nonpaper information flow in today's eWorld

Each action is detailed on the following pages. Use the tactical list of deployable how-to steps as a mental checklist (or physical if necessary) to ensure that you model powerfully positive managerial leadership behavior. Consider each subsection one at a time for personal advancement and in assisting the success levels of those around you.

As you reflect on each of the nine sections, the more versed you become with each, the more fluid your actions become. The more fluid you become at administrating each, the more proficient you are in engaging others, leading others, learning from others, and winning with others.

Micromanagement is the ineffective understanding and improper deployment of these nine actions or behaviors by senior- and junior-level management personnel. Reflect on each, and ask yourself the following questions:

- What level of the five organizational operational levels does this how-to tactic serve best?

- When is this how-to tactic best drawn upon and delivered, and when should it not be deployed?

- How do I coach others to understand this behavior and deploy it?

- By using this checklist, along with other industry-specific tactics, what might be the level of proficiency gained?

#1: Managing Attitude, Self-Awareness, Mindset, and Ego

The old rule that all workers must operate from like mindsets when it comes to the workplace is no longer valid. Management must realize that what motivates one player might do the opposite with another. To stimulate growth and productive participation among players on a team, management needs to realize how to feed the human ego.

Some people are hungry and need their egos fed on a regular basis to operate at peak performance; others seldom need ego-feeding and have low levels of outward ego gratification needs to operate on a professional basis. When it comes to ego gratification, consider the wide range of perspectives of what constitutes the need for it. Compare the professional application to feeding the egos of individual players on your team. When management looks at ego needs, what's being addressed are the unique motivators required by individual players to keep them content, happy, motivated, feeling needed, and feeling appreciated—and what factors stimulate greater levels of participation and ownership from players. By identifying the ego needs and stimulators for players, management can gain a better perspective on how to motivate and manage the team overall.

For example, a recent survey by Robert Half & Associates found that men recently promoted into a new position almost immediately ask: What are the expectations of being promoted again? On the other hand, a woman recently promoted into a position asks: What expectations are there of me to perform this position to the fullest?

From this insight, management can then develop techniques and the means by which incentives and motivators can be designed to gain maximum benefit for players, on an individual basis, without association of one's gender, race, age, culture, and so on. Remember, when push comes to shove in life, it's the ego (emotional psychology) that feeds one's physical actions—survival of the fittest!

In Figure 9.1, the **Attitude and Ego Management SAFETY Model** is presented as a thought-provoker for what may be some of the needs players have to keep their egos healthy and motivated.

The descending six levels of maturity are applicable to both the individuals you interact with and groups as a whole. Similar to Maslow's Hierarchy of Needs psychological association model, this model expands upon that from an organizational dynamics viewpoint. In my experience of working with commercial entities, associations, and the government, the hierarchy reveals itself in every environment. As an individual feels comfortable, secure, and fulfilled at one level, he or she naturally aspires toward the next. The people and the culture of an organization drive how it is reflected.

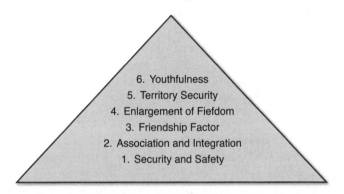

Figure 9.1 Attitude and Ego Management SAFETY Model

Some individuals are driven from Level 6 to Level 1 and interact respectfully with others to get there. Some are aggressive and leave many in their wake as they move onward and upward. Many times, it is the latter that leads to subtle erosions in organizations and individual relationships. Managerial leaders will be confronted with this as a conflict if it's not noted early and addressed diplomatically.

It's also important to recognize that not all individuals aspire professionally to Level 1 at all times. Some find themselves more comfortable in Levels 2 through 4 and may be proficient within those levels. It actually may be the stress and pressure of being forced upward beyond where someone's ego wants to be that can lead to managerial leadership challenges.

People in business settings are sensitive individuals, and their egos need to be considered. With some players, the ego has to be continuously fed. By identifying the level at which a player is operating, management can help to make him feel secure within that level and work to help move him to the next level in the matrix. Remember, all players seek SAFETY (the acronym formed by the first letter of each level in the pyramid model—going from the bottom to top) professionally within the business they are employed in and hunger for those situations, projects, and interpersonal relationships that feed their egos.

A managerial leader recognizes that professionally there are six levels of safety the individuals you lead operate from. Your ability to meet them tactically on their levels increases both your effectiveness and the yield from them.

- **Level 1: Security and Safety**—Here, the player concerned with job security is making sure she delivers what is expected, is mindful of responsibilities, and is willing to work additional time to make sure the job is well done. The player at this level is appreciative to have employment (which she applied for, interviewed for, and asked for) and sees everything beyond the paycheck as a bonus—insurance, time off, investment, freedoms, and so on. She avoids mindless conversation, gossip, and second-guessing others and is loyal to the organization. The job becomes a part of her identity and she appears as a leading advocate for it and you, her leader.

  If you examine your on-boarding practices, integration, and follow-up actions with new members to your organization and team, you can expedite this integration and reduce the period of cautious anxiety that a person may experience. A monthly check-up and check-in by key team members, colleagues, and management (benchmarking their efforts off of performance reviews is a great guidepost) is a great way to ensure on-boarding and integration success.

- **Level 2: Association and Integration**—Here, the player becomes more comfortable with his surroundings and the individuals he interacts with most directly. Socialization begins to develop; participation in additional job-related and organizational-related endeavors takes place—other committees, projects, cross-functional networks, community-related service projects, and so on. Players here assume more responsibility and are open to promotion and additional assignments. Individuals at this level begin a greater focus on intermediate financial gains, with more interest in pay raises, bonuses, investment vehicles sponsored by the organization, and so on. An interest develops in career options and aligning themselves with departments that appear to have a greater life expectancy.

  Again, if you examine your on-boarding practices, integration, and follow-up actions with new members to your organization and team, you can expedite this integration and reduce the period of cautious anxiety or blunders due to overconfidence that a person may experience. A continued monthly check-up and check-in by key team members, colleagues, and management (benchmarking their efforts off of performance reviews is a great guidepost) is a great way to ensure on-boarding and integration success.

- **Level 3: Friendship Factor**—Here players establish alliances with other individuals, begin to socialize more in the workplace with colleagues, take ownership in others' lives, and talk about what they are doing outside the workplace. They begin to forge cliques and participate in extracurricular endeavors with colleagues. Emotional connections begin to develop with individuals on both the professional and the personal level; others' pains become their pains. All this manifests in on-the-job distractions to the performance output experienced at Level 1.

Again, if you examine your on-boarding practices, integration, and follow-up actions with new members to your organization and team, you can expedite this integration and reduce the period of cautious anxiety or blunders due to overconfidence that a person may experience. A continued monthly check-up and check-in by key team members, colleagues, and management (benchmarking their efforts off of performance reviews is a great guidepost) is a great way to ensure on-boarding and integration success.

- **Level 4: Enlargement of Fiefdom**—The player here recognizes that making himself a subject matter expert in the organization, or having greater share ownership or at least possession of raw resources, materials, and even staff, is a perceived route to job protection, power, and increased authority. Here the art and science of networking have been perfected. The keen individual operating at this level can become abrupt, aggressive, and even arrogant in his people interactions, but he feels a degree of safety in acting out. At this level, the player actively pursues projects, alliances, and workloads that are perceived to make him more important and deliver what he believes will be greater job security and upward mobility. Many times, at this level, the conduct that may be observed by others rivals that of survival of the fittest.

Again, if you examine your on-boarding practices, integration, and follow-up actions with new members to your organization and team, you can expedite this integration and reduce the period of cautious anxiety or blunders due to overconfidence that a person may experience. A continued monthly check-up and check-in by key team members, colleagues, and management (benchmarking their efforts off of performance reviews is a great guidepost) is a great way to ensure on-boarding and integration success.

- **Level 5: Territory Security**—At this level, the player begins to settle into the flow and is actually seen as the spiritual, intellectual, and functioning subject matter expert or leader of her area. The player pursues endeavors (certifications, advanced degrees, association memberships, representative junkets, and so on) and even external interactions that establish her as the celebrity. The player is almost revered and is given allowances in performance and conduct that would never have been granted to an individual at Levels 1 through 4.

Again, if you examine your on-boarding practices, integration, and follow-up actions with new members to your organization and team, you can expedite this integration and reduce the period of cautious anxiety or blunders due to overconfidence that a person may experience. A continued monthly check-up and check-in by key team members, colleagues, and management (benchmarking their efforts off of performance reviews is a great guidepost) is a great way to ensure on-boarding and integration success.

- **Level 6: Youthfulness**—The player here once again arrives back at a level of unbridled enthusiasm for what he does and the organization. It was last really seen at Level 1. The player here is having fun once again and enjoys the job for what it is; he appreciates being a part of the organization and enjoys sharing and helping others. At this level, the individual works to get the job done, regardless of time required or what he may financially be compensated for. The player openly shares with others, mentors freely, seeks out opportunities to just help out to ensure the organization thrives, and is an advocate for both the organization and those individuals deemed to genuinely want to grow and become better.

This is the level of true entrepreneurialism even within an established team or organization and leads to greater momentum and success of the organization overall.

While evolving to this level may take an extended period of time, as with the other levels, if you examine your processes, you can expedite this integration and reduce anxiety or blunders. A continued monthly check-up and check-in is a great way to ensure on-boarding and integration success.

By observing a player or colleague, you can begin to determine at which level of the SAFETY Model she is operating; therefore, you can predict which level she will proceed toward once she has secured a hold on the level she is presently operating from. To establish better interacting relationships with people, help them help themselves via the six life levels—starting with Security and working ultimately toward Youthfulness.

Another way to look at the SAFETY Model matrix is to consider it a basic human motivator system. What is really the essence of a person, and from which level in life is someone operating? Psychology through the decades has identified many different systems from which mankind can analyze what motivators there are in life—what motivates people. The core basis of all these charts, graphs, systems, and theories is that motivators for individuals first must play off some degree of inward personal ego gratification need. For some, the need level is high and demanding, while with others the need level (while there) is not as demanding and doesn't override the majority of actions and thoughts.

With some individuals, the need levels also become more involved, complex, and educated, based upon one's conditioning factor and station in life, including age, sex, race, educational perspectives/ background, financial status/background, and professional perspectives/background. By understanding the individual person (refer to Chapter 6, "Analyzing Players and Prospects for Team Success"), the ego gratification concepts become more strategic, and your analysis becomes more focused.

Look at some of the players on your team and determine the levels at which they are operating. On the initial SAFETY Model diagram for this section, identify your team's transformers and mentally or physically plot them on the matrix. Determine how you can assist those players to secure their levels, and what can be done with them to move toward the next level. Plot your team's transmitters and terrorists; determine the same developmental course of action for each individual player. This exercise provides additional perspective on how to move a team closer to daily victories.

#2: Motivating Groups and Individuals

Imagine you have two cars in your garage to choose from for a trip. One is old; the other is new. The old one is tested and reliable, while the new one is shiny and trendy. One may have cost a lot; the other was less expensive to acquire and costs less to operate. One may get great mileage, and the second, not as good. What these two vehicles have in common, though, is simple. Without continually putting petroleum/fuel into them, neither will continue down the byways.

However you go about motivating individuals or groups (regardless of the incentive, bonus, rewards, perks, recognition, compensation increases, and so on), every individual requires, at some time, some degree of refueling.

Motivating the individual players on your team is the first step in motivating the team overall.

With a better understanding of the ego gratification need level of an individual player, you can begin to interact with your players to develop each individually (manager and coach time). At the same time, you can move a collective group of people (team) toward a greater good and organizational goal (growth). To design a winning team, all players must see a connection between their energy and involvement and where the organization is going. Each player has to see the results and appreciation of those efforts.

Given the generational segmentation breakdown, divergent cultures, ethnicity, and the independence people want to exhibit while claiming to be recognized as a cohesive unit, the old rules of how an organization could merely put forth one unified system or approach for motivating one player on a team may be counterproductive for another. And what may have been a way to motivate at one time now may not work—you must always be assessing the environment, and players individually, to determine whether your incentive plans and motivators are producing maximum yield.

The next time you or your organization needs to address or update this area of your organization (incentives, rewards, awards, perks, benefits packages, and so on), imagine that if you had a cross-section of each generational segmentation represented for discussion and brainstorming, what the diversity of motivating line items might be. Far too often organizations set themselves up for mediocrity or failure at the outset by having the conversation led and decided by a disproportionate age group not reflective of the entire organization.

Incentives are great as long as they work and don't have negative repercussions on management or among players. For incentives to work, consider the following points:

- Is this incentive cost-effective?
- If it works, can it be repeated?
- Does the incentive penalize any players or show favoritism?
- Does it meet a need level?
- Does it send the right message?
- How do I meet or beat this option in the future?
- Does it call attention to effort, work, or accomplishments that have gone beyond the call of duty and expectation, or is it paying a reward for merely doing one's job?

- Does the recipient of this incentive really appreciate it?
- Does the same person(s) receive the incentive reward more often than not?
- Does the presence of incentive plans create tension among players or within teams (departments, regions, divisions, and so on)?
- Have any of the players been involved in designing the incentive variables/plans?
- Are the incentives being used today the same as incentives used in the past? If so, how repetitive are the variables?

For incentives to work, they need to be thoroughly analyzed to make sure these types of questions don't come to mind later (in hindsight) and spell disaster.

In addressing the multitude of ways to motivate another individual or group, managerial leaders may feel pressured as to how best to approach it, and whether there are some guideposts for what to do. Consider this Managerial Leader Motivator Rule of Three in the design and implementation of any motivating system in the future:

- Does this item have meaning to the recipient?
- Will it have lasting impact on this person?
- How does management ensure it can repeat the gesture without falling into a position of one-upping it the next time?

Barring any restrictive, draconian organizational rules or union immaturity, an explosive means of identifying what really motivates a player and team is to have a team brainstorming meeting and solicit ideas for consideration as to what would motivate each member to greater levels of success.

You may want to qualify this session with the players if you were, for example, initiating this endeavor independently from the organization. Either have them offer ideas as a group, and solicit three ideas to be written down and offered to management for consideration, or design a cross-sectional team to work on this objective and report back to the whole team at a later time and date. When soliciting ideas or when working on this task independently, break down incentives into three categories:

- Incentives that cost no money or revenue
- Incentives that cost $20 or less
- Incentives that are more involved, and complex, and cost the team or organization some money

Designing incentives can and should be fun. Organizationally for a managerial leader, all direct reports that may be affected by this initiative should also have a clear understanding of the rules that constitute when someone may expect to receive such a motivator beyond the obvious "Good job" statement. A person's baseline compensation package is for him to excel at the job he applied for, interviewed for, indicated he wanted, and has been placed into. Let's not forget Level 1 of the SAFETY Model. Individuals must understand that the incentive is not awarded for showing up and doing what is expected of them. This reward does not happen automatically, like an annual cost-of-living index adjustment.

One way to accomplish the creation of a list of incentives is to ask each individual on your team to send an electronic Word file or fill out an index card. Place his name on the top. On one side, list all the items that to him would have meaning as *free* motivators the organization or managerial leader could deliver. On the other side, list motivators that may have financial value. The beauty of this task, once accomplished, is that as a managerial leader you now have an extensive list that adheres to the Motivator Rule of Three.

With this self-inventory from each individual in your group, you now have an easy reference list to use repeatedly in the future with each individual. While there may be some divergent items among one person's list and another, it is his own list, so mentally anguishing over what to do and how to repeat it has been removed.

Table 9.1 presents ideas or food for thought in designing your own player and team incentive program. These are examples of what motivates some players, collected from professional organizations across four continents during the past decade.

Whether or not you use any of the incentive motivator ideas presented in Table 9.1, are presently using similar ideas, or are designing your own, the use of incentive-based programs must be implemented with extreme caution.

Table 9.1 Incentive Idea Bank

Free	Monetary
Thank you	Certificates
Letter of recognition	Paid day off
Letter from CEO	Balloons
Increased authority	Flowers
New office	Concert tickets

Free	Monetary
New project opportunities	Pay raise
Team party	Increased benefits
Flex time schedule	Increased retirement
Merit points	Longer lunch
Recognition in newsletter	3-day weekends
Recognition in press	Training options
Temporary titles	Dinner with boss
Permission to dump a project/task	Weekend retreat
Inclusion in planning sessions	Shorter days
Extended job responsibilities	New office décor/furnishings
Call from CEO	Company car
Employee of the month award	Special parking spot
Unscheduled performance evaluations	Company merchandise
Team leader assignments	Memberships
Choice of own work	Holiday party
Suggestion box	New technology
Reduced delegated work	Ball caps
Horizontal job movement	T-Shirts
Vertical job movement	Cash bonus
Increased recognition	Entertainment prizes
Increased responsibility	Wall art
Mentored relationship	Breakfast/donuts
Learning and training opportunities	Coffee service
More time with C-level personnel	Expense account
	Clothing account
	Certificates to spouse
	Certificates for kids
	Plaques, trophies, etc.
	Business cards
	Pen set
	Medallion coins for excellence
	Book club membership
	Soda/H_2O supplies

An incentive program, once implemented, must accomplish its objectives for its intended purpose now. It must not be counterproductive to the long-term development of an organization. If the motivation garnered from the gesture is short-term, the given act may not have been truly meaningful. Also, remember: All motivators must feed the ego, in respect to the exact behavior you want more of.

An incentive-based program can produce outstanding results from a player or team. However, think about the players who don't make the incentive program goal accomplishments and don't receive the incentive reward or award. How will those players or that team feel? How will future productivity levels be impacted, based upon not receiving the incentive? What happens to their performance and attitude if they don't receive the incentive but find out that others who fell short of the goal, but were closer to the target, received the incentive? What happens to players' performance and commitment if everyone is receiving the same incentive, yet some are not pulling their weight, forcing others to compensate for the slackers and dead weight?

Incentives have to be appreciated by the recipients—or the hollow gestures will have a hollow welcome. Incentives have to have impact and meaning. Incentives have to be timely. Incentives should only be used as a way of saying a special thank-you for effort and results far above those expected from a player. Player performance in the norm is recognized already with a paycheck!

Consider your team and list some incentives you could use to stimulate additional growth and productivity.

In working to motivate a group (team, department, shift, line, unit, committee, project, and so on), here are six guideposts to follow as a managerial leader. The more you can do any one or a combination of these six actions, the better. A byproduct: The energy level, enthusiasm, and ownership level demonstrated by individuals collectively as a group will increase greatly. Consider the following:

- **Choice**—Allow individuals to make independent choices of work assignments as often as possible.

- **Decision**—Allow individuals to make their own decisions as to how best to administer the task they have assumed or been delegated.

- **Creative**—Allow individuals to be creative, bringing out increased energies. This deals with the "how" of actions, along with how the other persons want to do their work. If it's legal, ethical, and cost effective, stay out of their way.

- **Feedback**—Within group settings, individuals thrive on performance-based feedback on what is working and not working, and seek ways to keep moving forward.

- **Challenge**—As long as the work is appropriately challenging, individuals pull together and get excited.

- **Competition**—At a healthy level and balance, competition with something else, others, and one's self actually generates more team spirit and energy.

Along with the following team and player incentives, immediate response through praise is another powerful motivator for human behavior. In management, the act of genuine and sincere praise can ensure continued commitment from players in tough times and stimulate players when they have fallen into a procrastination rut.

For praise to be most effective, it needs to adhere to four basic ground rules:

1. It needs to be immediate.

2. It needs to be specific to the behavior exhibited and further desired.

3. It needs to be given by a person who commands respect from players and especially from the player receiving the praise.

4. It must be appropriate and have meaning.

Motivating and stimulating commitment from others through incentives and on-the-spot praise are major managerial leadership tools for winning teams.

Motivating players and the team can be accomplished through both monetary (extrinsic) and nonmonetary (intrinsic) rewards, as you saw in Table 9.1. Examine each player individually and your team overall to determine what motivates and what doesn't.

Self-Assessed Motivators/Incentives

As an effective manager of resources and leader of people, have each player (employee) brainstorm and write down the ten extrinsic and ten intrinsic motivators they would view as incentives or merit bonuses for work and energies that exceed expectation levels. Place each person's personalized list in his personnel file and draw upon his entries as needed (at the conclusion of projects, programs, work periods/cycles, appraisal periods, and so on). This list provides valuable insight into what motivates your team overall and what motivates each player individually.

Ultimate player and team motivation has to be focused on emphasizing what a player can do, not what a player can't do. Efforts have to be focused on building, strengthening, and fostering players' inner pride in what they do, and what they are about. The greater the player's pride and self-confidence factor, the greater the player's commitment factor will become. The entire team benefits from greater energies.

Giving Praise (Recognition) and Incentives (Rewards)

The fuel that maintains a winning team is effective and consistent recognition and rewards to its players. Individuals (groups of people together who form your teams in life) need psychological reinforcement that what they are doing is correct and meaningful. When attention is given in a positive and constructive manner, more of that behavior will be gained. If people are left to guess whether their work is being appreciated and is meaningful, typically their assumptions are proven wrong, and work levels begin to even out and then decline.

First, differentiate between praise (recognition) and incentives (rewards). *Praise* (recognition) is the act of spotlighting or acknowledging a behavior (publicly or privately) that has led to a success, accomplishment, or substantial gain by an individual or team. This activity gets the person or team in question to recognize and rethink what it was that led to that victory. By emphasizing this positive, an individual or team can then repeat the activity as necessary.

Incentives (rewards) are given for acts, service, or delivery of something that exceeds expectations and norms. Incentives must have direct meaning to the recipient and a level of value, meaning, and even direct financial gain for the recipient.

There are six critical factors to successful incentives and praise being delivered. Whether you are engaging an individual or a group, make sure you:

1. Emphasize the "can" and not the "can't."
2. Allow all involved to celebrate a success or accomplishment on a regular basis.
3. Give in a genuine manner.
4. Personalize to the recipient.
5. Make it appropriate to the act and the person, and present it in a timely manner.

6. Connect it in a clearly communicated way to the act/behavior being recognized, with reference to expected future performance.

#3: Managing Meetings and Huddles

Managing the amount of time players spend in meetings and reducing the number of meetings that take place within organizations is the aim of this section. So how much time do you spend in meetings each year?

The Wharton School of Business studied that exact question. The findings are shocking. It is estimated that by the time a member of management retires, if she held such titles as executive, manager, supervisor, business owner, that person would have spent roughly 33 percent of her working career sitting in meetings.

Can you afford to pay that much money to have your players sitting? Well, that is exactly what most organizations do. They pay staff to eat away every day by sitting in, blending in, and in some cases, sabotaging meetings.

Consider a typical meeting. They tend to be breeding grounds for terrorists. One shows up and works throughout the course of the meeting to undermine the core agenda and management. If allowed to go on unchecked, a terrorist can easily recruit other individuals and derail a meeting and agenda.

To efficiently manage a team and meetings, there has to be a structure that respects each player's position—yet keeps the meeting on course and guards against terrorists or misspent time.

To excel as a managerial leader of greatness, know that the essence of meetings is about starting, following up, monitoring, or ending actions. Meetings in and of themselves are not action events that produce profits.

Consider meeting management skills as a three-part approach:

1. Before
2. During
3. After

Before calling the meeting, consider an alternative when you actually need to gather your personnel talent in one gathering. Call a *huddle* instead, virtual online or face-to-face live. A meeting constitutes, among other things, a need to meet in a sitting environment. The huddle dictates no sitting. The power of a huddle is that you:

- Meet where there are no tables or chairs.
- Allow for all appropriate stakeholders to come face-to-face.
- Allow participants to be able to hold documents and exchange items.
- Allow participants to arrive with no beverages in hand.
- Give individuals the opportunity to meet on a regular basis to ensure everyone is briefed, interactions take place, and forward momentum is being maintained.
- As in athletics, this is a needed face-to-face meet-up, yet done at an accelerated pace as everyone has productivity to get back to.

When more than a huddle is required, proceed with the meeting. Again whether online in a virtual delivery or face-to-face live, adhere to the strategic vision of the Before-During-After action sequence to ensure staying on point and productive.

Before the Meeting

Before any meeting, there are several questions management must ask and several steps that need to be addressed to ensure that a successful meeting takes place and for on-time meeting management.

Self-Imposed Questions

Consider these questions prior to calling and arriving at your meetings:

1. Can the purpose of this meeting be communicated to the team and players by another means (email, voice mail, one-on-one, face-to-face with principals, or ignoring the reason for the meeting, and so on)?
2. Do I need the entire team for this meeting?
3. Am I calling a meeting for a limited scope of challenges that pertain to only a few specific players?
4. Is this merely a regular meeting? Is there really no purpose for this regularly scheduled meeting?
5. How much will this meeting cost financially?
   - Determine the average per-minute salary for each player in your meeting.
   - Multiply that times the number of minutes your meeting will take place.

- Add the costs of all associated expenses just for the meeting (location rent, refreshments, equipment used, handouts, support staff involved, other labor fees for participants, any travel and lodging for participants, and so on).

- Include the lost productivity and profitability times each active participant in your meeting.

- Add to this the lost add-on productivity or profitability for other individuals not in your meeting, and using as their inactivity excuse the inability to access you or others in the meeting.

Preparation Points

Consider these points prior to calling and arriving at your meetings:

- **Agenda/Action Guide (or whatever you want to call your game plan).** Design an agenda for the focus of this meeting. An agenda gives you the opportunity to mentally and physically plan, pull notes together, and obtain the facts/data and documentation necessary to accomplish your objectives prior to a meeting.

- **Transformers.** Identify the transformers on this team who would be in your meeting and interact with them prior to the meeting. Brief them on your objectives and agenda. Get their participation and buy-in to your position, as this will assist you during the meeting in pulling transmitters in your direction and neutralizing the terrorists.

- **Location.** Plan the logistics and location of the meeting site. If your traditional meeting environment is not conducive for success, or you find yourself competing with continuous interruptions, plan on a different location for your meeting.

- **Players.** Invite only those players who you need and who are directly impacted by this meeting agenda. If you don't need a player in a meeting, don't require him or her to be there. Remember how much you are paying each player per hour. Take that figure and multiply it for each player you will have in your meeting times how many minutes or hours they will be in this meeting. You will quickly arrive at the rough dollar amount for your meeting.

- **Best Time of Day for Highest Growth and Results.** Identify with your team what the most productive times of the day for meetings are and schedule meetings for those time zones, regardless of what others, especially terrorists, may say. Use time as a strategic success weapon in meetings, instead of time being the enemy. Ideally the best time of the day for any meeting is directly before something important. If there is nothing important or urgent on that specific day's schedule, always schedule meetings directly before lunch or the end of the day! These are the most important things to take place each day (going to lunch and going home at the end of the day) for most players. The positive of these two time frames is that everyone in the meeting understands what is to take place when the meeting is over, and the meeting's dominant talker gets peer pressure from colleagues to "shut up"! With a meeting scheduled directly before something important, all players will typically be present for an on-time start, unlike the first-thing-in-the-morning and right-after-lunch-type meetings, when there are always certain players arriving late and blaming it on traffic. Now, though, the players are present and can't blame the traffic for being late.

- **Facilitator.** Every meeting should have a designated facilitator to serve as the navigator for that meeting and to ensure that the agenda is being followed. It may serve the meeting's best interest if the facilitator is not the person who called it. This role can rotate from one meeting to the next.

- **Perceived Outcome.** You should have mentally mapped out your desired outcome for the presentation prior to holding the session. You may even want to write a note as reference for where the meeting needs to move to and to serve as a reminder of what your worst-case scenario may be for this interaction.

- **Three Types of Meetings.** There are only three different styles or types of meetings that management can call to order. They are information-sharing, information-gathering, and information-creation. With this understanding at the outset, you can plan for the best administrative facilitation style for the meeting. For information-sharing meetings, you would want to facilitate more as an autocrat; for information-gathering, a democratic style; and for information-creation, a laissez-faire style is best.

- **Forty-Eight-Hour Notice.** A written announcement should go to all players expected at the meeting. Even if advance calling or notice has been given, do so again 48 hours prior to a meeting to assist those who seem to forget advance notices of meetings. Mention by name all the players you need or whom you expect to present any type of report or update. This warning gives all players a chance to prepare and saves time in reports. This announcement carrying the specifics of those players who will be reporting also serves as a powerful way to tell the typical meeting terrorists to keep their mouths shut during the participants' reports.

When you use these kinds of actions you can facilitate the before-meeting needs more efficiently and increase your effectiveness during the meeting with all participants. These Before points serve as a preparation checklist for greater meeting participation, interactions, and overall meeting management success for the During stage.

During the Meeting

Once the meeting has started, it is critical to maintain balance within it and to enforce the structure you have put into place. Players in meetings are like children: They all start by seeing what they can get away with and what you are all about. If you let players have an inch, they will take a mile, and it will seem like you are running the distance to regain control of your meetings.

To ensure the highest level of productivity and greatest level of player participation, decrease terrorist attacks, and reduce the amount of time everyone has to invest in meetings, consider strategic questions prior to the meeting's commencement.

Self-Imposed Questions

Follow tactically throughout the session as well by keeping these questions in mind:

1. Have I established the proper structure for this meeting to be successful?

2. Are we on or off track in the meeting with regard to the agenda?

3. Are we on the right issue or are we jumping around on the agenda? If so, how do I get back on track?

Management Techniques/Tactics During Meetings and Huddles

Keep in mind the following techniques and tactics during your meeting:

- **Start and Stop**. Start your meeting exactly when you say you will, and don't wait for anyone. If you wait, that person will never be on time. Then everyone who is there on time becomes alienated and you convert them into pseudo-terrorists.

Stop your meeting when you say you are going to. Even if you are not done, you must stop and shut up! If a meeting is to be over at 10:00 a.m. and you still have items to discuss at 10:00 a.m., pause and make sure the players in the room are both mentally and physically with you. Most will have things planned at 10:01 a.m.; sitting in another of management's meetings is not on their lists! Ask a question to determine whether the team needs a brief break, needs to reschedule, or should continue on with an agreed-upon amount of additional time. If you stop the meeting flow and get the players back with you, the remaining minutes of the meeting will be significantly more productive.

- **Player Assignments.** Every meeting has several players who attend believing that they have an "unofficial" official role in it. Management can facilitate effective meetings with these players by putting them in a position where they are not challenging the meeting coordinator. At the beginning of the meeting, in front of all the others, ask these players if they would "officially" assist in the management of that specific meeting, by serving as the official timekeeper (signified by that colleague who typically attends meetings and maintains eye contact with the wall clock, or if there is no clock, takes his wristwatch off and places it before him on the table for all to see); and the official secretary (that colleague who takes notes during the meeting on everything that is said, and by whom). The timekeeper will keep the meeting flowing. He (not you) will now nonconfrontationally redirect any player who is off track. The secretary and his notes will become the official meeting minutes, so you can follow up your meetings with written confirmation of what was discussed and resolved. Each player is informed and you can now control post-meeting miscommunication.

- **Agenda**. All players attending the meeting should have a copy of an agenda so they can understand what to focus on and accomplish. The agenda serves as a map and should be visible to you as a tracking tool of where you are, and how much time you have invested in any specific item, therefore assisting the coordinator or leader in managing that meeting.

  If anyone goes off the agenda, you can now nonconfrontationally move the conversation and other players back to the purpose of the meeting, by comfortably pointing at the last agenda item discussed and redirecting the group's momentum back to that point.

- **Two-Minute Warning.** Every player mentioned in the 48-hour notice who is to actually give a report or make a presentation will be informed that each has two minutes only, at the beginning of the meeting, to either give his entire report or an overview of it. No Q&A will take place during or immediately after the two-minute reports. Once all identified players have given their reports, the first person will be called upon to complete his overview, and then the Q&A will take place. This cuts down significantly on senseless dialogue and questions, speeds up reports of facts and data, and cuts down on the volume of fluff typically presented in reports.

- **Forty-Five-Minute Limit.** No meeting should require participants to absorb more than 45 minutes on the same topic. If a meeting needs to go more than 45 minutes due to content issues (as often is the case), the facilitator should make plans for breaks, activities, or interactions to stimulate energy and counter agitation and daydreaming.

- **Three Types of Meeting Management Styles.** Depending on the meeting type you are calling and participating in, there are three different management styles you must assume to maximize that type. If you are having an information-sharing meeting, you should serve as an autocrat. If the meeting is information-gathering, act as a democrat. And if the meeting is an information-creation session, you act with laissez-faire.

- **Six Power Questions Stimulate Involvement.** If you find yourself in a meeting and are unclear on what is being said, proposed, or challenged, don't become defensive or engage in a war of words. Initiate a strategic series of questions that stimulate the other player into conversation, away from confrontation. This affords you additional knowledge and assists in designing your management response. The questions are W, W, W, W, W, and H. If these letters don't mean anything to you, go back to your high school English course. The person who asks the questions typically wins the interaction; the person who dominates the interaction and conversations ultimately loses. Still confused? Reflect on any interaction you have had with a four-year-old. The letters represent Who? What? When? Where? Why? and How?

- **Punch List.** During the meeting make a listing or chart of each issue addressed, with the status of each. The status should include action to be taken, date initiated, who initiated it, date to be completed, who is accountable, and comments. A copy of this chart should be maintained in an official meeting log and copies given to appropriate players.

- **Time.** At the beginning of any meeting with an individual or team, state how much time is allotted to it.

- **Know Player Workload Liabilities.** Realistically understand your present workload and that of the other players in a meeting. Be cautious not to overload a transformer or transmitter to the point that the productivity level turns negative.

- **Multiple-Layered Player Participation.** If you're going to have more than one management layer/level present at a meeting, meet *before* the meeting or presentation with those players and assign roles and responsibilities, so that *during* the meeting, management isn't fighting for power in front of the team. Lines of authority in this meeting need to be clear: Who is the actual facilitator, and whose meeting is it?

- **Mind Mapping or Growth Wheels.** Use alternative note-taking techniques in the meeting. Allow yourself to stay connected with everyone else, so you don't get caught up in taking notes and then miss some of the communication.

- **SMART Formula©.** Use the **SMART Formula** (see "#4: Delegation Dynamics") to ensure player understanding and buy-in to meeting issues.

- **Questions.** Make sure that all meetings have extra time budgeted for expected and unexpected questions from players.

- **End with Action Wrap-Up.** Given the complexity or length of a possible meeting, always make sure your last agenda item is a brief recap of what all the action items are/were, and reference who owns each.

- **Negative Participants.** When a negative participant appears in a meeting or challenges a position presented by management or another player, don't react; take immediate logical control and act. Consider the following techniques designed for tactical interaction with the negative player (that is, terrorist):

  ◆ **Empathy**—Immediately acknowledge his position or statement. You are not agreeing or disagreeing with him, merely acknowledging him. A negative person expects you to challenge, defend your position, or react. He doesn't expect you to be rational about the attack.

- **Stimulate a conversation**—Immediately upon acknowledging the other person, utilize one of the six questions (W, W, W, W, W, H) to get him talking to educate you, or for you to gain a better perspective of where the person is coming from. This gives you a better response position.

- **Demand an alternative**—No one has ever made him accountable for issuing a challenge. Don't let the employee off the hook. If a player challenges your position in a meeting, you must stop the process right then, keep the conversation (not confrontation) "issue-oriented" and not personality-oriented (which is what the negative player has come to expect and may even want), and demand an alternative from him. If you solicit an option or alternative from the instigator once and he has no offer, repeat up to three times, "What do you feel we should do?" And then move on, if he gives no options. If options are presented, objectively analyze and consider them.

- **Assign 100 percent accountability**—Place the project, task, or issue directly in his hands and make the player 100 percent accountable for it. Directly move on to the next agenda item.

- **Request write-up**—Ask the player to write up the point he wants to discuss and several alternatives for resolving it, and to get with you one-on-one later in the day or week. Then directly move on to the next agenda issue.

- **Avoid argument**—At all costs, avoid getting drawn into a debate with negative people in front of an audience. They seek these situations. Reschedule a negativist's issue for a one-on-one discussion, in private, after the meeting.

- **Setup**—If you know going into a meeting there may be a vocal objector, then go for him in your opening statement. Don't let the negativists attack you or attempt to steal the show. Professionally go for the negativists before they get a chance to come after you.

For example, "In considering the proposition of purchasing blue pens for the entire department, I would like to spend a few minutes to solicit feedback as to whether this is a good idea or whether there may be other options. If so, I would like to analyze each alternative pro and con as it is raised. Let's get this meeting going with a few ideas. John (perceived negativist, challenging person, terrorist), what are your feelings on the blue pen order?"

Management must maintain control over meetings or they will self-destruct right before your eyes. Those players who are transformers and/or transmitters may revert to pseudo-terrorists. This is due to management allowing a meeting to go off track and wasting their limited time.

After the Meeting

Once the meeting is over, there are several key requirements of that meeting's facilitator (manager) to ensure the outcome of it is actualized.

Self-Imposed Questions

Consider the following questions and points as a map for post-meeting success:

1. Did we accomplish what we set out to do in the meeting?
2. Did the terrorists or the transformers win this meeting?
3. Do I have a clear understanding of what the next course of action is? If I do, do the other members of the team have a clear understanding of what the next step is?
4. Did we follow the meeting outline as designed before the meeting? If so, how? If not, why?

Management Techniques/Tactics After Meetings and Huddles

Keep the following in mind after your meeting:

- **Self-meeting.** Make sure that you schedule some private time after a meeting to focus on what happened and what the next steps are.

- **Notes.** After every meeting, review your notes/minutes briefly, to ensure that the play-by-play notes you took while the meeting was in progress are accurate and whether additional notes (perspectives) are necessary to get those thoughts down while they are fresh in your mind. Then store all your notes and any other documentation from the meeting for historical purposes. Never throw away meeting notes.

- **Follow-up times.** Immediately transpose dates and names onto your working calendar for any follow-ups.

- **Mini-meeting.** If appropriate, after the meeting and on reflection of what transpired during it, you may feel it necessary to get face-to-face (once again) with a certain few players, to ensure that the issues addressed in the meeting are being initiated and that assumptions are not setting a stage from which problems will surface later.

- **Reminder gram.** In a nonthreatening manner, make it your standard operating process (save a template in your computer if appropriate) to always send a follow-up reminder email, memo, letter, or after action review (AAR) to all participants (and furnish a copy to any lateral and vertical stakeholders as appropriate) to ensure that everyone is on track for success. Politely invite open sharing of efficiency ideas among participants to aid in one person's increased success. By sending this communication (be brief!), it also serves afterward as a subtle documentation trail and can be a catalyst to motivate any potential terrorists into transformer action.

To maximize both your time and the time of each player on your team, consider turning these suggestions into a checklist for managing meetings.

#4: Delegation Dynamics

Effective delegation is both an art and a science. To effectively interact with other players and make requests from them, assign tasks to them, and have them willingly and enthusiastically pursue those tasks, is the ultimate management goal of delegation. Arriving at this point may, however, be another issue, and a stress-filled one at that, unless you objectively utilize the *Player Capability Index* model and what you know of the person you need to task management onto.

When a management tasks an individual who possesses the skill set and/or has prior experience with similar requests, that act can be called *delegation*. If a managerial leader tasks someone with an activity for which he possesses no skill set and in which he has no prior experience, this is not delegation; it is dumping. Dumping creates passive-aggressive poor performance, breeds terrorism, and can lead to the implosion of a player's attitude.

Let's examine some of the reasons why delegation may go off track. Some players seem never to get tasks assigned and delegated to them finished, while others seem always to be in the line of getting dumped on.

Delegation is a two-way interaction. For it to be effective and used as an educational development tool, management needs to be consistent about its approach and have a structure in place, so all parties involved understand exactly what the mission is. When delegation goes off track, confusion, tension, defensive behavior, and player posturing takes place. The costs to the organization associated with misguided delegation are financially dangerous. To the player's attitude and morale, they are killers, and to the overall effectiveness of the team they are extreme.

Misguided delegation may result in nonproductivity and a player on a team utilizing the following kind of response for work not completed. How many times have you heard: "Oh, I'm sorry, I didn't realize what you wanted"; "I didn't know I could do it that way"; "I didn't realize I could use that..."; "I didn't realize you needed it right now."

To reduce these traditional responses from players who don't perform and produce the results necessary from delegated tasks, consider using several of the following techniques with them (especially with terrorists and transmitters) in the future.

Delegation going off track may be attributed to several factors. If you can identify why this happens with a particular player, future delegation should include an additional management step with that player to guard against repeated excuses and/or mistakes.

Consider these six basic elements in delegation, with each step being presented at the time of the problem. Going back to a player after a task has been delegated/assigned and then establishing any one of the six core delegation steps will be seen by him as autocratic management and will imply a lack of trust. When trust between a player and management is impaired, the level of commitment and enthusiasm by the player on a task goes down dramatically.

Consider the following Delegation Dynamics Matrix®. Delegation is a systematic approach to entrusting something to another player. You need to approach the transfer of tasks from you to another as a one-step-at-a-time activity:

- **Goal establishment**—When you delegate, ensure that the other person clearly knows what is expected.

- **Empowerment**—Must be established. This step centers on the "how" factor—how it is or is not to be accomplished. Typically, all management should focus on is gaining an understanding from the other party as to how she will address the goal, based upon ethics, legality, and cost effectiveness. As long as the approach adheres to these three variables, don't interfere with her.

- **Checkup**—To attain complete consensus, ensure that the first two items are being understood and buy-in is taking place.

- **Access**—Access to any resources necessary for the attainment of the goal needs to be guaranteed. If you need to send an advance communication so that the delegated individual does not get derailed by a third party, then do so.

- **Deadline and follow-up**—This ensures the task gets done within the time perimeters you have. If the nature of the delegated task or the individual involved dictates that, between start time and deadline there be ongoing follow-up to ensure effective progression, call ahead and establish the schedule of checks, so all parties understand when this is to take place, and so everyone can anticipate this interaction. This removes perceptions of the follow-up being a checking-up encounter.

- **Review**—Reviewing all actions after the goal has been attained is important, so everyone involved can use the feedback as a learning opportunity, and individuals can use the experience as a benchmark for future endeavors and increased efficiencies.

Using this model requires that management slow down its interactions with players and assume a more systematic, step-by-step approach to the act of delegation. The Delegation Dynamics Matrix requires the following managerial leadership actions:

1. **Goal clarification**—Explain in detail **what** the goal or objective associated with the task you are entrusting to this person is. Communicate what it is you want done.

2. **Empowerment**—Outline how you feel the player should proceed with the goal and what he can and can't do in the pursuit of getting it accomplished. Explain, in essence, what authority he has directly associated with this goal, that the newfound authority on this task is limited to this task only, and that this authority is not universal. Qualify the authority and empowerment so as not to end up with a loose cannon on your team.

3. **Checking**—At this point you must stop the delegation process and make sure via auditory or written questions that the other person understands what the goal is and what the scope of empowerment is. Until you receive some degree of response you feel confident about from the player, do not proceed with the sequence. By getting an agreement from the player on the first two steps, you effectively eliminate the possibility of excuses.

4. **Access**—Make sure the player has it and can get it, for any and all resources needed to facilitate achieving the goal or objective. Make sure that all others know this player is working on this goal and has authority (empowerment) to access the required resources, without a lot of additional or traditional authorizations.

5. **Deadline and review**—Once you gain confirmation, via the communication interaction, that elements 1, 2, and 4 have been received and that there has been no miscommunication, you are ready to establish the due date and time frame associated with the task assigned to the player. Make sure the player has heard when the project is due; allow her to communicate any concerns regarding the deadline. If there are no concerns and you have gained confirmation from her that the deadline can be met, proceed to the review. After every delegation interaction (after the deadline has come and gone), every player and manager should invest a few minutes with one another to discuss and review what took place, pro and con. This review interaction is an educational growth opportunity, and allows both management and player to review successes and analyze any failures, so future actions will be more efficient and effective.

6. **Follow-up**—At the time of delegation, if you determine that the complexity of the task or that the player assigned to the task causes a need for regular checkups, then establish a follow-up sequence. If you schedule the follow-up before the player begins the task, it will be seen as a positive. However, if you don't discuss the follow-up and merely keep checking in on her unannounced, the player will quickly begin to feel that you are babysitting. This causes negative feelings and attitudes that will impact directly on the success of the task assigned (delegated) to her.

This is an auditory formula for delegation. If the situation or player warrants it, you should convert these elements into writing. With each of the six elements in the Delegation Dynamics Matrix established, qualified, and agreed upon by all parties, you can feel a greater level of confidence that the task assigned will be completed according to the previously described plan of action.

As management interacts with individuals and groups of people, the interaction itself can be an opportunity for conflict and confrontations. A powerful way to structure management interactions with players and with one another is to communicate and interact via a decision and commitment model utilized in the talent management industry for decades, the *SMART Formula*.

The SMART Formula (see Table 9.2) for interaction and communication in delegation can lead to greater levels of player participation and increased positive player performance. Consider this as a map to effective human relations when you need consensus, buy-in, and less denial. As you follow the elements in the matrix, keep the SMART Formula in mind as a behavioral map to improved relationships.

Table 9.2   The SMART Formula

S	Communication needs to be **specific**. It should not be open to differences of opinion at the time of initiation or at a later date.
M	Your interaction needs to be **measurable**. There should be ways to gauge whether you are on track or off, ahead of or behind schedule. These steps need to be mapped out in black and white prior to initiation.
A	Attain an **agreement** with each player on the preceding two and the remaining two factors, each independent of the other.
R	Inquire through questions and dialogue with the other players to see and hear whether they feel that what is being discussed and decided upon is **realistic, reasonable,** and **reachable.** If there is any negative feedback, it needs to be discussed, resolved, or set to the side, prior to progressing with any discussion and subsequent decisions.
T	Establish the **time frame** in which the decision will be acted upon. Any time-frame factors and deadlines need to be mapped out here.

Delegation should be seen as a positive means to growing and developing players so a team can come together and accomplish greater levels of success. Delegation is also a point from which priorities can be assigned to appropriate levels of players, so time being invested in issues and projects is efficient use of player time.

Management can only survive and grow toward market demands by letting go of work (delegation) that would have traditionally been addressed by management personnel.

Some players resist delegated tasks and attempt to divert attention and participation toward other projects to justify lack of or low levels of participation on issues and tasks that you assigned earlier to them. If a player can go unchallenged for not participating in an assigned issue, and management bails the person out, then management can expect similar behavior out of him many times in the future. If, on the other hand, management doesn't allow a player off the hook when a delegated issue, task, or project is not completed, then management can begin to change the educational process and hold players accountable for their actions.

Some players are also good at appearing on management's doorstep at the most inopportune times. Think about how many times you have observed a player waiting until a manager is on the telephone and then going to that person with questions and problems. If you watch what unfolds, the player has strategically waited for the manager to become involved in an auditory conversation. When she appears in the manager's office, neither party can engage in two such conversations. The manager asks the player in the doorway to wait; the player waits a few minutes and then leaves a paper stack on the manager's desk. The manager then quietly says, "Let's get back together on this when I'm off the telephone." Recognizing that now the stack is on the manager's desk and the player is gone, when does the manager typically see the player? When the manager goes on a hunt to find her.

In the environment of delegation, many times a player waits until the assigning manager is busy and then appears with dozens of questions or problems. These delegation techniques afford you alternative management actions with a player to ward off a large number of these typical problems.

Another managerial leader delegation technique that can be utilized to ward off the monkeys that land on your back is the Action Memo®!

There are two basic steps to tactically deploying an Action Memo. A manager can facilitate this in a number of ways. No, we are not suggesting that you create another memo for use with your team.

This is a powerful tool that can be used with any e-mail or voicemail system, or on a simple piece of paper. Consider the multiple applications for this instrument within meetings, delegation interactions, and as a simple productivity/efficiency device:

- Management can initiate the first step and assign players/individuals accordingly.
- Management can require that a player utilize an Action Memo at any time she needs to interact with a member of the management team.

An Action Memo allows the player needing management interaction to take a traditional auditory conversation or problem and convert it into a visual communication interaction. Management has to be careful not to alienate a player by refusing any of her inputs and to work for interaction and linkage between a player's ideas and solutions and those of management.

A typical memo, note sheet, text message, or email can be drafted in writing. An Action Memo simply asks an individual approaching you to be prepared to orally communicate only two items, that is, if she were to bring you a sheet of paper, there would be only two things written on it for discussion:

- **WHAT factor**—She simply writes down what the issue is; what the topic is; what the problem is; what the need is; what the opportunity is. The What factor is presented very clearly.

- **HOW factor**—Then, a minimum of at least two proposed solutions, antidotes, or courses of action should be presented.

Through the use of the Delegation Dynamics Matrix, the SMART Formula, and the Action Memo, a managerial leader can develop healthy and educated perspectives on players and what can and cannot be delegated to each individual. Through a player's participation in these techniques and management tools, a manager can begin to develop transformers from transmitters. A manager can strategically use a transformer to advance both her and the team's performances.

Consider the application of these three techniques and management tools as they specifically relate to a player on your team today.

The litany of techniques and management delegation tools that can be utilized to increase organizational production and decrease personal management workloads and stress is diverse. Subjectively, consider some other powerful ideas for effective management delegation within your environment. Consider the following delegation inventory and determine whether further management techniques can assist in team development.

Management Techniques/Tactics for Delegation

Design Departmental Workflow Charts. Analyze each department independently to determine delegation patterns. Some management players fall victim to delegating similar tasks repeatedly to static players, without regard to whether that is the most efficient use of those players in the team perspective. Also, by flowing work through departments, you can determine unnecessary steps and then work to eliminate wasted time and misused resources.

Develop Player Experts. Management should not have to play the role of expert on every task and job description element. Management should identify which players (see Chapter 6) are the experts (or have the high potential to become experts) on specific tasks or issues and develop those players to be the team leaders on given variables, thus reducing management workloads.

Train Technology Assistants. Train colleagues and customers (internal/external), when appropriate, to utilize other means of communication—email, fax, voicemail—to transmit work assignments, needs, and help requests. This frees your schedule for other one-on-one interactions and actually increases your production level on all tasks and assignments.

Combine Delegation Tasks. Low priority tasks should be grouped together for combination delegation of similar activities at the same time, saving player actions and reducing repetitive work assignments, trips, calls, and so on.

Start a Delegation Box. If people delegate up, horizontally, or even vertically to you, consider placing a box to the side of your desk or on your door for those assignments. This reduces the face-to-face interactions, interruptions, and socializing that may be associated with colleague interactions.

Instigate Write-Ups. Have players and superiors write the requests that they normally throw your way in transit, when you're walking or not at your desk. By asking them to write it down and forward it to you, many times the requests go away.

Use Player Logs. Maintain a quick reference sheet on each player you regularly delegate to. When delegating tasks to a person, make a quick notation on this log as to the task name, date given, and date expected to be completed. Review your logs monthly to determine patterns in level of ease or complexity of tasks delegated. Evaluate to see whether you are overloading some individuals and underdeveloping and thus underutilizing others.

Delegation is a powerful management tool, both for assisting management in addressing its top priorities and in developing players for a winning team.

While delegation is the single most powerful development tool in the manager/coach toolbox for organizational development today, it is also the most misunderstood and misused. View delegation as the fastest route to developing a player's level of self-esteem and for growing players both individually and as a group. Delegation allows for the proper transfer of work and decision making from one individual to another. Think of it as the means to increased successes and proficiency internally. Anything that can be pushed (meant as a positive management term) downward to another individual *should* and *must* be.

#5: Designing Decision-Capable Individuals and Groups

Designing a team of players and entrusting it with accountability and responsibility for making certain key decisions in the absence of specific management personnel allows a team to competitively function and eliminates the traditional management structure and layers that typically impede growth.

Decision teams should be directed by transformers (or identified high potentials within an organization) and should contain the appropriate cross-section of players to ensure educated discussions on challenges so decisions can be made and issues will not be placed to the side due to interaction requirements with players who are not members of the decision team and thus absent from dialogues.

Official decision-making teams should have the ability and authority (within reason) to make decisions on the run. Players need to be empowered to facilitate those decisions. Players on these teams should be educated and trained so they can perform up to the standards expected, as management has identified each to be capable of doing (as outlined in Chapter 6).

Each organizational level and individual department should have a designated decision team "online" in the event that a manager is offsite and a key decision needs to be made for the organization to continue production and meet market (customer) needs. But there are problems with these teams. Management must ensure that the teams have a map or systematically structured formula to analyze situations and develop options, prior to initiating a solution and committing organizational resources. This structure many times is not given to decision teams, and the team is first challenged with how to begin the process. Therefore, management must make sure the teams have some decision-making tools to start with.

When individuals are tasked with making decisions at any level within an organization, three variables must be weighed in an attempt to arrive at a decision with the highest value level. The factors that must be considered are risk, time, and quality.

The chart in Figure 9.2 allows you to graph these variables as they relate to you in any given situation within an organization (and in life as well). The point at which the two lines intersect is where you find the highest attainable level of value. It is then that a decision must be made for the ultimate good of an organization and its players.

Teams must recognize that there are competing factors that must be identified or associated with for any decision. Each factor needs individual attention, but players must know when it is time to move on, so as not to get pulled down by paralysis of analysis.

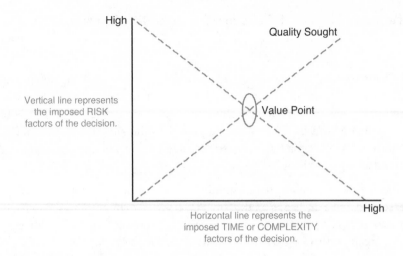

Figure 9.2 Graphing risk, time, and quality

Four risk management variables to consider in making a decision and to reference as a decision team ensure that all angles are at least briefly discussed:

- **Risk**—Thoroughly analyze all associated risk factors. Obviously, the more time you can invest in analysis the more you can reduce the risk factors (liabilities). However, if you invest too much time in the analysis of the risk factors, it may be too late by the time the team makes a decision.

- **Time**—Consider the reasonable amount of time available for this analysis before a decision and action must take place. Again, the team and each player must realize in the beginning exactly how much time is allowable or available for the issue being analyzed. Too much time invested can spell disaster.

- **Quality**—Identify the quality level sought or required. Obviously, the more time that can be invested in a cause (in theory), the better the decision. This is not always the case, however.

- **Value**—A realistic view of attainable quality or the Optimal Decision Point (ODP©) must also be identified, so as to know when to commit to a decision.

When players, management, and especially official decision-making teams balance these factors, sound and viable solutions can be designed. Weighing these factors when they intersect is the point at which the ultimate value will be obtained. To obtain the highest and most realistic level of value from decisions, consider the next formula.

Psychology explains a great deal to individuals in terms of how the brain processes information and then how it acts upon that data. In making sound decisions, the brain processes that data in systematic steps. When you interact with individuals on decision teams, these same steps are at work within each player's mind. To thoroughly manage the dynamics of a team approach to decision making, identify each step at the beginning. Each player can then reference the analysis points throughout the team's interaction. This also reduces the level of tension, defensiveness, and finger pointing, and increases effective interactions and ultimate decisions and solutions being acted upon.

How to Create and Lead a Team

In designing decision-making teams, there are a multitude of options. Consider these potential different team types:

- **Work group**—Designed as a collection of individuals necessary to task facilitation with limited low-level decision-making authority. Traditionally found within most organizations where individuals work toward a common goal with no tangible final decision-making authority.

- **Temporary team**—Designed to address a specific need that is typically not a normal event and has a limited life cycle. Once addressed, this team disbands and does not assume a new, longer-lasting life cycle. Thus decision-making powers are conditional, temporary, and may rotate among actual individuals and vary from what they would otherwise have within the organization.

- **Permanent team**—Designed out of a need that appears to be a new norm. Thus additional roles, responsibility, and authority are conditionally given to these individuals for those items that fall within the domain of the new permanent team charter or mandate.

- **Management team**—Designed for intermediate decision-making powers on the front line and throughout an organization. These individuals have been elevated into official managerial leadership and have assumed official managerial, supervisory, legal, ethical, formal, structured, and mandated roles and responsibilities as such. They have decision-making authority up to completion of needs and serve to manage and monitor workflow for an organization.

- **Cross-functional team**—Designed on a need-to-be basis, comprised of only the task-functional appropriate individuals from within and outside an organization. Decision making is structured, with subject matter experts on the team owning their areas of specialty and with authority limited or conditional to the situation.

- **Self-directed team**—Designed here to be independent and free flowing from a traditional organization hierarchy, with clearly assigned roles, responsibilities, and authority to facilitate their team's mandate. Individuals work with one another to get the job done, hold one another accountable, and assume all levels of liability for their decisions and actions.

The act of facilitating the decision process is all about a systematic approach. The brain wants to do only four things in making a decision, so put the process into business-speak and facilitate it. Here is a formula we designed for IBM in the 1990s when it was going through crisis renewal, and under the managerial leadership greatness of Lou Gerstner, Jr., reinvented itself. Like the phoenix, IBM rose from the ashes of near-death to reclaim its stature as a world leader. With this simple yet powerful four-step decision tool, its leaders were able to facilitate forward momentum at all times.

The four psychological thought-processing steps are building blocks on one another. To smoothly progress from Step 1 to Step 4, each subsequent step has to be thoroughly dealt with or players mentally digress back to an already-resolved step. The interactions continuously go back and forth, with no solution being attained in reasonable amounts of time.

Consider the map in Figure 9.3 for interactive analysis and decisions.

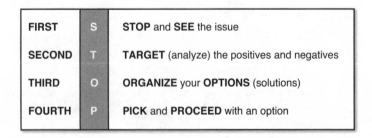

FIRST	S	**STOP** and **SEE** the issue
SECOND	T	**TARGET** (analyze) the positives and negatives
THIRD	O	**ORGANIZE** your **OPTIONS** (solutions)
FOURTH	P	**PICK** and **PROCEED** with an option

Figure 9.3 The STOP Formula for interactive analysis and decisions

When you face issues to which you dedicate analysis time, your brain focuses on one issue at a time. In essence, you need to dedicate both your conscious and subconscious brainpower to the analysis. Then you have to rationalize why you picked that issue or were tasked with it and explore all of the negatives and problems associated with it. Live and relive the traumas associated with what you identified. From this analysis step, you then move to exploring solutions and options. The key factor with the third step is that options mean more than one solution or idea must be available before considering an ultimate path upon which to proceed. When multiple ideas, solutions, and options are raised, player and team synergy develops. This may ultimately result in a more viable option being found and leads the decision process to the fourth step. From the brainstorming step (organize your options) you can identify one viable solution (pick and proceed) to implement (see Chapter 12, "Developing a Winning Habit Paradigm," for additional applications).

The **STOP Formula** leads an individual or team toward positive outcomes. Now there is a map to follow when discussion gets bogged down. With this formula you can work to maintain and make decisions issue-oriented, not personality-oriented.

You also can now focus energies toward positive outcomes and work to reduce the traditional Grief Cycle™ (refer to Chapter 5, "Five Differing Organizational Structures and Levels") of players with this technique. Collecting and stimulating ideas from players in a decision situation or from within decision-making teams is another challenge of management. Gaining ideas from players without criticism or judgments can be attained with proper management and ground rules. To stimulate input, consider the three minimum factors associated with every decision within organizations: risk, time, and quality. Along with these factors, it is also necessary to ensure realistic standards and expectations within the decisions.

Another powerful nonconfrontational technique that can be utilized to accomplish this is the SMART Formula (as presented in Table 9.2 in the "Delegation Dynamics" section).

In arriving at an effective decision, one in which most, if not all, of the players have participated and will therefore be more inclined to support, consider another application to this previous idea and what each letter represents in the acronym formula: SMART (refer to Table 9.2).

One effective way to stimulate thought and develop options in making decisions with a team environment (or by one's self) is a technique called the Crawford Slip Method. Professor C. C. Crawford, PhD, of the University of Southern California, structures decision sessions in such a way as to control interactions and idea fluency, while eliminating confrontations and criticisms through the method.

Essentially, you assign and transcribe individual ideas or statements onto separate pieces of paper, one idea per slip. When the ideas stop coming, you go back and look at the ideas or suggestions. By having them individually written down, you can now arrange them in some order. By looking at each idea on paper, in order, you have the ability to rearrange them. Also, by looking at what is written, you may also see patterns in your thinking and in what everyone is discussing. This slip method may stimulate additional ideas from participants or yourself—self-stimulated synergy.

When a team or player needs to make decisions where there may be some challenging personalities involved, you may also want to consider the three primary resources that impact the final decisions, as illustrated in Figure 9.4. You can have two of the following three factors in them, but never all three. Ask yourself if you were to make a decision and could only have two of these factors, how would this impact your decision, and how would the factors affect the actions you would expect from a decision? Which two factors would your supervisor prefer in making some of the pressing decisions within the daily schedules (if only two of the three could be had)?

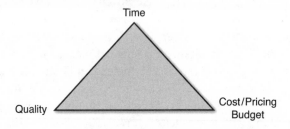

Figure 9.4 Primary resources that impact final decisions

Reaching a consensus on decisions is not always easy. Consider some of these ideas and techniques for your next interaction involving decisions with others. Put some structure into your interactions for success.

#6: Engaging Difficult and Challenging Personalities

Again, let's go back to one of the seminal minds of modern organizational business operations for decades, American management guru and author Peter Drucker (organizational management writer, consultant, and sociologist) studied organizations. He strongly felt that problems and challenges facing any group of people (team) today within any organization can be traced to two variables: systems and people.

It has been my research and experience with my clients globally that this is true.

The second variable—people—typically dominates the management scene and creates the most stress and tension among players on a team. Yet Drucker asserted that of the two variables, the percentage value attributed to the two is disproportionately weighted toward systems. Nearly 85 percent of organizational problems, challenges, and productivity issues can be traced back to systems, while only 15 percent of such issues are traceable to people.

85% equals systems.

15% equals people.

So forget the math—of these two categories, which of the two dominates your time and keeps you up at night?

These two variables are interesting, especially given the fact that it tends to be the people who cause the problems (on the surface) that daily dominate the managerial leader's time, not the systems that cause the tension and stress within a team. Therefore, techniques for managing the difficult and challenging person whom management comes in contact with on a daily basis will assist in facilitating the management styles (outlined in Chapter 4, "Six Alternative Managerial Leadership Intervention Styles") of manager, teacher, mentor, counselor, disciplinarian, and coach.

People challenging to you and your mission statement may be either external or internal. Management deals with people from the positive end of the spectrum to those players on the negative end of it. They may be customers, colleagues, clients, subordinates, or supervisors. They may be friends, family, or kids; they may be powerful or wealthy. It doesn't matter who they are, only that they are difficult and challenging. So, how can you interact with these people?

The fastest way to interact with them for a positive outcome is to change your typical approach to them; consider the appropriate Managerial-Leadership-Coaching Engagement Model, also known as the SA Model intervention.

In this section, a three-step process is proposed. Step 1 establishes the foundation from which the second and final steps develop. The three steps for managing difficult and challenging people for positive outcome are

1. Neutralize or condition the person or player by acknowledging her empathetically.

2. Interact with the person or player by taking ownership and communicating to her on a level whereby the worker understands that you want to engage and not fight.

3. Stimulate a change within the person or player by charting a course of action.

As you analyze these three steps, notice which one management typically jumps directly into when faced with a difficult or challenging person. Perhaps phrases like "crisis management," "conflict resolution," or "putting out fires" seem familiar. If they do, recognize this is a blend, because management and players are always jumping directly into the interact step or stage without ever neutralizing the other player.

To begin to change the paradigm of traditional interactions with difficult and challenging people, which turn confrontational and lead to heightened stress and team tension levels, consider conditioning the environment differently from what you might traditionally do and what the other player would expect you to do. By neutralizing the other player (reverse psychology), you condition her for a greater level of interaction, and that can lead to a more productive outcome—change!

To neutralize, establish nonthreatening ways to create a more relaxing atmosphere in which your interaction has a chance of being heard and thus accepted and acted (not reacted) upon. There are several ways to neutralize the other players in conversation, one-on-one situations, and when challenged in a more public environment where there are witnesses to the interaction. Consider a profession trained in the importance of neutralizing first to attain the desired interaction level and safe, productive outcomes: law enforcement. Does the management system parallel your environment and personal/professional interactions?

Emergency professionals (fire, medical, police) train weekly in special drills (manager role) so that when in a situation for which they have trained, the actions and responses will be automatic. By following your logic track and not your emotions, you can neutralize practically any situation.

Consider how law enforcement officers (troopers) position their patrol cars when making a traffic stop on the highway. They have learned through analysis and observation to position their cars on an angle—to serve as shields if necessary. There is then a process of logging in information about the vehicle they have engaged, and a video monitoring system, all of which are in play before they even get out of their own vehicles, thus giving them an element of neutralization.

If more than one person is in the vehicle the law enforcement officer has stopped, he requests one occupant at a time to step out of the car. He requests that hands be maintained at a level where they can be seen at all times. The person is instructed to move at a slow pace in one situation and a faster pace in another, given the situation. If the officer or trooper finds himself outnumbered and determines a need for greater levels of neutralization (control) for increased interaction success, the officer has the players assume a standard position against the vehicle and, one at a time, places them in handcuffs.

But if the officer/trooper was immediately interacting with the players beside the car and while the interaction was in progress he determined to handcuff them as they all stood within close proximity, can you imagine how difficult maintaining a neutral zone would be? Imagine how easy it would be for one of the players to incite a problem, a challenge, or a fight, or to run from the scene.

This is a process you will see in action yourself as you travel, if you become more observant of your surroundings. Now you, too, can become a student of others' actions and glean lessons that can aid you in your work environment, which is likely much less volatile.

The first step to people interaction has to be neutralization (and it goes without saying that if a situation or personality warrants make sure you consult with your human resource leadership or legal counsel before engaging these people).

Management Techniques/Tactics for Engaging Difficult Personalities

Use the following for engaging difficult personalities:

1. **Step 1: Neutralize** the challenging or difficult person before ever attempting to interact with him. Consider the following:

   - **Empathy**—Immediate acknowledgment many times defuses a negative, challenging, or difficult person. Acknowledgment means you recognize the person and his position. It doesn't mean you agree or disagree. Often, these challenging people feel they have to be difficult to get attention. Your immediate acknowledgment throws them mentally off balance and gives you management control.

- **Avoidance of challenging vocabulary**—When interacting with these people and in your initial attempt to neutralize the environment, avoid words that mentally poke a finger at them and solicit defensiveness. Words, such as *you, however, but, think,* and *opinion,* are all words that listeners feel compelled to defend their positions against, as they feel you have just attacked.

- **Use of ownership words**—These are words that send the message of "We are in this together" and "No one is trying to control anyone here." Use words such as *I, we, us, feel.*

- **Venting**—Let the other player vent 100 percent of what is on his mind. As he vents, take notes so the person can see that you are writing as he talks (or yells). Taking notes helps you to pay attention, track what he is presenting from a logical perspective, and helps the player keep his mouth closed (which typically opens and pulls you directly into the negativity).

- **Apology**—If the threat is an organizational problem, don't join in to point fingers or defend a known problem. Admit the negative point, offer a broad apology for the event, and then immediately direct the conversation (not confrontation) back to the person in question. Ask her for input on solutions.

- **Going it alone**—Increase the number of activities you do by yourself that would traditionally involve interacting with a challenging and difficult person. This degree of exclusion will bring about change in the person's behavior. You are being realistic with this approach. Think about how many times you end up doing the task yourself anyway—only with increased personal stress and tension.

2. **Step 2: Interaction** is the objective of dealing with challenging and difficult people. You don't want a personality grudge match, merely an issue-oriented interaction. By first neutralizing the other party, you increase the prospect of the following techniques being successful. Consider the following:

   - **Avoidance**—This is the most powerful technique for dealing with these people. You are cutting down your exposure to them and the ramifications of that exposure. It is easier to walk away from a negative interaction than to remain engaged in that interaction—easier said than done for most people.

- **Isolation**—Separate the challenging and negative players from the team and keep them focused and busy at what they are good at doing. If there are times when you have a person on your team who is difficult for the team overall, but his skill or knowledge is such that you need him, then refocus your utilization of that player and how you and others are exposed to him. Isolation can mean to isolate this person away from the team, or it could mean to isolate yourself away from the difficult person! This is a lot like two children fighting over which toy is theirs. You give a toy to each, separate them, and tell them to remain by themselves and play with their own toys. You then observe one of the players (who has been isolated from the other) make a behavior change to get back with the other.

- **Demanding an alternative**—When a player is causing difficulty and contradicting what others (or you) are saying, neutralize the situation via empathy and then demand (up to three times) that she offer an alternative. Don't turn this step into a personality interaction. Keep energies focused on the issues and don't let the player off the hook. Typically, people challenge this situation and the interaction becomes an instant debate. No one ever thinks to professionally require that the player who started this debate to offer alternatives or options.

- **Not rushing in with a response**—When a player becomes difficult, allow the use of silence to help you gain or regain logical control over the interaction to increase the success quotient.

- **Visual notes**—When you are challenged by a player, start taking notes while he is talking, venting, threatening. By taking notes, you assist yourself in remaining quiet and in determining what the root problem is under all the negative energy. He will see how out of control the situation is by watching what you are writing down. No one wants his bad language or out-of-control emotions documented via notes. These people slow down and calm down, and you will not have said one word!

- **Education**—Many times the reason for difficulty is differing levels of education and awareness on an issue. Determine whether you need more education—solicit it; if the other party needs additional information—provide it!

- **Seeking linkage**—Determine points of commonality between your position and the other person's, and merge those elements. It will be easier to interact when both parties see the commonality (linkage). Thus the challenge and defensive posturing will decrease and productive interaction will begin to increase.

- **Use of double standards**—Compare the issue the player has raised and a similar issue within your environment, so she can see direct association.

- **Asking questions**—When faced with an uncertain situation or player, don't initiate a conversation from the perspective of solving the presented problem. Instead, stimulate a conversation by using one of the six power words learned in school—Who, What, When, Where, Why, and How. If one of these words-turned-questions doesn't stimulate a conversation, don't rush in. Merely move on to the next letter, or word, or question.

- **One-on-one in private**—If a player remains difficult and challenging to you and the management structure, you must go one-on-one with her. Do so in private (put on the counselor hat outlined in Chapter 4). Consider what your objective is for this meeting, prior to meeting with the player. Consider trying to identify why she is negative, as the person may have a realistic position. Once you determine what the problem is, you will be able to start to work to neutralize her for better interactions.

- **Seeking consensus**—Before moving on to additional points of discussion, make sure that the people involved in the challenging interaction have attained an agreement point on the issue at hand.

- **Pain factor/pleasure factor**—Ultimately, another person will not change his behavior unless there is a reason to. If he experiences pain—more pain to do it his way than an alternate way—or if he experiences pleasure—meaning more gain doing it another way rather than his way—the person will change the behavior.

- **Subgroup dynamics**—Interact with your positive players before dealing with the challenging and difficult ones. By interacting with your transformers and getting their buy-in on an issue and their ability to persuade the transmitters to move in your direction, your interaction with the terrorists can be neutralized and a greater interaction level can be attained via peer pressure.

- **Notepad management**—When you are interacting with more than one difficult or challenging person, you have to manage those interactions and conversations more wisely. Move from auditory conversations to visual communication. If, for example, you have multiple bosses tasking you with issues and projects, take a piece of paper and, when one approaches you with a request, write out next to a number 1 her request and place her name below your entry. When the next boss approaches, get the same piece of paper and next to the number 2, write out his request, placing that boss's name next to or below it. Now the second boss has seen the order of work and who his colleague is who has also tasked you. The second boss may not accept the placement that you have assigned, but notice that thus far in the exercise, you haven't said anything. He will inquire as to what you are working on, and you will be engaged in a conversation, whereas traditionally you would be engaged in a confrontation.

- **Involvement**—Most importantly of all when interacting with challenging and difficult people, you have to get them involved in the process and decisions. The more involved the players are the less likely they will be to attack others and cause problems.

3. **Step 3: Change** develops when you neutralize the other parties and then interact with them from an issue-oriented, not a personality-oriented, perspective.

   By focusing your energies on conditioning the environment for efficient interactions, you can go about stimulating change without people really getting upset over it. First neutralize and second interact for a proactive response perspective (not reactive mode), and the changes will come about. If you, however, approach a player and immediately work to stimulate a change, it becomes manipulation, and everyone can sense when someone is trying to manipulate them.

Using an L-grid model, the Negativity Action Index, illustrated in Figure 9.5, you can mentally assess a potential engagement with a perceived challenging or negative individual to determine which of the preceding tactical approaches is best deployed. You can be sitting in a meeting and feel the need to respond to another person in a matter of seconds. Now look at your left hand and form the L-image with your hand, with thumb horizontally outward and the index finger pointing vertically upwards. Now, plot and respond.

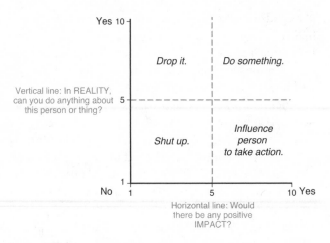

Figure 9.5 Negativity Action Index

Now imagine within that L-grid engagement model that you were to plot the axis lines from low to high. Imagine a scale of numbers, 1 through 10, on each line. With a score of 5 being the break point between a "yes" and a "no" indication, you can score people and situations in this index. With this model in your mind's-eye, you have four quadrants within the L-grid. Each quadrant directs you to the precise tactical action plan for engaging a negative person or terrorist for constructive managerial leadership behavior. The quadrants dictate:

1. **The lower-left quadrant** tactical response is to *shut up*. You have indicated that in reality, neither you nor anyone else can do anything about this person/situation, and the impact would not matter even if you could interact. So just shut up and move on. This does not imply that the difficult person wins and you lose. If you engage the person, you surely do lose.

2. **The top-left quadrant** tactical response is to *drop it*. While yes, you can in reality say or do something, in the final analysis the impact would not matter, so why stir up tension and animosity with others when it really does not matter? So the best course of tactical action here is to drop it and walk away.

3. **The bottom-right quadrant** tactical response is to engage the person who, in reality, has authority or power over this situation or person, and work to *influence* her to take action. If the person in authority were to do so, the impact would be positive, and in the end the

majority and thus the organization would benefit the greatest. Start planting the seeds with those who do possess the change factor, so you can harvest that influence interaction in the future—be patient.

4. **The top-right quadrant** tactical response is to *do something*. It is in this quadrant that you, in reality, can do something, and the impact does matter. Here is where you attain a level of transformer productivity.

How you tactically engage the challenging players within your sphere of influence or responsibility directly influences how others see you, respect you, and follow you.

Your team is a reflection of you as the managerial leader, and you reflect your team.

#7: Counseling the Difficult Player (Terrorist)

The reality today is that we have spent decades creating a public mind-set of, "Why work, when I can sue?"

So when you find yourself within the Managerial-Leadership-Coaching Engagement Model, also known as the SA Model, indicating the counselor or disciplinarian style of management, consult with HR or legal counsel, but do not abdicate this intervention. In many cases these people have never been held accountable, or it has been a long time since anyone has actually held them accountable, and that is why in many cases these people have become bullies—either overtly or passive-aggressively.

To compound this problem, we have negotiated away the reality that no one makes a person take a job with an organization. Yet it in many cases it becomes a marvel how, once hired, individuals begin exploring ways to make their lives better at the organization's expense. Hence minimal effort for maximum paycheck becomes a norm with many terrorists.

When this begins to show itself behaviorally in the organization, managerial leaders must take immediate action. Whether you need to assume a counselor or disciplinarian role, it must not be abdicated. Start by reminding yourself and all others of what our guiding values, vision, and mission statements are, as this may be the realignment variable needed to address derailment behaviors.

Interacting with the difficult, challenging, and negative player on your team for a positive growth outcome is the ultimate goal of every managerial leader in an organization. When that player becomes so difficult that the behavior, action, comments, and position of the terrorist is counterproductive for you and members of a team, management has to assume the style of counselor for first offense or interaction, and disciplinarian for the second interaction. Go one-on-one with that player.

The management cliché of "out of sight, out of mind" won't work in any successful growth organization of the future. The problem player may be out of the mind and sight of management, but all the other players on the team know exactly what is and is not happening. One negative player (terrorist) unchecked can cultivate additional negative players (terrorists) in your organization.

These behaviors can prove detrimental to an organization, both internally (with coworkers and other departments) as well as externally (with customers, vendors, and bottom-line perception of others about your reputation).

There are several ways management can approach this interaction, whether the aim is to educate and train a player back to peak performance, take corrective actions with this player, discipline the player, or work to eliminate the player from the team.

Worst-case scenario first! Ultimately, management (disciplinarian) has to be willing to live without a negative player, if he becomes disruptive enough to hold other players back from attaining results. If a player can be specifically seen as the negative spark plug in an environment, let him know up front that interactions are designed for a positive outcome or he will be removed from the team. Until the ultimate pain factor realization is levied, some players keep pushing management to see what they can get away with.

Given that the organization has invested a significant amount of time, money, and energy to get the player in question to the level of institutional and organizational knowledge he possesses, we need to approach the engagement with a mind-set of wanting to assist and keep the player, if possible.

Based on the analysis techniques presented in Chapter 6, your perspective of a player may or may not change. The analysis of a player is critical prior to going into a counseling session, as it may assist you in whether to have the session. If you are to have a counseling session with a difficult player, consider this subsection as a map of what to consider before, during, and after the encounter.

Before: Before the counseling session, consider the following guideposts for increased success and decreased liability.

Agenda. Develop what you believe to be the key issues that need to be addressed. Having them down on paper affords you the opportunity to secure all documentation necessary for this interaction. It gives you time to get your thoughts and notes together, and a chance to investigate your assumptions and positions to gather additional data, facts, and documentation necessary to keep this interaction issue-oriented, not a personality matter.

Location. Consider the most nonthreatening and conducive place for the interaction, where the other person is most inclined to open up and verbalize his positions without feeling threatened.

Time. Consider the best time for you (not him) to hold the session to further impact your missions. Is it at the beginning of the day or week, toward the end of the day or week, or directly before something important?

Observer. Consider having a neutral third party (your equal or superior, not the other player's equal) sit in on the session to take notes and observe. She is not there to lend her perspectives and comments, or to take sides. Pre-establish with this party her role before the session. Remember, in some work environments, the observers are posturing points, used merely to psyche out the other party.

Alternatives. Are there other options available to management for interacting with the difficult player to stimulate a change in actions or behavior, besides a formal or informal counseling session?

Third-Party Information/Leads. Many times problems concerning players on your team are not actually experienced by management. The concerns about a player are brought to management by another player (tattletale). For this reason, management must protect its position against "would-be" terrorists on a team. For those rare occasions when a player on a team may be instigating trouble and even trying to set up a particular manager, it's good to be cautious. If a player brings a concern to you about another person, ask the one talking to you to write down those concerns, citing specific issues. If she won't, be aware that the tattletale may be the problem player, not the person she is pointing a finger at. If the complainant does write down the concerns, you have a map for future observations. Once the informer writes down the specifics, ask that player to sign the paper. Once signed, you have an official document. If she won't sign it, let this be a second opportunity to analyze where the real problem is.

Solutions. Establish several options or strategies for working through the difficulty in case the player you're going to meet with becomes unresponsive. Then you can maintain control of the session and stimulate conversation between the two of you by posing your alternatives or options.

Pain Factors. Identify the penalties for nonconformance and nonchange. Determine the level of severity to take place in this session. Consider pain as the "leverage" you have to motivate them to address and work to change the behaviors that you have indicated as unacceptable to the organization. If you have exhausted all pleasure factors to this point and the difficult and challenging player is still refusing your position and authority, it is now time to get serious.

Elevation to Higher Authority. Based upon these reference points, always ask yourself at this point (prior to actually going one-on-one with the problematic individual) if this issue would be better addressed by someone in human resources, legal, and so on, due to the potential sensitivity or gravity of the subject. Potential clues for checking before you proceed would be any history with this individual that suggests he can be less than ethical, may be litigious, or may have any ethnicity, gender, or generational implications.

During: During the counseling session you are primarily there for your own benefit (as you represent the organization) and not for the difficult or challenging player. The interaction needs to be highly professional, structured, and focused. Consider the following techniques for maintaining a productive, controlled session:

Agenda. Start off by presenting the other people in the session with a copy of your agenda so that everyone can visually see what this meeting is about. With an agenda, everyone knows what is to be discussed, and therefore, what is not to be addressed. If someone goes off the agenda, you can point at it (not at the person) and make a directed comment focusing energies and the conversation back to the next item on the agenda.

Expectation Statement. Your opening statement should contain a reference to what your expectations are for this session. By doing this, the other player(s) understand your level of seriousness, commitment, and what this session's goal is. An explosive way to start the session is with a statement like, "We are here today because of choices you have made."

Time. Make an immediate reference to the amount of time allocated to the session. By doing so, all players know how much time has been budgeted for this agenda, and if anyone gets off track, you can reference time as another factor for getting back on schedule.

Neutral Third Parties. If you have an observer, introduce the person and discuss what his participation will be; then move directly on to the agenda. Always have a third party who is your peer level or higher in any session where there is history with a player who dictates to do so, for a liability or safety purposes. If the individual you are meeting with would have someone in the session as a representative (in union environments, for example), be sure to have a third party present on the company's behalf.

Follow-up. Establish what the follow-up plan and schedule will be for the agenda items about to be discussed. If the player in question knows up front that there will be a follow-up plan, and that he will be getting back with you face-to-face in a limited number of days to measure the progress made based upon this meeting and what is discussed and agreed upon, the follow-up date also serves as a motivator for the player(s) in question to stimulate some change.

Mini-Agreements. During the session, work through the agenda items one at a time and work to obtain an agreement on each individual issue, as to what it is and what will be done jointly to resolve it. Obtain an agreement on the battle plan before moving on to the next item. By establishing these mini-agreements, you will be able to manage the overall session more wisely. Also, if the session breaks down, you can go back to the last point where the parties had an agreement and begin again from there.

Taking Notes. Everything the other party says, suggests, or claims needs to be documented and attached to the agenda at the end of the session. Whenever a player in a session talks, as long as he is on the agenda, don't interrupt him; merely take notes. This note-taking helps you understand his perspectives and serves as documentation of what took place within the session.

Solutions. Several solutions to issues raised should be discussed before making a decision on the course of action. Stimulate a conversation with the other player to solicit solutions. If none are presented, suggest some of the solutions you designed before the session and get the other player's feedback.

Confidentiality. Discuss and agree upon what will be expressed to other members of the team after the session, if they inquire.

Silence. Use silence as a tool to reinforce your seriousness on issues and to stimulate responses from the other person. Don't let the other person be unresponsive in this session.

Agenda Manager© System. Consider formatting a piece of paper as your document flow for the agenda presentation of your concerns to players (see a sample form in the following sidebar). Have all parties sign the agenda in the appropriate places. After the session, each participant should leave with a copy of the agreed-upon agenda items and solutions. This documentation is another powerful means for stimulating change.

Using this system is easy and serves to facilitate a session from a structured and professional perspective. The steps for using the Agenda Manager system template are

1. Identify across the top of the page the core issue or subject matter to be addressed at this counseling session.

2. List the actual date and time of the session.

3. Write or type out the individual item(s) or issue(s) to be addressed under the item/issue section. Note each additional item with numbers, so all parties can focus on one numbered variable at a time.

4. At the bottom of the form, identify all the names of the people in the session. This serves both as historical documentation and as a reminder of all the players in the session if your mind blanks out.

5. On the far right side of the form, place your initials. The player in question should place his initials adjacent to each line item discussed, when it has been finalized and a course of corrective action has been mapped out. If the player refuses to sign, be aware that he more than likely has not resolved that issue and further conversation is required. If he still refuses to sign each item, make a vivid note of that fact. Then move on to the next line to be addressed.

This system is designed to allow all parties involved to maintain professional controls, and for all parties to address issues one step at a time for positive outcomes. Should the player in question (or in some environments, the player's representatives) refuse to participate in the Agenda Manager there is a serious issue of lack of trust among the entire group, which should serve as a topic of conversation in another session.

Sample Management Productivity Group (MPG) Meeting Agenda

1. Three-minute SWOT brief by each **division** leader. In this MACRO brief should be an update/report of all actionable items for self and team accountability needs; this should also contain a profit center update.

    a. Identify **one** power action item for next 7 days to increase/save revenue.

2. Three-Minute SWOT brief by each **department** leader. In this MACRO brief should be an update/report of all actionable items for self and team accountability needs; this should also contain a profit center update.

    a. Identify **one** power action item for next 7 days to increase/save revenue.

3. Regroup for further presentation and/or Q&A from each division/department leader (only as needed).

4. Recap any action items from meeting.

5. Announcements of any successes/wins that week and collaboration opportunities for immediate sales.

6. 15–30-minute self-development module.

7. Next meeting set/agreement.

After: After the counseling session, you must invest a few minutes away from the team, your colleagues, and the players just in the session with you, and also away from interruptions to finish the third and most critical step in the successful facilitation of a counseling session. To ensure greater levels of transformation with the difficult player you just left, and to ensure no liabilities later, consider the following:

- **Agenda**—Review your agenda to ensure that all items listed were addressed and that nothing was overlooked or short-changed. Look at the Agenda Manager and make sure all points were addressed and initialed.

- **Notes**—Make sure that the play-by-play notes you took during the session make sense to you in retrospect. If you need to add additional perspective or edited notes so they will make sense to you six months or a year later, do so.

- **Observer's notes**—Take the observer's notes and review them. In a second color of ink (noted as your additions), add any perspective to these notes, if necessary, for future understanding.

- **Follow-up**—Make sure that the agreed-upon follow-up sequence is maintained. If necessary, put notes in your professional daily calendar of those future dates and what you are to be doing. If you want the session's observer to participate in the follow-up activities, coordinate that now, not later.

- **Player formal/informal follow-up**—Immediately after the session, make a photocopy of the Agenda Manager page. Write a follow-up postscript note to all parties to reinforce the session's issues and remind the player(s): This is what we discussed and agreed to, and this is when we get together to measure our progress. Hand-writing the note still conveys the message, yet it is less threatening than a typed follow-up note.

- **Creation of a packet**—Once completed, take a copy of the agenda, any notes taken in the session, the follow-up note, the Agenda Manager (if used), and any organization-specific forms and bundle them together (or staple). Maintain one set onsite in an appropriate personnel file. Also have a duplicate set offsite for your own insurance—and never purge this file.

- **Send a nonconfrontation solution email**—In essence send an email after the interaction, speak to the severity of the situation that served as the purpose of the meeting, reference the specific call-to-action next steps, reassert your commitment to the solution implementation, and CC all other appropriate parties to leverage the other names to motivate the behavior change and create layers of documentation accountability.

The only real difference between a counseling session and a disciplinarian session is in a counseling session, there is much more interaction, dialogue, managerial leadership discretion, and desire to move forward. In a disciplinarian session, the individual you are meeting with is clearly instructed that this is the final time this matter will ever be discussed, the documentation is much more finite, and the only alternative to not changing her behavior is termination. Ideally, craft your documentation so it articulates that continuation of said behavior/actions on her behalf constitutes immediate "resignation from the organization." Then, along with her departure, it becomes more difficult for her to apply for and receive unemployment benefits.

Consider these tactical ideas when planning your next managerial leader counselor or disciplinarian sessions.

#8: Dealing with Procrastination and Burnout

Infusing energy and experiencing the rebirth of a player on a team who has digressed from participation and contribution to the organization to liability and procrastination is possible. Most players (including yourself) fall victim to procrastination for simple reasons. Left unchecked, this state of procrastination can digress further to a state of burnout.

When procrastination occurs within an organization, it causes low levels of productivity, which can spread or lead to players' tensions and difficulty. When burnout occurs within an organization, it causes work shortages, accidents, errors, apathy, and player turnover.

So what causes procrastination? Consider procrastination in players on your team and determine whether any of the following factors apply. Procrastination occurs due to

- Dislike for tasks being delegated routinely to player
- Dislike for the players around them
- Dislike for the specific task assigned to them
- Degree of confusion over how to begin
- Uncertainty whether enough data is available from which to make an accurate decision
- Fear of making the wrong decision on their own, and a fear of interaction with management necessary prior to final action
- FEAR, representing degrees of False Education (or evidence) Appearing Real, and psyching oneself out of action

Management can work to deter and even avoid situations that lead to the state of procrastination. By avoiding procrastination, management can avoid significant numbers of burnout situations with players. Start by applying the Player Capability Index formula in real time to a situation and person; you may recognize that the burnout may be due to not effectively utilizing your human assets. Once you do this, then consider the following management techniques.

Management Techniques/Tactics for Procrastination

Fear. Most procrastinators will hesitate to act because something is making them feel uncomfortable. Management needs to interact to identify what that factor is, deal with it, and then move on. Most players' fear factor is based on

---

False Education (or evidence) allowed to Appear Realistic. And this factor is what is preventing them from moving forward.

Deadline. Establish a specific deadline associated with the task the player has been assigned. Many times a specific deadline serves as the motivator or stimulant to get a person who may otherwise procrastinate to either come forward with questions or become productive. Unfortunately, management will at times be dealing with a procrastinator and request something by the end of today. Is that deadline specific or general? Does "end of today" mean 3:00 p.m., 4:00 p.m., or 5:00 p.m.? And then when management returns at the end of the day and it is not done, tension and conflict are the outcome.

Schedule Enough Time the First Time. Many times, management tasks a procrastinator with something and requests it back in a certain amount of time. Next time, in light of the player you're interacting with and the issue you are interacting on, schedule enough time the first time. If a procrastinator takes one hour for something, and in your estimation it should take 45 minutes, then schedule one hour. If the player gets it done in one hour or less, he will be in a positive mood, which means greater quality results. However, if you schedule 45 minutes and the player takes one hour, he will be in a bad mood, and will be behind schedule because of another project.

Schedule It to Later in That Day. Take the issue that has you stuck or another player stuck and set it to the side for a few minutes or hours. Place a note strategically where you will keep seeing it as a reminder to go back to this certain project later on. A procrastinator would push it to the side also, and say, "I will get back to this later." Only problem is, he doesn't define when "later" is. Here you are defining the "later"! If, for example, it is 10:00 a.m. and you find yourself stuck (wasting time, daydreaming, getting upset, talking to yourself, and so on), take that project, set it to the side somewhere, and write a note reminding yourself to go back to it at 2:00 p.m.; then attach that note to your telephone. Consciously move on to another project with a different mental perspective. Every time your eyes scan past the telephone and you consciously see the note, you are telling your subconscious mind to work on that issue. When 2:00 p.m. comes around, recognize that what had you stuck earlier in the day is easily dealt with in the afternoon!

Asking Questions. When you find yourself or someone else in a procrastination state, identify how the situation came about and what has caused productivity to come to a stop. Once those answers can be identified, management can work to avoid similar situations.

See-Say-Do. Instead of showing a player what needs to be done (see) or telling a player what needs to be taken care of (say), have her do it! Next time when you find a player procrastinating, have her show both of you that she can do the job. The next time she is tasked with something, the player's last mental point of reference will be that of success, and therefore she can do it again.

If management does not interact with a player on a team who seems to be a procrastinator, even if just a casual procrastinator, that player, over time gone unchecked, can revert to a person who feels burned out. When a player hits this stage, there are a limited number of options available to management.

Management Techniques/Tactics for Burnout

Do Something Different. Have the player do something completely different from his norms. Don't have the player continue to do more of the present task, as there is a good chance he doesn't like any of it. This could mean something different professionally (assignments, tasks, duties, trips, interactions, volunteerism, and so on) or personally (community activities, social involvements, sports, and so on).

Delegate Something Different. Consider what the burned-out player typically receives from management with respect to tasks. To stimulate life and energy in this player, delegate something completely different to push her out of the norm.

Volunteer for Something Different. Assist this player in getting involved with something different, either through volunteering or not allowing him to volunteer for the usual things. The point here is to get the player into a new habit and to spend his time in different activities.

Move. Have the player make a lateral or vertical move to stimulate a new psychology. Get her professionally out of her routines and into something new, challenging, and different.

Mentor. Have the player serve as a mentor to new players and gain energy from new life. This will at the same time give the older or burned-out player a new mission and feeling of worth.

Dealing with procrastinators or burned-out people takes energy from management and from other players. To maintain your level of organizational success and guard against falling into one of the same traps, you have to consider a few universals with both kinds of players. Consider a few ways to ensure productivity and work to stimulate subtle changes in these two kinds of players at the same time.

Management Techniques/Tactics for Combined Procrastinators and Burnout

Avoidance. Work to avoid direct interaction with these players if you know of alternative ways and means to accomplish your objectives. This reduces both stress and tension levels (yours and theirs). Also, by avoiding these difficult situations, you are reducing the volume of negative strain on their psyches. Everyone wins, and now the other players can focus her energies on being productive.

Education. Increased education and training on your behalf or the other players in question reduces the volume of unknowns that leads to nonproductivity.

Pairing Up. Strategically place the team expert on an issue with a player who is typically slow or nonproductive, to see whether the mini-teaming stimulates positive interaction and productivity. Observe to see whether the procrastinator or burned-out person learns from your team expert and whether that player increases his levels of efficiency.

Reassignment of Tasks. If procrastination continues, reassign the typical workflow so that the procrastinating player you want to keep on the team is no longer in the receiving line for those negatives.

#9: Managing Time, Time Wasters, and Paper Information Flow

Gaining control of time in the workplace seems to be a never-ending pursuit. Imagine being able to save time and place it in a time savings account, so when you need additional time you can make a withdrawal. Unfortunately, it doesn't work that way.

Again, having the right human asset in the right place and at the right time can go a long way in addressing this issue.

Saving time now, for utilization in the future, is the reason management needs to work to eliminate as many time-wasting activities as possible. The Law of the Competitive Edge states that if you could save just one hour a day, or regain one hour a day of misspent time, over the course of the year that one hour daily would add up to more than 45 eight-hour days of time!

Gaining that one hour a day is the objective of this short course on organizational time management, project time management, personal time management, and people time management.

To manage that time, first recognize that three different types of time environments encompass your daily professional schedule. Only in one of those three do you have 100 percent control. When you are within the other two, you don't have control capabilities. At best, you can manage these two environments.

Consider the following three different professional time types for a better understanding of where time is allotted, and percentage-wise, how much time you spend daily in each.

- Boss-imposed time =
- System-imposed time =
- Self-imposed time =

There are three time types each professional day. Consider what these three environments are all about: Boss-imposed time is a situation where your boss places demands on you and there is no recourse; you cannot change the situation. System-imposed time is the time constraints and demands placed upon you by the procedures, regulations, policies, laws, customers, vendors, and culture within your professional environment (system), which you have no control over and more or less have inherited. Whereas in the self-imposed time environment, you have direct control and power of choice and actions over what you are doing. This is where you typically find peak performance (and for many is thus defined as before work, during lunch, after work, and on the weekends).

Based on how you feel your time is spent or invested each day, you can maximize the time falling within the three environments, especially the self-imposed time.

One powerful way to determine objectively what the time wasters in your environment are is to utilize a daily time log (sort of a time and motion study of yourself) for an entire day. At the end of the day or the following day, invest some time in analyzing where you spent your time, and thus where wasted time may be lurking. To successfully decide which time management techniques to utilize from this section (and from throughout this text), you must first have a clear perspective of where you spend time. The daily time log shows you exactly that.

If you use this time log, remember it is for your edification only. No one else needs to see what you're doing throughout the course of the day as you log onto the chart, nor does anyone need to see the finished daily log.

Consider building your own time log with 30-minute increments for your normal day along a vertical axis and then create a list of action activity entries for both what you should be doing and also known time wasters across a horizontal axis. Then for a series of days, aggressively use it by placing check marks in the appropriate columns for what you are doing every 30 minutes.

Through the utilization of a time tracking chart like the one in Table 9.3, you can determine where your time was spent negatively and where specific time wasters may be within your environment. Once you can identify the time wasters in your three environments, you can strategize ways to regain productive usage of that time.

Table 9.3   Sample Time Tracking Chart

	6:00	7:00	8:00	9:00	10:00	11:00	And so on...
25 New Daily Contacts Reached							
10 COI/VIP Contacts							
2 Appointments/ Presentations							
10 eDM Direct Connections							
2 eMedia Kit/eProposals Sent							
Admin Time (Morning Preparation)							
Area Canvassing (Selling/ Prospecting)							
Database-Leveraged Activities							
Lunch							
eFU/CBs							
Professional Development							
Database eDM Campaign(s)							
Phone Power							
Close-Out Admin							
SEO and Social Media Connectivity							
IP Development							

	6:00	7:00	8:00	9:00	10:00	11:00	And so on...
Mail-Outs, Packets, Contracts, Invoicing							
Website Review and Updates							
Affiliate and Partnership Networking							
Time Wasters							
Internet							
Long Lunches							
Socializing							
Breaks, BS, and Trajectory B Pathways							
Drive Time							

The purpose of the daily time efficiency log is to aid you in determining what you have and have not been doing, every 30 minutes. By logging onto your personal chart every 30 minutes (or so), at the end of the day you can reflect on what the day contained for you. By identifying any patterns in your behavior (or others') that lead to either a productive day or major downtime, you can plan accordingly.

Ultimately, from physically using a time efficiency log, you are able to objectively answer the two major questions that management reflects upon for hiring, keeping, or dismissing a player from a team. The two questions that every position must answer are

- How can this position and player make the organization money?
- How can this position or player help the organization save money?

From the utilization of a daily time efficiency log you can determine two answers:

- How did I spend my time?
- Who else spent my time and how did they do it?

The answers to these four questions are the powerful answers that Peter Drucker outlines as management's requirement to be able to maximize people as valuable resources in an organization. These responses and answers also prove valuable in managing time and dealing effectively with time wasters. The remaining pages of this subsection assist you in maximizing your time within some of the major time-wasting environments.

Management Techniques/Tactics for Managing Time, Time Wasters, and Paper Information Flow

Telephone and Emails. Telephones and emails never seem to disrupt you when you have free time or when you are between projects. They seem to come alive when you have no free time, you're late on a project, and you're dealing with a crisis, or when you are alone in the office and trying to handle several things at one time. Some general rules to live by to turn the telephone into your power time-saver tool are discussed in the following items.

Voice Mail. Activate voice mail or your answering machine once each morning and once each afternoon, for 30 minutes of time uninterrupted by the telephone. Focus your energies on critical work tasks. Leave a personal message for the caller so he knows what is happening. ("Thank you for calling; this is Jeff and I am working on a critical project for the next 30 minutes. At the tone please leave your name, a short message, and the best time to return the call. I will be checking these messages at _____. If it is an emergency, dial _____ and ask for _____. Thank you.")

Hold Button. Don't use this function until you have asked and received an answer from one of two powerful questions: (1) "May I put you on hold/can you hold, please?" or (2) "May I take your number and name and call you right back, as it will take me a few minutes to obtain this information?" Otherwise, the caller is restricted at his end as to what he can and cannot do. If that caller is upset or hostile, the entire hold time reminds the caller of his level of negativity. And when you return, the person on hold is even more upset.

Chunking. Gang up all the emails, voice mail messages, texts, and phone message slips of people you need to return contact or calls to and return them at one time. For example, if you know that during the last few minutes in the morning before lunch certain people will be less likely to socialize, call those people right before lunchtime (or use the same philosophy and call them at the end of the day).

Outbound Phone. Determine which people you need to contact have voice-mail or answering services/machines. If they have an alternative phone message system, ask yourself whether you need to relay information or to talk with this person live. If message relay is the objective, never talk with her live.

This substantially reduces the volume of time you spend on the telephone, while at the same time increases productivity.

Outbound Email Response. Determine whether you really need to create the next great piece of prose or whether you can simply place your cursor next to the questions within the received email and type your answer back in a different color. This saves volumes of time.

Subject Line. Sometimes you can respond or send an email to someone and use the subject line to communicate your entire need. This saves time and energy.

Emails, Social Media Posts/Requests, and Paper Stacks. The volume of correspondence (paper) in the professional organization today is unbelievable. No matter how electronic your environment is or becomes, there is and will always be paperwork, paper flow, paper stacks, and paper collecting in file cabinets and drawers. To manage paper more efficiently, consider the following idea.

RAFT. Invest the first few minutes upon arriving at your work environment to immediately RAFT your stacks each morning. When you return from breaks, lunch, or meetings and look in your in-box, for example, in essence all about you is paper looking for a stack to call home.

Any paper stack can be rafted in a matter of seconds with this technique. You pick up the main stack and ask yourself one of four key questions as you touch each item. The answer to these questions as you are touching each item directs which substack the item belongs in. Once you have converted your primary paper stack into four substacks, you can manage paper and work to eliminate stacks from collecting around you.

The four power questions for managing and eliminating paper stacks and dealing with emails from your life are

- **R = Refer**—Can I refer this item to someone else?
- **A = Action**—Does this need my action?
- **F = File**—Does this need to be filed?
- **T = Toss**—Can this be recycled or tossed away?

You have now broken the primary stack down into four substacks. From these four substacks, set to the side those two that can be dealt with at any time (the "R" and "F") and focus on the immediate items for action ("A"). With the two substacks to the side, you can deal with them at your discretion and also utilize them as props should someone corner you during the day and begin to waste your time. Grab an "F" or "R" and proceed noncon-frontationally with that stack as you disburse them and interact accordingly with others. As for the other person, invite her to assist with your endeavor.

Correspondence. How many times have you read a letter, fax, memo, or contract and had no idea of its contents on second reading? Now you invest time again to glance over or read it again.

Even if you use a system such as the RAFT formula, the material you sort through and place in the appropriate stacks is only half the issue. Establishing your own note-taking system on the paper and documents for easier future access is necessary. Several powerful techniques you can utilize to increase your comprehension of written materials and help yourself with the filed paperwork activity are

- **Growth wheels**—A type of mind-mapping note-taking that assists you in becoming a whole brain communicator. As you read a letter, for example, underline or circle all power points within the text. Upon finishing the text, go to the upper right-hand corner of the paper and draw a circle. In that circle, in your own words, write down what the major point the text was about. Off that circle place lines and transfer the names, figures, dates, and so on from the text of the letter to these new lines at the top-right corner. In essence you are creating your own condensed note section for every letter or document you read. Placing these notes in this area of the paper and in this manner assists you in finding information contained in letters. As you reference a paper stack or file folder within a cabinet, all you need do is look at the upper right-hand corner of each page until you reach the desired one. Then you can open the entire folder and pull that individual page out for further reference. You can eliminate the time spent looking over and through every piece of paper to find one specific item.

- **Immediate Action Correspondence Turnaround (I-ACT)**—Imme-diately upon receiving an email, text, letter, memo, fax, document, or any visual piece of communication from another person who requires your reply, consider the level of formality that must be maintained. If the level is low or the relationship you have with the sender of the communication allows, save considerable time and resources by merely writing the answer directly on the document sent to you. Return the document or a copy of it immediately. Consider whether you can merely handwrite the information or response to the sender directly on the letter sent to you. Write your reply on the bottom por-tion of the letter where space is available, or on the reverse side of it immediately after reading it. This saves valuable formal writing time by merely replying on the sender's paper. If you need a copy for your files, make a copy of the original letter with your reply written on it.

With an email, for example, you could respond with a simple one-word response. Or send an email to someone with the entire question as the subject line to maximize impact and save time.

- **Reading file**—Place low-priority letters and correspondence in a reading file and review this file at regular times. If you travel, this file can be saved and read during trips to maximize traveling downtime.

General Time Management. Consider alternative management techniques for dealing effectively with other time zappers as well. No matter how effective you are, there is no getting away from paper stacks, paperwork, people who like to socialize, getting yourself and others organized to accomplish the top priorities, and endless file folders carrying projects. Consider the following techniques for increased effectiveness.

Delegation Dynamics Matrix. Consider the delegation formula presented in the delegation dynamics section.

Action Memo. This is a powerful technique for removing the monkeys strategically placed on your shoulders by others. Review the "#4: Delegation Dynamics" section for a step-by-step approach to this management tool.

Quadrant Manager. This powerful prioritizing system can be utilized in concert with any other day planner system or as a stand-alone tool. Break daily work into one of the four appropriate work categories and focus energies accordingly. Refer to Chapter 7, "Sustaining Your Professional Success Quotient," and Figure 7.1 for a detailed approach to this technique.

Tickler System. Save your memory for important items. Utilize your electronic calendar system (computer, PDA, and so on), desk calendar, day planner, or file system, and write down the people to call and things to do on the appropriate dates. Once logged in, concentrate on other issues and don't worry about remembering lower-priority items.

Electronic Management Systems, such as PDAs and desktop systems, should be deployed as appropriate to the environment and individual. Systems can be synced into organizations' intranet systems and accessed externally via the Internet. Whatever level of functionality you deploy, remember the system should eliminate redundancies and increase efficiency, or it is not a system worth adhering to.

File Folders and File Folder Management. These are the most obvious tools for managing projects. Each project needs and deserves its own folder. Don't try to manage work by zigzag stacks on your desk. Place each project in a separate file and then use the next three steps for file folder management:

- **"Next step is"**—Whenever you leave a project for another task, always grab a piece of paper or sticky note and leave a brief note to yourself as to what your next step is. This saves you valuable time later when you return to a project and attempt to determine what you're supposed to be doing. This also allows you to refocus your mental energies to where you were when you left—instant creativity!

- **File folder/project management quadrant manager**—Use the upper half of the inside cover of every file folder to design a quadrant manager as it relates to that specific project or task. By designing the specific do/see/call/write tasks, you can monitor each project individually to determine whether you are on track. This system also affords you the ability to delegate a project and allows the other player to have a starting point or map of that project; right there inside that file folder are your notes as to the minimum course of action required to facilitate that project.

- **File folder/project Growth Wheel©**—Use the bottom half of every file folder to design a specific growth wheel with your notes that will assist in accomplishing this task or project. As each item on this map of notes is accomplished, put a check mark next to it, designating that it is no longer relevant. This also serves as a fast-track glance as to what is next. Use these specific time management savers along with the ideas presented throughout this chapter as additional ways of dealing with time wasters.

Managerial Leadership Bible Lesson Nine

Every managerial leader participates in nine core administrative functionalities regardless of stature or industry. The better equipped that person is to facilitate that task with as little disruption as possible and as much fluid forward momentum as she is capable of, the better is the hallmark of a great managerial leader who yields great results for the team and the organization that she shepherds.

Review Questions

The review questions accompanying each chapter or section are designed to assist you in achieving the learning objective stated at the beginning of each chapter. The review section is not graded; do not submit it in place of your final exam. While completing the review questions, it may be helpful to study any unfamiliar terms in the glossary in addition to course content. After completing the review questions for each chapter, proceed to the review question answers and rationales.

1. Employee incentives should be the same for every employee so they don't feel jealous.

    A. True

    B. False

2. What should a manager consider in creating an effective incentive?

    A. Can the incentives be used as tax write-offs?

    B. If it doesn't work, who is to blame?

    C. If it works, can it be repeated?

    D. Does the incentive create competition between employees?

3. An incentive should be provided if an employee:

    A. Works overtime every week.

    B. Comes to work on time every day.

    C. Takes shorter lunch breaks than given.

    D. Exceeds expectations.

4. The power of the huddle is that you:

    A. Get to shout your company's mission statement.

    B. Meet where there are no tables or chairs.

    C. Allow employees time to relax and chat.

    D. Plan for more meetings.

5. What is the first question you should ask yourself when planning a meeting?

    A. What size room will need to be reserved for the meeting?

    B. Should the management provide coffee and snacks?

    C. How can the meeting allow employees a "breather"?

    D. Can the purpose of this meeting be communicated to the team and players by another means (email, voicemail, one-on-one, and so on)?

6. How should a manager plan for a meeting that will take longer than 45 minutes?

    A. Make plans for breaks or other activities to reinvigorate employees.

    B. Tell employees that the meeting will be longer.

    C. Ask one employee every 10 minutes to give a presentation.

    D. Keep friends from sitting next to each other.

7. Which is an effective way to deal with a negative participant at a meeting?

    A. React

    B. Argue

    C. Empathize

    D. Disagree

8. _____ is a systematic approach to entrusting something to another player.

    A. Designation

    B. Delegation

    C. Dismissal

    D. Deterioration

9. An _____ simply asks an individual approaching you to be prepared to orally communicate only two items.

    A. Agenda

    B. Actualization Assessment

    C. Action Memo

    D. Alert Note

10. Which tactic for delegation involves analyzing each department independently to determine delegation patterns?

    A. Train technology assistants.

    B. Develop player experts.

    C. Start a delegation box.

    D. Design departmental workflow charts.

11. After investigating other factors, a decision-capable individual or group should identify the _____.

    A. Risk

    B. Time

    C. Optimal Decision Point

    D. Quality

12. A _____ team is designed to address a specific need that is typically not a normal event and has a limited life cycle.

    A. Management

    B. Temporary

    C. Workgroup

    D. Cross-functional

13. The four psychological thought-processing steps are not in any particular order.

    A. True

    B. False

14. How do you neutralize a conversation with a difficult person?

    A. Acknowledge her empathically.

    B. Validate her with compliments.

    C. Disagree with her and end the conversation.

    D. Nod your head and pretend to listen.

15. How do you avoid procrastination among your employees?

    A. Make them keep a daily chart of what they've accomplished.

    B. Play energizing music through the office's intercom.

    C. Establish a specific deadline.

    D. Create a "buddy" for each employee to keep them on task.

Review Question Answers and Rationales

Review question answer choices are accompanied by unique, logical reasoning (rationales) as to why an answer is correct or incorrect. Evaluative feedback to incorrect responses and reinforcement feedback to correct responses are both provided.

1. Employee incentives should be the same for every employee so they don't feel jealous.

   A. Incorrect. The flexible manager must realize that incentives change from employee to employee and over time as well.

   B. Correct. Incentives should be weighed by a variety of factors to consider individual needs.

2. What should a manager consider in creating an effective incentive?

   A. Incorrect. These incentives are about the employees, not just the company.

   B. Incorrect. The manager should take all ownership of designed incentives.

   C. Correct. If an incentive is too expensive or takes up too much time, the employees might be disappointed if you can't repeat it.

   D. Incorrect. While some healthy competition is effective, incentives should not create jealousy between employees.

3. An incentive should be provided if an employee:

   A. Incorrect. Not every employee would be capable of this, and such a practice would suggest better work delegation is needed.

   B. Incorrect. This should already be done to meet normal expectations.

   C. Incorrect. Employees are allotted breaks to make them more effective. An employee should not be rewarded for ignoring his or her physical and emotional needs.

   D. Correct. A paycheck is an employee's incentive to meet expectations; exceeding expectations should result in an incentive.

4. The power of the huddle is that you:

   A. Incorrect. That is a sports huddle, not a business one.

   B. Correct. This keeps the time of the meeting down to a minimum.

   C. Incorrect. This is the exact opposite of what a huddle should do.

   D. Incorrect. Huddles are for avoiding long meetings.

5. What is the first question you should ask yourself when planning a meeting?

   A. Incorrect. The first step in considering a meeting is if there is a need for a meeting at all.

   B. Incorrect. The first step in considering a meeting is if there is a need for a meeting at all.

   C. Incorrect. Meetings should be for increasing efficient work, not relaxation.

   D. Correct. To be a time-effective and cost-effective manager, meetings should be cut considerably.

6. How should a manager plan for a meeting that will take longer than 45 minutes?

   A. Correct. It is difficult for people to concentrate on one subject longer than this.

   B. Incorrect. Informing employees will not make them more attentive.

   C. Incorrect. Presentations should be given at the beginning of the meeting.

   D. Incorrect. While this may draw individual attention from the meeting, it will happen regardless of meeting time.

7. Which is an effective way to deal with a negative participant at a meeting?

   A. Incorrect. This could lead to an argument.

   B. Incorrect. Not only will this interfere with your reputation as a manager, it will accomplish nothing.

C. **Correct. A terrorist will anticipate you reacting, not trying to understand his concern.**

D. Incorrect. Disagreeing is the same thing as attacking the participant. Open discussion is necessary, not outright dismissal of ideas.

8. _____ is a systematic approach to entrusting something to another player.

    A. Incorrect. This means assigning a name, not a task.

    B. **Correct. This is essential to effective productivity.**

    C. Incorrect. This can refer to disagreeing with, or firing an employee.

    D. Incorrect. Deterioration would occur if you could not delegate properly.

9. An _____ simply asks an individual approaching you to be prepared to orally communicate only two items.

    A. Incorrect. An agenda may contain many items.

    B. Incorrect. This term is not used in the textbook.

    C. **Correct. An Action Memo keeps employees from confronting you with a hundred questions when you are otherwise occupied.**

    D. Incorrect. This term is not used in the textbook.

10. Which tactic for delegation involves analyzing each department independently to determine delegation patterns?

    A. Incorrect. This is a task involved in developing player experts.

    B. Incorrect. This step is on a micro level.

    C. Incorrect. This is for manager reference.

    D. **Correct. Before completing any of the other microtasks, a manager must understand how each individual department delegates its workload.**

11. After investigating other factors, a decision-capable individual or group should identify the _____.

    A. Incorrect. This is only one factor that contributes to the ODP.

    B. Incorrect. This is only one factor that contributes to the ODP.

C. **Correct. This allows the group or individual to know when a decision has to be made.**

D. Incorrect. This is only one factor that contributes to the ODP.

12. A _____ team is designed to address a specific need that is typically not a normal event and has a limited life cycle.

   A. Incorrect. This group is used for intermediate decision making on an everyday basis.

   B. **Correct. Once the specific need or event is addressed, there is no longer a need for a temporary team.**

   C. Incorrect. A workgroup is an everyday group with little to no final decision making ability.

   D. Incorrect. Although this is a special type of team, it is made up of a variety of experts inside and outside the organization with authority limited to the situation.

13. The four psychological thought-processing steps are not in any particular order.

   A. Incorrect. The steps are building blocks on one another.

   B. **Correct. Each subsequent step has to be thoroughly dealt with or players will mentally digress back to an already-resolved step.**

14. How do you neutralize a conversation with a difficult person?

   A. **Correct. A person who expects you to automatically disagree with her will be pleasantly surprised if you listen and empathize with her.**

   B. Incorrect. Compliments may be seen as a distraction from the issue at hand.

   C. Incorrect. This would only escalate a situation and cause more confrontation.

   D. Incorrect. Without paying attention, how can you come to any conclusions?

15. How do you avoid procrastination among your employees?

    A. Incorrect. This might be waste of employee time.

    B. Incorrect. Everyone has different musical tastes and almost everyone would find this distracting.

    C. **Correct. If you leave assignments open, that opens the door for procrastination.**

    D. Incorrect. This is a waste of employee time.

10

Improving Interactive Communication

Communication and access to knowledge (information) will be the key to power and influence for the future.... Communications impact—it is not as much what you say, as it is how you say it that directly impacts the response others have to your message!

—Nido Qubein

Learning Objective

After completing this section of the course, you will learn that communication is a major factor in management success, and you will learn how to communicate effectively.

Communication is the vehicle for motivation and management. Through communication, action and reaction take place. People can express and share ideas, feelings, and thoughts. Interaction can be understood, whereas through assumption, communication problems can develop. Communication, the ability to communicate clearly and nonconfrontationally, is the hallmark of an effective managerial leader today.

Nearly forty years ago, Peter Drucker profiled that problems within an organization can typically be traced back to two sources (and it still holds true today). One source is problems with systems, and the second is problems with people. Of these two sources, systems account for nearly 85 percent of all organizational problems. People account for roughly 15 percent. Of these sources, it is typically the people source that leads to the dominant trauma and tension with players—not system problems!

It is estimated that nearly two-thirds of all inner-office problems are communication related: poor communication, overcommunication, undercommunication, negative communication, miscommunication, and so on. It is no wonder that communication is a major factor in management success.

For communication to become more interactive and successful, the sender of it has to make major changes in behavior accountability. One can no longer merely send a signal and view his responsibility as completed and believe that it is the responsibility of the receiver (the listener) to receive, understand, and act upon that signal. If the receiver doesn't act accordingly, it should not be his (the listener's) fault and problem.

Interactive communication implies that the parties involved are interacting with positive signal transfer, and that each is equally assuming 100 percent accountability for the signal exchange. Each has to maintain control over the entire communication interaction, and neither party (especially management) allows assumptions to play out, either internally in one's own head or aloud with another player.

Interactive communication depends on the sender of the signal and its receiver (whether you serve in either position) taking the communication as a step-by-step process.

There are three phases to interactive communication, and the senders must ensure they have been accomplished completely prior to moving on to the next phase. This confirmation can be solicited either through verbal or nonverbal feedback. Using the communication pyramid model shown in Figure 10.1, you can see the natural progression of how the exchange must evolve.

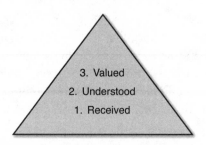

Figure 10.1 Communication pyramid model

Interactive communication rests upon the foundational model shown in Figure 10.1. Information must pass through three phases for it to be acted upon. As you nonconfrontationally move from one phase to the next, you have to become interactive to facilitate the communication process for the success of all parties involved.

The first responsibility of the sender is to ensure that the other party actually gets the message: **received.** Once this first phase is attained, the receiver must comprehend the signal: **understood.** Only when the signal is received and understood is there an opportunity for the receiver to mentally digest it and for there to be any sort of action. Therefore, for the receiver to be motivated by the signal and for action, the action must be **valued.**

As the signal is received by the receiver (listener), it can be intentional or unintentional, linear or interactive. The receiver's perception (not the sender's intentions) of the signal is all that matters. Intentional communication signals are logic driven and calculated. Unintentional communication signals are emotion and feeling based; they are driven and transmitted outbound without the sender realizing it. Traditional management communication, in most cases, is linear (one-way).

In one-way-based linear communication, the sender sends the message and does not feel obligated to follow up to ensure it was received, understood, or valued. The exchange is thus linear. Linear communication typically leads to miscommunication and further organizational stress. On the other hand, interactive communication suggests that the sender and receiver assume 100 percent accountability to ensure that a message sent is received, understood, and valued—zero assumptions.

To reach the level of interactive intentional communication, the mechanics of communication need to be analyzed. Every time you communicate outbound to someone else (the technical term for this is *encoding*) or receive a signal inbound from someone else (the technical word for listening is *decoding*), there are three basic psychological steps to effectiveness.

Improve your communication ability with others and reduce negative communication by reflecting upon what these three phases (or steps) have to do with the exchange. Consider the following diagram:

STEP ONE: ENCODING	STEP TWO: DECODING	STEP THREE: CHANNELS

This model outlines the process through which outbound and inbound communication works. Step one is encoding. As ideas and signals surface with the sender (you), they are shaped by what you think (logic) or feel (emotions) and given your six core filters that are discussed later in this chapter, which condition and shape individuals to think and feel the way they do. Based on the initial thought, you then move toward step two, decoding. Pause and reflect on what you know about the other person and his filters before you send the signal. This may serve as an insurance policy to protect you from a communication error.

After reflecting on what shapes the formation of the signal, its sending, and how it is received and digested, you are then ready to send it to the other person(s) via step three: channels. There are three channels you can utilize to send the signal from your brain to the receiver's brain: visual, auditory, and kinesthetic (VAK). Peak performers use all three channels, if possible, when transmitting signals. Start by sending the signal via the channel you are best at, and then follow up with the two complementary channels. The more effectively you send the signal via these channels, the greater the interactive communication impact will be.

The process of sending signals via the three channels and the ways to interactively communicate in any one of them is explored in greater detail later in the chapter. To successfully communicate to another person within an organization (or outside the organization), consider strategic ways to ensure success in each of the three phases or steps of communication (via the communication pyramid model).

Making sure that the signal has been received is the first and most critical step or phase in interactive communication exchanges. Think of the number of experiences in your own organization when it was assumed that someone else received a message, note, letter, or document, and only when it was too late did the players involved realize that the assumption of receipt led to the crisis.

Consider some of the following ideas as a means of ensuring the signal is being received:

- **Checking questions**—Immediately after communicating to another person or forwarding a message to him via some vehicle, develop the habit of asking to make sure he received the signal. This only takes a few seconds and may result in the saving of valuable minutes.

- **RSVP**—This is a return mechanism or request that the receiver acknowledges receipt of the message/signal.

- **BRC**—Use a business response card or return response letter with an enclosed stamped, self-addressed envelope. Some visual means of receiving something from the receiver of your signal that indicates he received your signal is invaluable.

- **Electronic squeeze page or BRC**—Use your website and search engine optimization options to draw a person electronically into your message or website, via an offer or promise. Some visual means of receiving something from the receiver of your signal that indicates he received your signal is invaluable.

- **Half-day rule**—This directs you to follow up any signal you have sent outbound to another person and make auditory contact with her to ensure receipt. If the answer is yes, you have accomplished the first phase. While you are talking with her, you can inquire about any questions concerning the signal and nail down the second phase of the communication exchange. You can make this technique the half-hour rule or the ten-minute rule. It doesn't matter what the time delay is. What is critical is that you assume the responsibility to follow up quickly to ensure receipt of the signal.

- **Phone call**—Make a quick phone call to the receiver of your signal. In this instance, if you are short on time and have sent a visual signal, you merely access her voicemail or answering machine and leave a message to follow up. If the receiver has neither, then leave a follow-up auditory message with one of her colleagues and direct the receiver to the signal you sent earlier.

- **Repeat**—Have the receiver occasionally repeat what you have said. This affords you the opportunity to hear her perspective on what you are saying, and to confirm whether the listener received and understood you correctly.

Once the signal has been received by the player(s) involved, then, and only then, should you concern yourself with ensuring that it has been understood. Before you even send the signal, there are elements to be considered. Plan and organize your thoughts, so that when you present them, they are systematic and each idea flows into the next. The well-planned signal is always easier for the receiver of your signals to understand.

To ensure the signal is being understood, consider some of these techniques and ideas:

- **Clarify**—Occasionally in the communication exchange, you need to stop and clarify points that are obvious to you but may not be so obvious to the other person.

- **Feedback**—Gain some sort of verbal or nonverbal response from the intended receiver; ensure that what you have intended the signal to be equals what the receiver's perception is.

- **Ask questions**—More specific questions are used in this second phase to ensure that the elements of your signal are being understood by the receiver. The more information and individual details attached to your signal, the more important it is to ask strategic questions to accomplish your objectives. You may consider four specific types of questions:

  - ◆ Probing questions to solicit additional information to further assist you in your delivery and to mentally decide what needs to be expanded upon for the receiver.

  - ◆ Evaluation questions to make sure that what you have sent is what has been interpreted, as well as questions to measure the responses to make sure that you understand them.

  - ◆ Advice questions to allow you to ask questions while giving additional direction.

  - ◆ Interpreting questions allow you to digest responses to your signal to ensure that your understanding is equal to the receiver's.

- **Obtain signatures**—While you are interacting with the other person(s), devise a way to have him sign off on what the two of you have discussed. If the receiver doesn't understand you, he will hesitate to sign something. You gain the feedback necessary to accomplish level two.

- **Nonverbal signals**—Look at the nonverbal signals the receiver is sending as you interact. Look at his face, body language, nodding head, and breathing patterns, to help in determining whether he is following you, understanding you, or is lost or irritated. All these factors impact the effectiveness of step two.

- **Create mental imagery**—As you communicate, use words that paint a mental picture. The more vivid your words, the greater the mental impact on the receiver, and thus the greater the interaction will become. This helps you gain understanding.

- **Use visual aids**—As you communicate, consider the opportunities to increase interactive effectiveness by incorporating visual aids into your exchange. These could be charts, folders, diagrams, brochures, maps, business cards with additional notes written on them, pictures, and so on.

  There are only two rules to visual aids. First, use one only if it is appropriate. That means the visual is timely, is in good shape, assists and reinforces the signal, and presents a quality message. Second, don't use a visual if it doesn't aid the signal. Don't use a visual aid if it is in bad shape, poor taste, outdated, or detracts from your message.

  The Wharton School of Business in Pennsylvania studied the issue of communication exchange and information retention on signal receivers (listeners); it determined that a message heard once is 68 percent forgotten in 48 hours. Within 30 days, less than 10 percent is retained. However, if the same signal is communicated with the complementing use of visuals, you can increase retention (understanding) of it by as much as 73 percent.

- **Reinforce the signal**—There are many ways to reinforce what you have sent. The use of visual aids is one. You may also want to send a follow-up fax or electronic message. The use of examples, statistics, analogies, and stories can lend further impact and actually help the receiver understand what is being sent. With the signal received and understood by the other person(s), the exchange now proceeds to the most important phase of all: value. Only when the receiver senses some degree of value in your signal will there be any degree of action on it. There are many ways to ensure value is received from your signals. Consider the following points:

  - **WIIFM and WIIFU**—When sending signals to other people, keep focused on the underlying psychological motivator in human behavior: All people are tuned to a constant psychological radio frequency WIIFM, "What's In It For Me?"

    In group situations, leaders are tuned into a wider frequency, which tells them to focus on "What's In It For Us?" (WIIFU). Remember that people read signals with WIIFM. Some people are loudly focused on this frequency; others have it on as quiet music in the background and only occasionally refer to it.

- **Timing**—Consider your timing when sending the signal. The wrong time of day or week may impact its reception. Whether distracting activities are taking place in that recipient's personal or professional environment may also impact reception.

- **Territorial Issues**—Your sensitivity to the other person's traditional territorial concerns also impacts the value of the signal you send. Territorial issues, for example, are those areas (territories) that if violated prevent the other from listening. He may be looking at you while you continue talking, but he won't be listening.

  Territory is like education. You may need to interact with another person on an issue dealing with a subject that person feels versed in. However, you need to interact with him on that subject from an instructional standpoint. Approach the subject matter with guarded caution so you don't violate his education and cause confrontation.

- **Messenger**—Sometimes you can increase the value of the signal by reconsidering the person who delivers it. Use other people to deliver your signals when necessary to accomplish your objectives.

- **Enthusiasm**—You have to believe in the signal you're sending and have genuine energy and motivation if you expect the recipient of it to become motivated. Remember, the "iasm" in enthusiasm stands for "I Am Sold Myself!" Ask yourself if you're buying into this signal prior to delivering it. If you're not, it will be written all over your face when you deliver it. Your enthusiasm for a signal sets the stage for how the recipient receives it.

- **Tie-In**—Establish the linkage between your signal and how the recipient will benefit from it. Establish how it will help develop her in the progression toward professional goals. Many times, if the receiver can see the tie-in between what you're communicating and the bigger picture, she sees the value and is motivated to action.

- **Ownership words**—Focus on the "we" and not the "you" in conversations. Ownership words are words that, as used, imply all parties are in this together, and no one is pointing fingers at the others. Ownership words are words such as *we, us, team,* and *I.*

The importance of maintaining a step-by-step approach to communication is that you can control the flow of it and measure whether the signals you are sending are being received, understood, and valued.

Another aspect of interactive communication and attaining peak performance states within management is reflected in the percentage of your signals that the recipient internalizes.

Some studies explore the three phases of communication and the model of how the signal flows from the sender to the receiver. All of what the recipient receives and internalizes (understands) for interpretation (value) breaks down into three different elements of the signal.

> 7 percent = the WHAT factor of the signal
>
> 38 percent = the HOW factor
>
> 55 percent = the WHY factor
>
> 100 percent = the outbound communication signal

Interactive communication also rests upon how effectively you merge these percentage values as you send the signal. The three factors combined make for the total signal that you send outbound, and directly impact the value seen in your message.

Communicate to the Receiver's Sensations

You can obtain greater impact with your signals by flexing the three channels and using variations of them at different times. Consider the following examples of communication via the channels to gain immediate reception, faster understanding, and precise value with your interactive communications.

When communicating outbound, consider which channel the brain needs to receive the signal through to effectively receive, understand, and value it. If you are communicating outbound via the visual channel, focus the signal so it stimulates the visual senses. Use phrases, such as "six feet five inches instead of tall"; "fire-engine red instead of bright red"; "Can you see what I am saying?" instead of "Does this make sense?" In essence, use vivid and visual words. As you talk or write your message, paint a picture in the mind's eye of the recipient.

When you communicate to a visual person or through the visual channel, play off the eye. Incorporate more visual aids as you talk. Use charts, pictures, diagrams, and documentation; write out key points as you talk them out; leave a visual reminder with people after you go regarding what was discussed. This way, it can be seen later visually.

With an auditory person, use words that play off the ear: words that convey sound and noise to reinforce a message. For example: "Did you hear what

I said?"; "Does this sound like something you would be interested in?"; "It sounded like a window being shattered!" These words convey an image, and that image is of sound. In auditory channels of communication, reinforce any visual correspondence with a follow-up telephone call, for example, or leave a message in a voicemail or answering machine system, so the receiver hears as well as sees the signal.

With the kinesthetic person, adjust the signal to play off feelings and emotions, as this channel conveys the feelings of the signal. You want to be more interactive face-to-face with this channel and with kinesthetic people. Use phrases, such as "How do you feel about this idea?"; "Does this set well with you?" And make your statements flow like this: "The caller used a very soft and soothing tone of voice. It was like being in a doctor's office and having a friendly mother-figure assisting as nurse."

Becoming more effective as an interactive communicator in management (and in life overall) takes a systematic approach and a quick intellect. Make adjustments, as necessary, to attain desired results with each interaction.

To become a whole communicator, a manager must assume 100 percent accountability, with respect to the three psychological steps of communication and must target each of the three levels. To increase your communication effectiveness, there are specific actions a managerial leader can consider:

- Reflect upon how your filters shape how you feel and think as you encode the signal.

- Reflect on how the other person's filters shape how she feels or thinks while decoding your signal(s).

- With this reflective insight, decide which channel(s) would best transmit the signal from your brain to the receiver's brain.

- Once the signal has been sent, it is your responsibility (especially as a management player) to ensure that it has been received (phase one), understood by the other party (phase two), and that the receiver senses a degree of value attached to your message (phase three).

Loyola University conducted a study that reflects the accountability factor in communication. It solicited the quality or traits most sought in a good boss or organizational leader. The dominant response: Being a good listener! This is typically the same trait you seek in your best friend and closest relationships.

Improving interactive communication can have the single greatest impact upon increasing organizational efficiency and reducing player stress. By focusing energies on improving the listening activities within interactions, you can improve all communication interactions. Communication is your responsibility.

The greatest debilitator to communication within business today is when managerial leaders fail to establish a thorough reason for "why" they have communicated, "what" they have communicated, or "how" they have communicated.

Management spends countless hours exploring what individuals do daily and how they do it. Hours are spent determining why changes should or must be undertaken, and then equal time is given to the new what factors and ways of how to do the new endeavors. But little or no time is given to why management decisions have been made when communicating them to the organization. Yet this is the immediate focal point for players when they finish reading a new change memo, while listening to a change initiative via their voicemail, or even when sitting in a meeting and hearing about new directives.

Effective communication starts with clearly articulating at all times to all people the complete set of 5-W and 1-H we all were taught in school. The same lesson plan applies in the workplace of today.

Managerial Leadership Bible Lesson Ten

Whether you communicate or choose not to communicate, as a managerial leader you have just communicated. Effective managerial leaders choose their words wisely and use them with passion and emphasis for impact.

Review Questions

The review questions accompanying each chapter or section are designed to assist you in achieving the learning objective stated at the beginning of each chapter. The review section is not graded; do not submit it in place of your final exam. While completing the review questions, it may be helpful to study any unfamiliar terms in the glossary in addition to course content. After completing the review questions for each chapter, proceed to the review question answers and rationales.

1. When discussing communication, what does "behavior accountability" mean?

    A. Once you communicate something, it is the other person's responsibility.

    B. You must ensure that everyone listens to you.

C. You must be held accountable if what you have communicated creates confusion or misunderstanding.

D. Everyone is accountable for his reactions to what is said.

2. The first responsibility of the sender is to ensure that the other party actually gets the message.

   A. True

   B. False

3. Traditional management communication, in most cases, is very _____ (one-way).

   A. Intentional

   B. Unintentional

   C. One-on-one

   D. Linear

4. Which type of questions allow you to digest responses to your signal to ensure that your understanding is equal to the receiver's?

   A. Probing

   B. Evaluation

   C. Advice

   D. Interpreting

5. There are two guidelines for visual aids. First, use one only if it is appropriate. Second, don't use a visual if _____.

   A. It doesn't aid the signal.

   B. It is not available in color.

   C. You are talking about numbers.

   D. It isn't on PowerPoint.

Review Question Answers and Rationales

Review question answer choices are accompanied by unique, logical reasoning (rationales) as to why an answer is correct or incorrect. Evaluative feedback to incorrect responses and reinforcement feedback to correct responses are both provided.

1. When discussing communication, what does "behavior accountability" mean?

   A. Incorrect. The exact opposite is true.

   B. Incorrect. Even if a person listens to you, she may not understand what you are trying to communicate.

   C. Correct. The responsibility for an effective communication is in the speaker, not the listener.

   D. Incorrect. Due to misunderstandings, people may behave in a way that seemed logical to them given the situation.

2. The first responsibility of the sender is to ensure that the other party actually gets the message.

   A. Correct. This is the first of three stages for interactive communication.

   B. Incorrect. As discussed in Question #1, the responsibility of message transmittal is in the sender.

3. Traditional management communication, in most cases, is very _____ (one-way).

   A. Incorrect. The message can be intentional or unintentional, but the communication itself is not.

   B. Incorrect. The message can be intentional or unintentional, but the communication itself is not.

   C. Incorrect. Management traditionally can speak to groups or individual employees.

   D. Correct. Communication flows in the direction from manager to employee with little or no interactive feedback.

4. Which type of questions allow you to digest responses to your signal to ensure that your understanding is equal to the receiver's?

   A. Incorrect. Probing questions provide insight into the communication.

   B. Incorrect. Evaluation questions are used to ensure the correct message has been received.

   C. Incorrect. Advice questions allow you to ask questions while giving additional information.

   D. Correct. These questions allow you to "interpret" signals between you and the receiver to make sure they are the same.

5. There are two guidelines for visual aids. First, use one only if it is appropriate. Second, don't use a visual if _____.

    A. Correct. If a visual does not aid understanding, why use it?

    B. Incorrect. Visuals can be displayed in a variety of ways to gain understanding.

    C. Incorrect. Often numbers are especially in need of a visual aid for people who think numbers are abstract.

    D. Incorrect. Visual aids can be as simple as a note on a business card or brochure.

11

Interviewing, Hiring, and Promoting the Right Person

Imagine the level of performance output individuals and organizations could yield, if only capable individuals were involved.

—**Jeff Magee**

Learning Objective

After completing this section of the course, you will be able to provide tools and strategies for better hiring procedures.

Each year organizations spend millions of dollars on scoping a job/position, promotion of job openings, and the interview and hiring process associated with bringing a new player onto a team. And every year organizations experience new player trauma when they hire a person who develops a substantially different personality and work ethic from that projected in the initial interview phase—the Dr. Jekyll-Mr. Hyde complex. How do you counter this epidemic? Start by overhauling the interviewing, hiring, and on-boarding process.

Problems in the hiring process are compounded by the reality of today's workplace by governmentally mandated data collection requirements on applicants that apply and/or are hired to organizations. These mandates attempt to ensure in many situations that a governmentally dictated or desired diversity be applied to your organization, regardless of the massive incompetency of individuals or laziness of candidates.

One powerful way to counter this issue and to increase your self-awareness and personal accountability to find the best, recruit the best, and forget the rest is to apply the Player Capability Index Model to interviews, benchmarking the job description off of candidates, and reflecting on your immediate, intermediate, and long-term employment needs with a candidate.

Keep in mind that in many places local, state, and federal regulations restrict a prospective employer from asking the types of questions necessary to find a peak performer. Many laws actually protect the mediocre and pathetic individual at the expense of the organization and peak performers. So you must become educated in the entire process of on-boarding prospective or new individuals to your organization. This chapter focuses on some ideas and strategies for countering the sea of rules and regulations that work against interviewing. It also focuses on identifying some current interviewing behavioral patterns you have and ways to change self-defeating activities.

The estimate of what it costs to go through the process of exiting a poor performer from your team, and of then getting another person online and functioning at the performance level of her predecessor, was once estimated by Robert Half & Associates for the Department of Labor as ranging from 1.5 to as much as 11 times a person's salary.

To maximize an interview session and increase the number of productive new hires, this chapter presents several techniques and models to complement the efforts that you and your organization already deploy.

Start by evaluating what you are really looking for in a successful candidate for your team; develop a *people description*, rather than just a job description, and use the Player Capability Index Model as presented in Chapter 6, "Analyzing Players and Prospects for Team Success."

Then measure that response against what you are presently doing in the interview process. You may determine that you are investing time in interviews asking the wrong questions, or are not listening effectively enough to all that is revealed by the candidate. These answers are the clues management needs to design and build cohesive, working, productive, winning teams for future growth and success.

Let's take the process one step at a time. Start by evaluating what you are looking for in an ideal new individual for your team. Determine what talent acquisition you are seeking to augment and complement your existing talent pool. Consider the following models for improved performance and success.

Model One: Winning Player or Ideal All-Star Player Profile

Create the people description via the winning player or ideal all-star player profile as a model, as presented next in this chapter. Think of it this way: Create an inventory of an "ideal new employee" as an example or an "all-star player profile." On a sheet of paper or in a Word document, simply start writing down all the ideal attributes, behaviors, and characteristics (ABCs), traits, abilities, and so on, in the candidate you seek for the specific need and position that is open. Repeat this same drill independently of your work with all those who will have the greatest degree of interaction with this position. You may also request that your core customers provide similar feedback on this position, if appropriate. Now, with this compilation of data points, combine them as a template for your interview and use that as a benchmark for interview questions and measurement.

To make these ABCs even more powerful, for the determination of what you really seek in an all-star player and what variables are most critical, consider the following paragraph.

With the responses written down, go back and qualify or measure each one with this measuring key to determine what you are really looking for. Score each entry that you have written down as either a letter "A" for attitude or a letter "S" for skill. From this collective answer you can then see whether you have been asking questions to determine the "A" trait/characteristic or the "S" trait/characteristic in your interviews and hiring procedures. Most organizations have been conditioned to invest disproportionate amounts of time asking questions about the S factor and completely overlooking the A factor. However, from your inventory, you will probably recognize that you have more than likely listed significantly more "A" characteristics as those of an ideal new employee for your team.

So, what do the A and the S represent? On the inventory, go back and put either an A or an S next to each entry. Each one can have only one letter beside it, so make a judgment call for each. If it could only be described as one or the other, which one does it tend to be?

A represents attitude traits/characteristics.

S represents skill traits/characteristics.

From your personal overview, did you determine that attitude is more critical in a winning player than skill? Most management teams working through this exercise determine that to be so. From this overview you and your interviewing teams may want to have an in-house retreat and pursue this exercise in greater detail. The team's (or your) collective responses to this exercise give you greater insight as to the questions to focus on in the interviewing process.

As you ask questions of candidates, listen to the responses you get. Each answer or response actually carries two answers with it. If you listen closely to everyone, you can measure each candidate's attitude and skill levels. How do you hear two answers to each response? Easy! The skill portion of the response comes from what the candidate actually says (the 7 percent factor, from Chapter 10, "Improving Interactive Communication," of the person's actual words). The attitude portion of the response (the 38 percent factor) comes from how he responds, through his tone of voice, as outlined in Chapter 10.

This winning player matrix is one way to determine whether you have really been focused in your interviewing and hiring efforts. Many times management teams realize they have been so focused on pursuit of the right technically skilled candidate, they overlook the fact that a person's personality (attitude) is the factor that will be interacting with others. Hire or promote the technically qualified candidate with poor people ability (attitude), and there will be tension, frustration, and anxiety within the organization.

Model Two: Position/Employee Personnel Performance Appraisal Assessment Instrument

Another objective way to assess a candidate for internal promotion or an external candidate that you would introduce to your team is to use the exact position or employee assessment instrument or appraisal instrument that they would be measured by if hired in the interview. Hand the candidate a copy of the reference instrument and say, "Hypothetically, if you were a member of our team, this would be the organization's official instrument that you would be measured from on a 30-60-90-120 day repeat basis. Let's talk through each section. I would be interested in your feedback on each...."

As you go through the form, be mindful of both his verbal responses and his nonverbal actions and reactions. His nonverbal cues will be more revealing of how he might perform if hired, so keep note.

(See the Performance and Development Assessment template in Chapter 12, "Developing a Winning Habit Paradigm.")

Model Three: Rule 80-10-10, Who Are They?

Another way of looking at candidates in the interviewing process is for you (as the manager and organization) to be selfish. Look at the present workload, work requirements, and tasks that you want to be able to delegate (but presently are not), and determine the skills and attitudes needed. With this collective thought, set out to find candidates who will meet these needs!

Design a profile of what the ideal candidate looks like, and what the minimum requirements you are willing to accept are, and don't accept anything less. Anything less will only serve as trouble in the future.

As you review candidates, consider whether each person has been a transmitter, transformer, or terrorist (refer to "Three Subgroups in Life—Rule 80/10/10" in Chapter 2, "Five Mission Statements for Ultimate 'New View' Success"). Advancement should go to transformers and transmitters, when there is a feeling that a person could become more assertive and proactive with the right training and conditioning. To advance or hire a terrorist or typical transmitter only allows you to maintain status quo—at best!

Model Four: Position Competency Task-Traits Index

An explosive means to improved interviewing is to create a template that you can populate with appropriate traits for a position. Then assign a scale of importance for each trait to the functionality of the position sought. With this template you can facilitate an objective and thorough interview by going down the list and discussing each with the candidate, getting her feedback, and then evaluating and scoring her relationship to each. This will guide you in determining, if that candidate is promoted or hired, the level at which you will have to assume the six differing managerial leadership engagement styles with her on a daily basis.

The methodology here is simple. On a sheet of paper (or in an electronic Word file), establish at the top center of the page the title of the "position" sought, the "job" needing to be filled, or the "function" needing to be assumed. Then down the center of the page, list the mandatory and ideal traits necessary to administer and facilitate that position. On the top-right side of the page, label the organization score, on a scale of 1 through 5, with 1 being least important and 5 being most important for that trait, in relationship to executing that position or job. Then you prescore each entry on your form before the interview on this master trait template. The top-left side is labeled candidate score. In the interview, you circle for the candidate the level of ownership she indicates she has for that entry.

As you engage the candidate, conversationally discuss with him, starting at the top of the page and working downward, his explanation and self-assessment testimonial for each.

When you are done with the interview, you will have raw objective data from which to make an informed decision. If you are interviewing in teams or in rotation, each interviewer should have a copy of this master template, and then afterward compare one another's assessments to your ideal needs to avoid making an emotional hire of an inferior candidate.

As you assess your candidate and score the level of proficiency for each targeted trait, a low to high score gives you valuable insight as to the level of managerial leadership engagement necessary to maintain her at peak performance, or get her to peak performance. For example, if you hire a candidate with a low score on a trait that you have scored as high, there will be a required degree of manager or teacher engagement necessary for that candidate to become proficient, and for you to be able to take a hands-off approach to her and the workload. On the other hand, if you hire a candidate with a high level of proficiency, you can expect to have less interaction time with him. More of a coach or mentor engagement style may be all that is required with such a candidate.

A sample form for your use may look like the following.

Position Competency Analysis Grid

Do not hire someone that fits into your team, hire someone you need for your team! This is a classic mistake organizations make. To make sure we continually set people up for VICTORIES (*remember the Ownership Model application and the Player Capability Index Model*), consider the following grid, the three categories of data needed within it, and how to use them throughout the employee life cycle development process for greater ownership possibilities:

Position/Project/Task Name

Candidate		**Organization**
1-3-5	_____	1-3-5
1-3-5	_____	1-3-5
1-3-5	_____	1-3-5
1-3-5	_____	1-3-5
1-3-5	_____	1-3-5
1-3-5	_____	1-3-5
1-3-5	_____	1-3-5
1-3-5	_____	1-3-5

Candidate		Organization
1-3-5	_____	1-3-5
1-3-5	_____	1-3-5
1-3-5	_____	1-3-5
1-3-5	_____	1-3-5
1-3-5	_____	1-3-5
1-3-5	_____	1-3-5
1-3-5	_____	1-3-5
1-3-5	_____	1-3-5
1-3-5	_____	1-3-5
1-3-5	_____	1-3-5
1-3-5	_____	1-3-5
1-3-5	_____	1-3-5
1-3-5	_____	1-3-5
1-3-5	_____	1-3-5
1-3-5	_____	1-3-5
1-3-5	_____	1-3-5

KEY:

1 = Does Not Meet Expectations

3 = Meets Expectations

5 = Exceeds Expectations

Model Five: Player Capability Index

Another effective technique for objectively analyzing either a task needing to be addressed or a player to be interviewed prior to adding him to your team is the Player Capability Index, previously presented in Chapter 6. Refer to that chapter to use the index to analyze a potential new hire.

Every letter within the formula can serve as a Q&A template over the telephone, via Skype conference call, during one-on-one interviews, and with team-based interviews. The formula also serves to guide the categories of questions on an evaluation application form and serves as a vetting assessment of the individual for the immediate, intermediate, and long-term future needs. The formula is as follows:

$$C=(T2+A+P+E+C)E2 \times R2 = R$$

Model Six: Personal Mission/Value Statement

Engage the candidate by asking him to submit a written perspective on his personal mission or values statement. See if there is synergy and commonality between the two of you or whether there are some early indicators here of possible derailment if you proceed.

Model Seven: Social Media Analysis

Review what the person's public social media presence says about him, and identify what he projects as his personal brand identity. Review who the person keeps company with. Of course any one factoid is not conclusive of itself in making a final decision, but it could provide you insights needed at the time of interviewing to do a better job at hiring or on-boarding individuals.

For example, review what the candidate's LinkedIn profile indicates and benchmark that against her resume, application, and what is revealed in an interview. If she has changed employers every year or two, proceed with caution; you need a serious Q&A with the candidate and explanation of the movement. If the candidate is unemployed, what does she say on social media? Benchmark that against what she tells you in the interview process. This may save you significant HR issues later and a significant amount of financial headache!

Model Eight: Boss-Peer-Subordinate Perception

Explore how you can get feedback on a candidate from his previous employers (his boss or rater of his performance), peers, and direct reports to see the candidate through the lens of others.

Model Nine: Ask for Copies of Past Performance Reviews

Evaluate the person through the lens of her last job performance by asking for copies of the previous employment position performance reviews. Or ask for client referrals or endorsement letters of the person you are interviewing if she is a solo practitioner prior to interviewing with you.

Model Ten: Application Analysis

Make sure any online or hand completed application actually tracks the data you need to make an informed decision to bring someone in for an interview.

Apply the Player Capability Index to your application process if you have one. Recognize all the usable skills, abilities, attributes, characteristics, and so on that we can call the DNA you ideally want a candidate to possess that you probably are not asking about right now. Ask the "list the highest level of education attained, where, when, and in what area" question. Also ask the candidate to list all the self-development, self-study online courses or workshops completed in the past five years. This second question is a form of letter T in the Player Capability Index and typically represents technician types of education a person has attained that can be immediately applied to the workplace, but if you don't ask you will not know and you miss the opportunity of increased DNA to your team.

Model Eleven: Job Description/ Expectation Document

Utilize the most current version of the position job description that should detail the expectations of an individual in that position and use each item as a conversational reference point. For each expectation responsibility, the conversation should focus on the traits, skills, and abilities needed to execute that expectation line item. Determine for the candidate being interviewed what her level of capability is for each expectation line item. Evaluate for strengths and weaknesses, so if you select the candidate for the position, you as a managerial leader will know what her on-boarding developmental and accountability pathway needs will be.

Remember that the job description relevance to hiring, on-boarding, coaching, performance reviews, and overall organizational effectiveness: To attain great performance feedback exchange and drive improved performance behavior, start the performance review conversation by ensuring everyone understands the definitions and expectations being analyzed and documented. For example, a clear, concise real-time relevant job description should be used as the baseline measurement for the Meets Expectations evaluation. This is neither a bad nor good word; it simply is what it is—what a person was hired or promoted to do. Therefore, any other measurement benchmarked against the performance review criteria is easy. If someone is not performing what is written down as the job description, in that given area he is below or not meeting expectations, and if someone is performing more than what a job description spells out or is providing greater value to the organization, he is obviously exceeding expectations. The traditional problem with performance reviews is that they are not forward focused and developmental on the strategic or tactical behaviors and intellectual energy an organization needs. Also, the definition of what is being measured is always too subjective, so if you simply use the job description, then the measurement is simple. Another challenge is that far too often the review process is disproportionately a historical snapshot of past tense with no future focus and commitment. Let the job description serve as the benchmark to what you measure.

Your performance reviews feed any future Professional/Performance Development Plans (PDP) that allow a person to accelerate in his job description or ascend to another job description. The language makes it clear as to the expected performance standards.

Facilitating the Interview

The action of interviewing, hiring, and promoting is a process. And as a process, management should take a step-by-step approach to the activities associated with interviewing. Consider the following subsections as ideas to approach and facilitate the process for win/win outcomes for management, the organization, present members of the organization, and the new prospect to be added to the team.

Management techniques and strategies to consider in the hiring and interviewing process:

Agenda. Design your agenda so you can mentally and physically see where you are and ensure that the key skill and attitude traits/characteristics are being sought.

Location. The physical environment has a lot to do with how the candidate acts, feels, reacts, and responds (opens up) to the process (questions and interactions). You may consider the first meeting in a neutral office (meeting room, break room, boardroom, someone else's office, offsite at a restaurant, and so on).

Logistics. How the interview room is set up also impacts the interaction. Some people get into psychological games of setting up the room, positioning chairs and people. Don't invest much time in these games. Focus on the purpose of this session and aim toward that.

The room should be relaxed, so all parties can open up, and so management can see the candidate physically and verbally. Look at the nonverbal signals being sent by the candidate, as well as listening to the actual responses to questions.

Time. Decide how much time to allocate for the session prior to initiating it. Position a clock, watch, or timekeeper to ensure that you stay on time. Consider the best time of the day and week for the session, as people perform at different standards depending on their inner energy cycles. Your time constraints are impacted by what is happening in your environment. You don't want to schedule an interview and then have to compete with constant interruptions. This becomes distracting to both you and the candidate.

People. Consider who should participate in the initial and subsequent interviewing sessions. You may want to delegate the first screening session to another team player or a small controlled team. The key players of a team or department need to be involved in the session(s). It becomes hard for people to point fingers and blame management for hiring a terrorist if they, too, were involved in the screening and decision process. You may want to have specific groups, teams, or departments go through the winning player matrix exercise. From the group's analysis, you can develop your profile for interviews.

If you hire a player who meets the team's designed profile for new members, and that player turns out to be negative, it becomes harder for the people on the team to blame management. This issue now becomes a team issue, and all members can be utilized to work with that difficult player, educate him, or eliminate him altogether.

Feedback. Make sure that you don't dominate the interview. Keep notes of what the candidate says during the session and make sure that you solicit feedback on what you discuss. Those notes assist you in further analyzing candidates objectively. When the candidate talks; listen. Try not to interrupt a person in an interviewing session. These sessions are typically uncomfortable and intimidating to some; if you interrupt the interview, she may not open up again.

Pose Situational Questions. Reflect on some realistic situations that have caused stress among players, and pose questions to candidates to solicit their responses to these situations. This gives you additional insight into how candidates think, analyze, and rationalize situations. Remember, this is a person you are considering investing money in to hire, train, insure and so on.

Give the candidate a homework assignment with one of your real-time challenges, and see what mental DNA she brings back to interview number two.

Pose Qualified Questions. Increase your ability to get cutting-edge insights in a precise way to allow you to get the real mental DNA read on a person you may consider adding to your team. When you ask a question, listen for both "what" the fact tangible response is (for insight into his Skill/IQ) and listen to "how" that answer is presented (for insight into their Attitude/EQ).

Be mindful that state and federal governmental agencies and laws are designed to protect the mediocre and make it challenging to find the rising stars, but with clarity and models you can get the insights you need and avoid HR challenges later in the employment life cycle.

Questions can come from:

1. **Player Capability Index**—Use the formula and use each letter to drive questions. Regardless of the response, always ask the follow-up question if you don't get an in-depth answer. ("Can you tell me more about what you just said?")

   - $C = (T2+A+P+E+C) \; E2 \times R = R$

2. **Job Descriptions**—

   - Review and scope any position job description you are creating for a new or existing position you already have that needs to be filled.

   - A job description serves as a reference benchmark of macro and some micro expectations of what an occupant to a position is expected to perform.

   - Keep job descriptions relevant and real-time focused for future execution by occasionally having a person serving as an all-star in a position keep them updated.

   - As a template reference point, access any trade association tools/templates/guides/samples/and so on, and any best-in-industry contacts you have that would share like job position descriptions as a guide for what you could be asking.

3. **Performance Review**—

   - Pull your actual organization's position/job performance evaluation assessment form/tool/instrument and incorporate that into the interview process as well. Talk the candidate through the measurements and conversationally discuss what each means if she were hired and solicit her feedback.

4. **Trajectory Code**—

   - Vet a candidate to determine whether their trajectory pathway "C" KPIs are congruent with yours or whether there are potential pitfalls in alignment.

5. **Three Time Intervals for Questions—**

- Immediate, intermediate, long term
- How can you provide value to the position and team in the immediate time frame (you define your need, maybe 30-60 days)?
- How can you provide value to the position and team in the intermediate time frame (you define your need, maybe 3-6 months)?
- How can you provide value to the position and team in the near long-term time frame (you define your need, maybe 1-2 years)?

Your Expectations. Share with the candidate what the expectations are for a successful new member of the team. Management needs to establish what its expectations are. The manager should also share personal and professional expectations for a successful new member. From these, solicit the candidate's feelings. Eliminate misunderstanding of expectations in this initial interview, so all parties have the opportunity for expanded dialogue here. In far too many cases, misunderstanding of expectations is not realized until the candidate is hired and on the team. It is then more difficult to get rid of the player than it is to keep him and shuffle him from one team or department to another.

Candidate's Expectations. You need to determine exactly what the candidate's expectations are. There are several that you need to determine right at the beginning and make sure you write down. These are as follows:

- Expectations of management
- Expectations of you as manager
- Expectations of fellow team members
- Expectations of where the candidate wants to be within the organization in six months, one year, three years, and five years

If the candidate is hired, these statements will be measurement gauges during the six-month and subsequent reviews. Both of you will be able to see whether you are on track or off track, with respect to where you started in the initial interview session for hiring or promotion.

Job Sharing/Rotation. This concept refers to moving team players from one position to another. Leaving each player in a position for a period of time and then advancing him to another helps each gain a better understanding and respect for others' positions and responsibilities. By rotating players, management can avoid stagnation, procrastination, and burnout. This movement stimulates productivity and ingenuity. By exposing a player to a cross-section of job-related tasks, both the player and management can determine career direction better and thus both can work accordingly.

Commitment Level. Ensure success for each interview or review session by having prewritten objectives, and therefore, specific commitments that you and the organization are prepared to make or offer. Don't allow the energy or emotion of the session to force you to make further commitments. Defer those additional decisions to a later call (via the telephone) or subsequent sessions.

Any commitments made in a session need to be written down and signed by all parties involved. This avoids any party having a misunderstanding of the offer or agreement.

Worst-Case Scenario. Always discuss with the other party what the recourse would be if the new candidate is hired and things don't work out. This provides management with a unique perspective about the candidate's mindset. If there are no recourse perspectives to your "what if" questions, give additional consideration to whether you will be in a positive or negative position, should you hire this candidate and then have to terminate her for some unforeseen issue.

Ultimate Measurement Assessment. Prior to the session, design objective ways (measurement models) to identify the candidate's abilities and capabilities. From these answers, you can measure whether she will be able to meet the needs of management. Refer to Chapter 6 for several measuring models that should be aggressively used in interview sessions.

Profile Comparison. In the interview session you can measure a candidate's potential and fitness for your organizational and management needs by profiling the most positive winning player already on the team. Go over the names of those on your team who are ideal team members, and draft a description of what makes each such a winning player. In essence, develop a winning player matrix of the traits and characteristics of each.

As you observe what makes these players such positive contributors to your team, use those traits as a map to monitor whether your interview efforts, screening process, or questions are allowing you to interview candidates well. Utilize the opportunity to add new members to your team as both a luxury to fill a player ability level presently lacking, and also as a way to add to your transformer base.

Gaps and Cracks. Look for inconsistencies, chronological gaps, and candidates' previous experience on resumes.

Ask for References and Discuss Them. You really should ask the candidate for several references while you are face-to-face and discuss what the context of each reference name would be that they provide to you. Ask them what that person might say when you call them. What is more revealing during this activity is not so much what the candidate may say, but what his body language may be yelling if you pay attention!

Gaining a better understanding of current team members and prospective new members through interviews and on-the-job rotations helps to decrease employee turnover and increase team unity and individual player productivity. Player profiles need to be designed and developed for each player to determine his capabilities and potentials before placing him in a position and then finding out that he lacks the ability, skill, education, determination, or desire to perform as management needs.

The combination of placing and promoting existing players into positions and adding new players is an art to be undertaken with great consideration for future gains and advancements. The promotion or addition of the wrong player into the wrong position can spell disaster for players, management, and the organization overall. The interaction of formal or informal questioning in the interview process has to be planned and carefully tracked.

The interview process should allow you to determine perfect (or near-perfect) fits between organizational needs for present and future growth and candidates' ability levels (whether or not those candidates are already on staff or are to be brought in from outside sourcing). Poor candidate hires, typically, can be traced to one or a combination of eight key factors, according to Martin Yates, former National Director of Training for Dunhill Personnel Systems, Inc., in his classic book *Hiring the Best: How to Staff Your Department Right the First Time.*

Consider these factors as you design or redesign your interview process from start to finish. The eight poor candidate hire factors are as follows:

- Poor analysis of job functions
- Poor analysis of necessary personality-skill profile
- Inadequate initial screening
- Inadequate interviewing techniques
- Poor utilization of "second opinions"
- Company and career/money expectations are conveyed inappropriately or oversold
- References not checked

Your face-to-face time (the informal or formal interview), therefore, needs to be strategically designed to afford you maximum productivity. While the interview process can become intimidating for some, or even easy to get off track from your objective, it has to accomplish certain goals. Those may vary depending on the position you're interviewing for. Therefore, script critical data as needed via questions for the interview.

Questions. Develop minimum questions for each candidate to consider and respond to, based on the position being interviewed for. The more technical the position, the more technical the questions should be. The more consumer or customer service–oriented the position, the more customer-focused the questions should be. There are four categories of questions to be asked, and you can expand them to any degree necessary.

1. Professionally oriented questions help find out about the candidate's work background.

   Use the job description in the interview and actually read line-for-line and ask the candidate what credentials he has that could be applied to each line item or how he could accelerate each line item expectation. Take notes, and document his responses directly on the job description you use as a template. Put the candidate's name at the top, have him sign the document when you are done attesting to its authenticity.

2. Personally oriented questions help gain a perspective about the person you're hiring and how her personality will impact her performance on the job.

   Again use the Player Capability Index Model as a template of questions that could be asked to ensure you drill deep into her background.

3. Business-oriented questions help determine a candidate's specific experience and background, as they relate to the position you're interviewing for and your organization.

4. Pressure-oriented questions help determine your candidate's ability on the spot. Present the prospect with situational questions or a mock situation and ask her to explain to you what she would do. Watch body language and listen to what the candidate says. You can gain true insight into your interviewee, and thus whom you would have on your team, if this candidate were hired.

Consider the employment agreement template later in this chapter as a model for you to use in your organization to ensure that the next hire you make understands the ground rules for success. This gives you the power necessary to maintain her commitment and success in the near term and affords you the leverage necessary if she needs to be removed from your team in the long term.

Can you imagine the level of performance output individuals and organizations could yield, if only capable individuals were hired, promoted, empowered, and allowed to perform without managerial leaders micromanaging them?

Managerial Leadership Bible Lesson 11

Far too many organizations are held back due to emotional decisions around hiring and promoting individuals. Compounding these bad decisions is when organizations feel compelled or obligated to hire, promote, and accept individuals as transfers into positions based merely on seniority and no competencies. Organizations and individuals would be best served, and thus greater rewards yielded to the customer, by having truly capable, caring individuals on the payroll. It is incumbent upon future managerial leaders of greatness to make sound decisions from objective criteria, and this starts at the hiring line.

On the following pages you find additional templates for interviewing effectiveness and a proposed employment agreement for your consideration. If you want these in electronic format, contact DrJeffSpeaks@aol.com and request them, free of charge.

Note that this template merely serves as a tool to give you data points for consideration. Knowing this data would be beneficial in strategically considering an applicant for a position within your organization/team for maximum integration and overall productivity. These data points should serve as merely a starting point for your interview and for gaining a better understanding of a candidate/applicant. You should delete any areas that you deem inappropriate and add any data points to this matrix that would benefit your overall team success. You should recognize that in some locations, organizations, and businesses, some of these data points may be deemed illegal. Please be sensitive to the fact that many legislators, bureaucrats, and some legal scholars who have never held a real business job will work to impede your capitalistic desires!

Application for Position Template

Biographical Data:

DATE SUBMITTED:_____

NAME, LAST (PRINT): _____

NAME, MIDDLE (PRINT):_____

NAME, FIRST (PRINT):_____

PHYSICAL MAILING ADDRESS:_____

APARTMENT/SUITE: _____CITY: _____

STATE:_____ZIP CODE (+4):_____

HOW LONG AT THAT ADDRESS:_____

WHERE GEOGRAPHICALLY DID YOU LIVE
PREVIOUSLY?_____

PHONE: _____ CELL PHONE:_____

PERSONAL EMAIL ADDRESS:_____

SOCIAL SECURITY NUMBER: _____DOB:_____

SINGLE/MARRIED: _____ SPOUSE NAME: _____

WHAT DOES SPOUSE DO? _____

CHILDREN:_____

OTHER:_____

Educational Data:

HIGH SCHOOL NAME/GED: _____

CITY/STATE: _____

YEAR COMPLETED:_____

UNDERGRADUATE COLLEGE DEGREE/MAJOR:_____

NAME: _____

CITY/STATE: _____

YEAR COMPLETED: _____

GRADUATE COLLEGE DEGREE/MAJOR: _____

NAME: _____

CITY/STATE: _____

YEAR COMPLETED: _____

POST-GRADUATE COLLEGE DEGREE/MAJOR: _____

NAME:_____

CITY/STATE: _____

YEAR COMPLETED: _____

List any significant classes, workshops, online programs, symposiums completed, CD/DVD/LMS or certifications that you possess, which raise your personal/professional stock value to others:

Professional Historical Data:

Please attach a current copy of your resume with specific emphasis on your immediate and past employment history.

Climate Data:

The position you are applying for is an integral component to our organization. We are excited to share this opportunity. Can you briefly tell us a little bit about yourself and your background?

1. What are your short- and long-term goals if integrated with this organization?
2. What motivates you to put forth your greatest effort?
3. Tell me about a tough decision you had to make and how you handled it.
4. What two or three accomplishments have given you the most satisfaction and why?
5. What computer systems have you worked with, including software?
6. Would you consider yourself a self-starter and why?
7. Do you like supervision, and can you share a time when you needed it?
8. How do you feel you handle pressure or stress?
9. Do you feel that you take direction well and why?
10. What are your hobbies, and why do you enjoy them?
11. Tell me about a time when you failed at something. How did you handle it?

12. Do you feel you are competitive and why?

13. What are your motivations to excel?

14. What are the three priorities in your personal life?

15. How do you feel that your former job experiences have prepared you for this position?

16. Do you feel you are a goals-oriented person? If so, tell me about a goal you have achieved and one that you did not.

17. What are some of the goals you will set for yourself if you become a part of our organization?

18. Do you feel you can work with minimal supervision and why?

19. Why should we hire you for this position?

20. Tell us about a time when you disagreed with your boss and how you handled it.

21. Tell us about someone who inspired you and why.

Employment Agreement Template

1. **Proprietary Information.** All information, industry, and company-specific financials, relationships, products, database, spreadsheets, research, and contact names (thus deemed "property") engaged will be considered proprietary information and the sole property of this company/employer should employment be terminated/ended in any fashion.

2. **Salary.** Base salary shall be set at $X,000 monthly and paid via direct deposit. Salary increases are not tied to performance appraisals or a calendar. It will be at your supervisor's discretion and with management's concurrence. Your work habits will be reviewed on a daily basis, and your performance will be documented. Periodically, you will be given a performance review. Salary increases will be given at the discretion of management and when appropriate.

3. **Commission.** Commissions shall be paid on sales as follows: percent commission on all net sales from any preexisting client or contact in company/employer database, above and beyond what they are and have historically done. Zero commission on any existing account that is serviced. A percent commission shall be paid on any new business.

4. **Health Benefits.** Company/Employer shall make available to all full-time employees, after the 90-day probation period, company

health insurance. This insurance will be in the way of an HMO or PPO health care provider. This benefit may be changed or eliminated without notice, at the discretion of management.

5. **Financial Bonus/Investment Packages/401(k).** From time to time, company/employer may make these available. Occasionally, company/employer may provide opportunities around sales campaigns where management will pre-announce additional financial performance-based earning opportunities. Company/Employer reserves the right to terminate these at any time.

6. **Work Hours—Daily/Weekly Work Hours.** Normal work hours are from 8:00 a.m. to 5:00 p.m., and it is expected that these hours would be aggressively worked, with some additional time required on Saturdays. This, however, does not mean that it may not be necessary and expected that you may need to work beyond these hours or on weekends/holidays to get the job done in the best interest of the company. As appropriate to ensure maximum peak performance, the financial industry is open for business from 7:00 a.m. to 4:00 a.m. CST and one should execute their professional responsibilities appropriately.

Lunch Break. Currently we are operating on a "situational" lunch break time frame. The timing of the lunch break may be adjusted as necessary so that someone is always available to handle customer calls and customer visits at all times. If management does not provide you with your selected lunch time, then common sense should be used in determining when to take a lunch break and how long is necessary; however, management reserves the right to select whatever lunch time may be in the best interest of the company.

Attendance/Personal Medical Appointments/Vacation Days and Holidays/Absenteeism. We have hired you for a specific purpose and we expect you to appear for work every work day unless other arrangements have been made in advance. Any personal nonemergency medical appointments that need to be scheduled should be scheduled for the last hour of the work day, to be taken and not counted as a sick day or vacation day. Each employee receives one week paid vacation each year, plus the one week around Christmas. Observed national/state holidays are discussed and agreed to at the end of each year for the forthcoming year and posted. If you are unable to appear for work at the assigned time, you must personally speak with your supervisor. Excessive absenteeism is grounds for dismissal/resignation.

7. **Educational Support.** Company/Employer encourages the active participation in the ongoing development of personal and professional endeavors. Company/Employer will provide ongoing educational opportunities and will budget a limited amount of resources for reimbursement. Company/Employer encourages the self-development of every member of the organization, and with management approval, the employee is encouraged to build his or her own professional personal development library to include one of each management-approved item (book, audio [CD/cassette], DVD, video, magazine, accessories, and so on) from our own company/employer resource product line at no cost to the employee.

8. **Environmental Issues—Dress Code.** We deal with the public on an irregular daily basis and are irregularly frequented, both scheduled and unscheduled, by persons with whom we do business. It is important that we put forth the proper image. Business casual clothing, which is considered to be ordinary and proper, should be worn to work. We trust that you will use your best judgment in selecting what seems to be proper attire, by observing what your fellow workers are wearing. If you know that you will be interfacing with clients, then it is expected that you will dress in business formal attire. If you are in doubt, ask your immediate supervisor. All clothing should be clean, in good repair, and free of wrinkles. Your hair should be neatly trimmed and fashionable. Shoes should be in good repair, clean, and shined. In the summer, management may choose any attire deviation and communicate that to the team. The summer dress code will be strictly adhered to and any violation/disrespect of this policy will result in it being terminated.

   Smoking. The company/employer is committed to complying with federal, state, and local rules and regulations pertaining to smoking in the workplace. Except where required by regulations, smoking is permitted only in designated smoking areas within the company. Smoking is not considered a permitted reason to take a break. The designated smoking areas are outside front door bench area, your car, or offsite.

   Personal Phone Calls and Personal Visitors. The receiving and making of personal phone calls should be limited to emergencies and to calls that cannot be made or received before work hours. Personal long-distance phone calls should be made from your home. If you find it absolutely necessary to make a long-distance personal call, that call must either be charged to your home phone, or on your personal long-distance carrier's telephone credit card, and such calls should be made during approved break periods. Any deviation of this must be worked out with management ahead of time and will be done on an individual basis. All company phones are subject to recording or monitoring. The excessive receiving or making of personal phone calls during your scheduled work hours is grounds for dismissal.

Personal (noncompany issued) cell phones are highly discouraged from use in the workplace. We understand the need for today's employee to be reached in the event of an emergency and would hope that you instruct your family and friends to contact you only in the event of an actual emergency, and for this reason they should be given your work phone numbers. Please limit your calling out to your break time. If it appears that you are violating the cell phone policy, it will be brought to your attention by your supervisor. To avoid potential distractions and disturbances in the workplace, personal visitors are discouraged. If you must have someone visit, such visits should be limited to your lunch period. The employee is responsible for the conduct and safety of his or her visitors.

General Housekeeping. Everyone at the company/employer is expected to do his or her part in keeping our facilities and work areas clean, neat, and as organized as possible. We all spend a great deal of time here. A neat and clean workplace is a much safer, more attractive place to work. Everyone is responsible for cleaning up after themselves in the common areas such as the bullpen, lunchroom, and restrooms.

Confidentiality of Records, eFiles, HR Records. Any documents in file cabinets, file folders, mail systems, accessed electronically, etc., that don't pertain to you are deemed confidential and should not be opened, read, downloaded, or copied. Management reserves the right to do what they feel appropriate with any said documents/records. ANY violation of this policy by an employee is grounds for dismissal/ resignation.

Conversion of Property and/or Money. The unauthorized taking of property or money from the company/employer will not be tolerated. Each instance of missing property and/or valuables will be thoroughly investigated by both the company and/or the local law enforcement agency. It is the philosophy of company/employer to prosecute all who illegally take property and/or valuables.

9. **Termination Resignation Statement.** One's inability to execute these performance behaviors/acts will be deemed not cause for termination, but deemed as one's automatic "resignation" from company/employer and one's desire to pursue other employment interests. Accordingly company/employer can accept and execute this "resignation" clause at any time.

As agreed to on this _____ day of _____, by

_____   _____

John Doe, CEO Name

Observer/Witness_____ Position_____

Review Questions

The review questions accompanying each chapter or section are designed to assist you in achieving the learning objective stated at the beginning of each chapter. The review section is not graded; do not submit it in place of your final exam. While completing the review questions, it may be helpful to study any unfamiliar terms in the glossary in addition to course content. After completing the review questions for each chapter, proceed to the review question answers and rationales.

1. Instead of focusing only on a job description to prepare for interviewing, create a(n) _____ description.

    A. Salary

    B. Education

    C. People

    D. Gender

2. You may want to delegate the first interview screening session to _____.

    A. Employee(s) who will work with the new hire

    B. A hiring consultant

    C. The highest level management

    D. A terrorist employee

3. Which of these is often a key factor in poor candidate hires?

    A. Poor employer benefits

    B. Poor utilization of "second opinions"

    C. Poor location of newspaper advertisements

    D. Poor attention to dress code in interviews

4. Of the four types of questions to be asked in an interview (professionally oriented, personally oriented, business-oriented, and pressure-oriented) business-oriented questions are the most important.

    A. True

    B. False

5. Far too many organizations are held back due to _____ decisions around hiring and promoting individuals.

    A. Affirmative Action

    B. Corporate policy

    C. Team

    D. Emotional

Review Question Answers and Rationales

Review question answer choices are accompanied by unique, logical reasoning (rationales) as to why an answer is correct or incorrect. Evaluative feedback to incorrect responses and reinforcement feedback to correct responses are both provided.

1. Instead of focusing only on a job description to prepare for interviewing, create a(n) _____ description.

    A. Incorrect. This is often a part of the job description.

    B. Incorrect. This is often a part of the job description.

    C. Correct. As we have learned thus far, personality and attitude can be the deciding factor for a successful new hire.

    D. Incorrect. This is illegal for choosing prospective employees.

2. You may want to delegate the first interview screening session to
_____.

    A. Correct. Employees will have ownership in the decision to hire someone.

    B. Incorrect. This type of person may know little about what your company is actually looking for.

    C. Incorrect. Upper level management should meet with the prospective employee later in the process.

    D. Incorrect. Such an employee may suggest another terrorist to help them!

3. Which of these is often a key factor in poor candidate hires?

    A. Incorrect. Benefits should be discussed during the hiring process and not surprise the candidate.

    B. Correct. It is important to listen to everyone who met with the candidate. These additional opinions allow for a better candidate choice.

    C. Incorrect. This could possibly affect the number of candidates who applied, but not necessarily a poor choice in hiring.

    D. Incorrect. Appropriate dress is only one small factor in the interviewing process.

4. Of the four types of questions to be asked in an interview (professionally oriented, personally oriented, business-oriented, and pressure-oriented) business-oriented ques`tions are the most important.

    A. Incorrect. Asking all these questions will create a well-rounded assessment of the candidate.

    B. Correct. Each type of question is important.

5. Far too many organizations are held back due to _____ decisions around hiring and promoting individuals.

    A. Incorrect. While some people may believe this true, there is no foundation for such claims.

    B. Incorrect. Those policies are probably there for a reason and should only be disregarded in special situations.

    C. Incorrect. A team decision is the best decision to make.

    D. Correct. A "gut feeling" is not reason enough to hire someone.

12

Developing a Winning Habit Paradigm

The future belongs to those who believe in the beauty of their dreams...those who know where they have been and can measure how to get to where they desire to go.

—Eleanor Roosevelt, American stateswoman

If you can't measure it, you can't manage it. If you can't manage it, you can't change, fix, or improve it!

—Anonymous

Learning Objective

After completing this section of the course, you will be able to describe and put to practical use the techniques to develop a winning habit paradigm.

In the face of market chaos and competition, the internal changes and challenges that players and management alike encounter, the ability to systematically measure work, activities, projects, and progress is critical for success and growth. And the ability to measure this in such a way that systems and people can be held accountable is even more critical to true performance improvement.

A managerial leader's ability to make these changes or shifts in performance and behavior for greater effectiveness and efficiency is the focus of this chapter.

The need for these winning habit paradigms (maps) and the need to change some paradigms is the business operating norm. Organizations and management can no longer operate from the perspective that bigger is better and technology alone is the secret weapon. Some of the greatest failures in this past century came from looking at the back rooms of the leading colleges, universities, and Fortune 500 organizations that violated the people factor. Even though they dominated their fields through most of the last century, many of these organizations started falling apart in unison, and major economic and employment trauma was seen in business and industry implosions into the early 2000s.

Why? Violation of the people factor and avoidance of *The Managerial Leadership Bible* ideology and methodologies are the explanation.

Business leaders once revered were exposed for building their greatness through mergers, acquisitions, and spinning off unforeseen potential of a strategic business unit, not for actually creating anything internally of their own merit. Once the ability to keep the merger train moving forward became evident to them, these executives left quickly, only to leave to their successors the work of cleaning up the actual trauma their energies created. Being able to maintain, sustain, or increase growth by an organization's own creations and commercial transactions is a more objective mark of managerial leader greatness.

Lack of values, vision, and focus is mostly to blame.

Investing in your people and listening to each other, matched with systems of measurement, lead to greater levels of success.

As a managerial leader, your ability to interact with individuals in times of change, or even in maintaining daily centers of efficiency, the need to engage each player's safety needs (see Chapter 9, "Nine Tactical Steps to High-Impact Leadership") and fluidly move them through the six stages have a lot of commonality.

Team-oriented change can occur with utilization of the ideas and with a management commitment. Players on the team always look toward management for the lead. If management is committed and walks the line it talks, players will fall in line as well. However, if management is not 100 percent committed, players will sense this, and their level of commitment to the team will be reflective of management's!

Systems of measurement deal with personal and organizational assessments. This chapter centers on measuring systems—how to design them, when to use them, where to implement them, and who should be involved in them. One general rule of management is that what gets measured gets dealt with. Measure it and then you can deal effectively with it. Therefore, in management everything needs to be measured! The fundamentals of a quality measurement system start with an understanding of what it is that you, the players within an organization, the senior management team of the organization, and the organization itself, want and need to sustain life and ensure growth.

Before approaching the available measurement instruments and tools consider your point of professional reference in conjunction with some national and international statistics. How you rate yourself against your own potential and in contrast with these statistics may also give some perspective as to why your organization experiences its unique level of successes and failures. Consider some international levels of excellence and measures of achievement:

- According to a CNN/Gallup Survey (1995), workers in Europe and Japan spend on average 22 percent of work time each year engaged in some sort of on-the-job or offsite educational activities, while the working counterparts in America spend on average 2 percent of their annual work time engaged in educational training programs. In 2014, a follow-up CNN/Gallup Survey revealed little change in nearly two decades.

- Harvard University polled Fortune 500 firms for the inner organizational traits and characteristics that led to their success. The dominant response was attitude.

- A recent USA Today/Gallup Survey of thousands of businesses found that 56% of workers are disengaged from their workplace, 15% are actively disengaged, and only 29% are engaged in the workplace.

How do people and organizations excel? The new team (made up of the employees/workers from the previous team) realize that they are all a part of the same team, and it is in their best interest to operate from a position of ownership, mutual respect, and a need to interact. All members take on roles of leadership and teaming.

How do you rate in comparison to other organizations and management challenges nationally? Consider the available organizational measurement instruments for analysis for increased management-level interaction and increased effectiveness.

Quality is not only right, it is free. And it is not only free, it is the most profitable product line we have.
—**Phillip B. Crosby, Sr.**

As you consider the following measurement tools and their application to your organization and your management style, realize these are what Crosby calls the Four Absolutes of Quality Management:

1. Quality means conformance to the requirements.

2. Quality comes from prevention.

3. Quality performance standard is zero defects.

4. Quality measurement is the price of nonconformance.

This last absolute is powerful, and what this chapter addresses. As you work toward quality, ultimate quality management, and a quality organization, measurement is necessary. Ultimately, an organization moves to an environment where quality is built in to every phase and each individual step. Each player also inspects quality in each step, and the ultimate need for quality measurement and inspection soon is not needed.

An immediate assessment tool that can be utilized at any time and within any level of organizational dynamics is the survey. Surveys are fast ways to obtain feedback for immediate course corrections or to confirm that your present management actions are strategically on track. For your surveys to be most effective, consider the following guidelines:

- Start with a clear understanding of what the vision or goal is (the first two mission statements presented in Chapter 2, "Five Mission Statements for Ultimate 'New View' Success").

- Solicit feedback from only the vital few in your internal or external business circle. The *vital few* are defined as those individuals vital to your business and without whom you would experience significant pain. Many times surveys fall flat because management solicits feedback from the useful many. The *useful many* are those around you who may be involved in your business but are not critical or vital to your success. Solicit feedback via surveys from those who have a direct impact on your mission.

- There are four ways to move organizations forward and maintain market advantage. Surveys can assist management in assessing how to meet and exceed expectations of others' perspectives. There are four ways to distinguish yourself from others; surveys will assist in identifying where you are. You either have to give others *more* do it *better*, do it *faster*, or do it significantly *differently* than others to win.

- To obtain the highest response rate there should never be more than three questions (or three sections of questions) on a survey. Make the questions positive in nature to obtain maximum response of positive and negative feedback; otherwise, the questions will draw responses from the most negative and upset of players.

- Ideal questions a survey may present are (1) "What am I doing well?" (In essence, start by soliciting information to a "like" based question.) (2) "What could I do better?" Then sequence into "add" types of questions: (3) "What should I consider doing that I am not presently doing or offering?" Always end with any critical, negative, or "stop" types of questions.

- Measure what needs improvement and what is new.

- Design a response mechanism for the respondent to use that makes it easy for him to return your survey. Consider making the response a fax number, a voicemail system (so he doesn't have to talk with a live person), a survey response card that can be mailed back, or a letter survey that can be filled out and placed in an enclosed, stamped, self-addressed envelope.

- You can obtain higher response rates from individuals by tailoring the response vehicle to be used. For women, provide a return envelope for the survey versus a simple response card that is filled out and mailed back. (Women are more private than men when it comes to survey responses.)

For measuring ongoing projects and involved and complex ones, consider using a *growth wheel* note-taking technique. This allows you to place more notes and data in one place with less writing. Here's how it works:

1. Take a piece of paper and draw a circle in the middle of the page. Inside the circle, write down the main issue or topic you are dealing with (like the traditional note-taking formula that uses a Roman numeral "I" to indicate the main point).

2. From the circle, draw lines outward. Upon each primary axis line, write down each point or issue that needs to be addressed to facilitate the main point within the circle. (This would be like writing a large capital letter A and subsequent letters to indicate a supporting point to the I.)

3. Any points, data, information, or specifics that relate to any primary axis point can be attached to the axis line via subaxis lines to each. (This would be like the traditional note-taking formula that calls for the numbers 1, 2, 3, and so on to follow each letter A, B, C, and so on.)

4. From a measurement perspective, this technique allows you to identify the individual elements of a project being monitored. Write them out and assess each at any point to determine present status. This also allows for synergy and ensures against hindsight management. It also works well as a cause and effect diagram.

When it comes to tracking entire processes, the involvement of individual players, and where possible problems may lie, consider traditional flow charts. There are some basic guidelines to consider for maximum benefit from flow charts.

- Never plot more than one major issue. If there is more than one, break each out on separate charts.

- Never have more than three to five major subpoints to a flow chart. The more there are, the more likely you are to overlook something. In the process stage of a flow chart, if there are more than three points, break the additional ones out into their own tasks, charts, and responsibilities.

- The flow chart allows you to graph the actual steps being followed. And it allows you to chart the steps that should be followed in an ideal situation. The comparison allows for adjustments and measurements for improvement and greater levels of success.

- This chart allows you to create a pictorial of what is happening and what needs to take place, what the flow is, who is involved, at what levels, and to what degree. This allows management at least one more tool in ensuring productivity at an effective and efficient level.

- With a flow chart you can analyze decisions and their impact on the process and actions. The decision step of the chart therefore is a never-ending step in the process.

Using a growth wheel as a planning device is fast, explosive, and exceedingly thorough. It also is a low-tech, low-labor instrument and involves no technology (yes, one could adapt this model into a software program if desired!). Start by drawing six lines off the circle (in any order); inside the circle you merely label the lines with the project name, goal, or objective desired. Then on each line, one line at a time, put the following letters and corresponding words. Off their respective lines you can then place sublines with appropriate corresponding support data.

W "Who" will represent the people appropriate to the circle.

W "What" will be clarity of the goal, objective, end point desired.

W "When" centers specifically on the intermittent checkpoints, deadlines, and the final deadline.

W "Where" the actions will be designed and where they will be implemented must be considered.

W "Why" deals with nonpersonal logic-based reasoning and rationalization, for the endeavor that feeds all stakeholders' mind-sets.

H "How" details the specific action plans and processes to be undertaken to accomplish the "what" factor.

This is perhaps the single fastest and most comprehensive approach to planning or project management. A simple checklist of six letters can aid in avoiding a significant amount of trauma. Imagine the next time you task someone, or someone tasks you, if you were to take a simple piece of paper and jot down these six invaluable letters on the left side of the page, with a dash next to each. Now this can become your conversational template for a chronological and thorough Q&A to take place.

If you're looking at the organization from a historical perspective, consider *histograms*. This tool compares consistent variables from the past with what you are doing now for the future. These charts allow you to plot classes of data and determine whether there are similarities in what happened before with what is taking place presently. You can easily see patterns in process and players' participation with histograms. A typical chart may resemble a bar graph.

The most widely utilized management measurement tool is the *check sheet*. With a check sheet, you graph data to determine an answer posed from a challenge or problem management faces. Consider these pluses:

- Through observations you can detect specific activities that may or may not be impacting an outcome that you view as a positive or a negative.

- Through observation on a check sheet, you identify the categories of data needed, and identify how many times something happens or how many of something you may have.

- This technique gives you a brief snapshot observation of an issue, which can then be dealt with accordingly.

- The issue to be plotted or observed needs to be representative of what typically takes place. If your observations are directed toward something that is not representative of the norm, the results will be skewed.

- In making your observation, ensure that you or the players conducting the observations have adequate time to accomplish a thorough analysis and data-gathering search.

In developing a winning habit and identifying the models that work for you and others you may want to modify and adopt, the ultimate requirement is that the measuring system used be realistic and applicable. One of the major destructive points for businesses and managers is when they force themselves into a measuring system that doesn't take the specific environment into consideration.

When you are measuring factors—for change, improvement, modification, or elimination—consider the impact of the measuring system upon:

- Your people
- Your structures
- Your financial capabilities
- Your product or service

As you measure these factors, make sure the point that you are measuring is comprised of equal variables of "then" and "now." All factors must be equal for the measurement to deliver accurate data and findings. If the data are not equal, then build in allowances for the variances.

The continued growth of an organizational operation is dependent upon someone taking the responsibility to measure, analyze, monitor, and offer modifications for future efforts. Forecasting future needs is based upon current activities, customer demands, market trends from the past, and organizational capacity and abilities, along with management abilities and commitment, all of which impact life within the organization. Another measurement factor deals with the performance of the players in an organization.

Integrating these systems of measurement can serve as a mapping strategy to mark where you are and what you are doing, and thus serve to guide your actions toward where you need to be. Designing a winning habit paradigm starts by analysis and continues by designing safeguards against paralysis of analysis.

Measuring your progress, activities, and net results against what the market, an organization, or customers need is critical to organizational dynamics. In management, a powerful tool for measurement in tracking the growth and development of a player, a system, machines, groups of people, products, or services is to benchmark them against another tangible statistic.

Benchmarking is merely a tool of measurement whereby one identifies what is perceived to be the best in a market (whether a product, service, employee performance, and so on), and then uses that data to gauge one's own performance. This enables management to determine many important factors. Consider these ideas:

- Measure your reputation against others in similar positions.

- Gather data on other factors or competitors and then determine any gaps that you can play against and improve upon, for marketable advantages and team development.

- For effective benchmarking, follow these three steps:

    1. Collect data and information.

    2. Convert that data and information into systems of measurement between you and the other party.

    3. Look for those areas where you can improve, and for areas of uniqueness—customer expectations met.

- Benchmarking allows you to determine where others and your organization may be meeting or exceeding customer needs, and therefore, where and how you can compete—reverse engineering. Start with someone else's known success story or industry standard setter, break it down into its component parts, analyze what it is that has led to her success, and then improve upon it with your own efforts (see the section "Creating Reengineering Laboratories" in Chapter 15, "Putting Together a Winning Management Game Plan.").

- Data has to be written down to be measured and to measure against. Data and information gathered on perceived "bests" in industry are what you always measure against.

One of the most comprehensive and systematic approaches to analysis is the application of the STOP formula (presented in Chapter 9). The act of facilitating the decision process is all about a systematic approach. The brain wants to do only four things in making a decision, so put the process into business-speak and facilitate that process.

The four psychological thought-processing steps are building blocks on one another. To smoothly progress from step one to step four, each subsequent step has to be thoroughly dealt with, or people will mentally digress back to an already-resolved step. The interactions will continuously go back and forth, with no solution being attained in reasonable amounts of time.

Consider the following map for interactive analysis and decisions:

1. **S** = Stop and See "WHAT" is the issue to be added.
2. **T** = Target and Think through "WHY" that is the issue for attention.
3. **O** = Organize Options of "HOW" to proceed.
4. **P** = Pick and Proceed with the option most viable, so that all parties will understand "WHEN" forward momentum is to take place.

When you face an issue to which you dedicate analysis time, your brain has to become focused on that one issue at a time. In essence, you need to dedicate both your conscious and subconscious brainpower to the analysis (step 1). Then you have to rationalize why you picked that issue or were tasked with it and explore all the negatives and problems associated with it (step 2). Live and relive the traumas associated with what you have identified. From this analysis step, you then move to exploring solutions and options (step 3). The key factor with the third step is that having options means that more than one solution or idea must be available before considering an ultimate path upon which to proceed. When multiple ideas, solutions, and options are raised, player and team synergy develops. This may ultimately result in a more viable option being arrived upon, and will lead the decision process to the fourth step. From the brainstorming step (step 3) you can identify one viable solution (pick) and proceed to implement it (step 4).

The STOP formula leads an individual or team toward positive outcomes. Now there will be a map to follow when discussion gets bogged down in planning sessions, project management meetings, presentation situations, or self-discovery. With this formula, you can work to make and maintain decisions that are issue-oriented, not personality-oriented.

Designing Employee and Team Performance Appraisals

Expanded systems of measurement also include objective and consistent systems from which management and leaders can measure the development and growth of the players on the teams they are accountable for. Management personnel and team leaders have to move away from traditional annual employee evaluation or appraisal systems, and move toward regular and immediate ones.

To maximize human growth and organizational development, players need immediate feedback on what they do or how they participate—good or bad. Tracking tools can be easily used by management, for both the documentation process for such appraisal meetings, and to maintain organizational objectivity for true performance improvement purposes.

There is a psychology to appraisals that needs to take on a paradigm shift itself. Remember, that which gets documented or measured gets addressed; that which gets addressed gets improved upon!

Management and employees alike typically have a negative predisposition toward appraisals and appraisal meetings. This is based on many factors that have been allowed to grow and persist over years within an organization. Negative feelings are based on what the other party will think if critical elements are raised in a session, what legal ramifications can occur from these sessions, how one's confidence or lack of confidence plays into the way the session is conducted, and what real issues are addressed. These are just some of the factors impacting the negative fallout of what should otherwise be a positive and productive opportunity. To maximize the appraisal process, manage your actions and lead the other player toward growth and success.

To maximize your time and that of the players involved, when it comes to appraisals and the appraisal meeting, break down the employee development cycle into three distinct phases: Before the Appraisal, During the Appraisal Cycle, During the Appraisal Session. Appraisal sessions need to be held, as a minimum, on a quarterly basis (monthly if possible), to ensure mutual participation by management and employees. The sole purpose of an appraisal or appraisal tool is player development and growth; the appraisal is not an instrument to invoke pain, conflict, and confrontations.

Performance appraisals are a historical snapshot on performance to calibrate future performance effectiveness.

Before the Appraisal. Management and organizational leaders need to ensure that they are using consistent and objective tracking and measurement systems or tools for the entire team. For that matter, documentation is critical to ensure that personal feelings don't cloud the interactions and the overall development of the players in question.

Collection of data as it happens throughout the cycle and before the scheduled and impromptu sessions can be accomplished in the following manner:

- Maintain a logbook for each player in his personnel file. As events happen (good or bad), log in a short note to that effect (with the specifics, date, time, and outcome of that action). These are the events observed and documented throughout a cycle.

- Scan the Performance Outcome Position Statement© prior to a session to determine whether players are on course or off course in relation to the initial objective.

- Break the player's performance down into manageable categories for measurement. Some of those categories should reflect assignments/tasks assigned, self-management, vertical relationships, peer relationships, management abilities, leadership initiative abilities, and communication abilities. Each of the main categories may then reflect multiple subcategories, as they relate to your environment, organizational dynamics, and protocols.

- Prior to interaction, scan previous documentation (from personnel files) and review for consistencies and inconsistencies in behavior, for improvements, and for recurring problem areas.

- Visit with any colleagues, peers, or superiors on issues to be discussed, to gain a greater perspective on both issues and ways to improve and enhance the player's abilities.

- In final preparation for the review, you should draft the key issues to be discussed with key incident or fact points for each. These items can be drafted on an agenda manager (as presented in Chapter 9 in the "#7: Counseling the Difficult Player (Terrorist)" section).

  This system will assist you in guiding the conversation from point to point or issue to issue. As the parties involved in the appraisal session address and resolve each issue, that issue on the agenda manager can be initialed by each party. This documentation system is also effective because you can manage the conversation and avoid any confrontations, insinuations, or personality differences.

- Design a few suggestions for how to improve upon the present situation or behavior as a backup for conversation, should the other person become silent in the appraisal and review session.

- Review what you drafted as the issues to be addressed in the appraisal session: any concern areas, supporting documentations, and associated solutions, as well as all positive areas for praise and continued improvements.

- Schedule adequate time for the appraisal session (on average at least one hour per player) in a suitable environment with ample time for self-preparation prior to the session with that player.

During the Appraisal Cycle. Between traditional and/or scheduled organizational appraisal or review sessions, it is critical for management and effective leaders to maintain a positive rapport with the players in the organization. As they interact with one another and perform their primary responsibilities during this period, management is given multiple opportunities to track, trace, and record player performance.

Impromptu appraisal sessions are also a valuable tool for employee development and team growth. Management and effective leaders draw upon every opportunity afforded them by a player to interact and share guidelines and suggestions for peak performance. Whenever a player does something that warrants a positive word of praise, management needs to pursue that interchange as aggressively as it would when a player causes a problem or has a difficulty.

There are two easy ways to approach tracking player performance between sessions, so that when it is time for a scheduled organizational appraisal session, the session itself will be more meaningful and easier for management to facilitate.

- An Action Memo (as presented in Chapter 9 in the "#4: Delegation Dynamics" section) is a fast tool for documenting a player's actions, either accomplishments or problems, throughout a cycle. Merely take a piece of paper and write down two items: First, what the issue or topic is; second, what he did that was positive, or what he could have done to avoid a problem. Then place this sheet of paper in his file or on a Player Analysis Log© (PAL).

- A Player Analysis Log would be either any organization-imposed tracking form you are requested to use, or your own design of a simple template that allows for the systematic and objective chronicling of essential data on all employees you want to coach to peak performance. This sheet is a formal tracking device that management can keep in every player's personnel file. Team leaders can access the file and utilize it as well. This log allows management to formally track key incidents, issues, and actions, as witnessed by management and leaders throughout a recording period.

During the Appraisal Session. Maintaining positive conversation and energy flow during the session is a must for effective management between the player and leader. There are several key factors to keep in mind. Consider these steps:

1. Review the Player Analysis Log prior to the session to familiarize yourself with the player's performance and the specific areas of interest for this review. This allows you to mentally prepare.

2. Prepare a copy of the session agenda (agenda manager) and give it to the player at least 24 to 48 hours in advance, so she has time to review her record (for example, strengths and weaknesses/growth and development areas/areas for continued growth/concern areas/what she does best) and the appraisal session objectives before arriving.

   The purpose of the session is to serve as a developmental tool to review the player's performance and outline the next best courses of action, for either improvement or ways to maintain effective and successful performance.

3. Engage in dialogue with the player to obtain his feelings and views on your agenda. Practice active listening while he responds to your questions and the items on your appraisal.

4. Explain your position, research, and observations, and how you arrived at your impressions and/or conclusions. Express your willingness to listen to her views as well and state that the appraisal session is a give-and-take situation. Should a critical position that you have presented be inaccurate, you must convey to the player that you are prepared to revise it, based upon tangible evidence that she may present.

5. Establish with one another and mutually agree to the time for the next scheduled appraisal session at the conclusion of this one, and leave on a positive note.

6. Ensure that every measurement opportunity is an opportunity to include a *Performance Development Plan (PDP)* component that is immediate, intermediate, and long-term focused for the individual's development in both the position she is responsible to and for her career pathway aspirations.

The employee appraisal or performance review is the single most problematic area within American business. It is either not done or is not done as effectively and thoroughly as it should be, according to management guru

Edward Deming. An ancillary problem to an improper review is that it takes an employee as much as six months to recover from such a review. This impacts behaviors, attitudes, and ultimately performance and productivity of both players and organizations. If the core purpose of a performance review is to enhance performance, then a culture must be created organizationally whereby all participants (appraiser and appraisee) invite and look forward to these meetings. With this attitude, the appraisal process should take place on a "regular" basis for your organization and area of responsibility—a formal setting on a monthly basis, and an informal one daily.

For example, imagine you are the head coach for a professional football team. You shoot film of every practice and game; you take notes of every player's actions on a regular daily basis and during the big events, if not physically, at least mentally. You mentally workshop continuous ways to improve, as you look at your team of individual players as your people assets. Now, would you keep all of that data to yourself, and only share it with the team as a whole and with individuals one-on-one at the end of the season? Amazingly, most businesses operate with that exact mind-set of one annual review period, and yet want to have an all-star winning team!

The appraisal review is a critical aspect of the manager role of a leader (given the six alternative management roles or hats used in leading and guiding the people on one's team).

An effective appraisal system allows management to monitor a player's performance and exert precise advice, guidance, or counseling as necessary to attain peak player performance for the immediate as well as the long-term needs of both player and organization.

The appraisal tool also allows management to leverage its position with the employee or player on its team, and to obtain higher levels of participation and commitment toward training purposes, promotion opportunities, professional development needs, pay raise opportunities, and overall development from a human resource perspective for the employee. The appraisal allows management and player to draft an action plan for future activity.

In designing your next player performance appraisal, address the activity as a directional interaction opportunity afforded to both management and employee. Become a leader of your team by utilizing the appraisal process as an instrument for growth and positive feedback. In essence, the appraisal system allows management to become effective mentors, guiding both the individual player and organization alike.

The Ultimate Leadership-Directed Appraisal System. A combination of the power of the most effective player development appraisal systems can actually be made in today's fast-paced, high-demand environments. Consider combining three appraisal systems into one joint effort for maximum player, management, and thus organizational development.

First, start by requesting that the employee or player to be appraised conduct a self-analysis, and submit that personal analysis in writing to management 48 hours prior to the scheduled face-to-face review. The areas of interest you should direct the player to respond to might be questions like:

- What are your three most powerful strengths within this position?
- What are your three greatest (personal) challenges within this position/organization? Areas for concentrated improvement could be...?
- What is your greatest accomplishment or contribution within this past appraisal cycle?
- Where do you see yourself growing in the next appraisal cycle?

Second, request a peer review from those other players who have the most direct interaction with the player (vertically or horizontally) on a regular basis (within or outside his specific area/department/divisions, and so on), to be submitted 48 hours prior to the scheduled session. This peer review can address the same sequence of observational questions presented previously (or others) and should be submitted to management with a copy to the player in question. Each colleague participating should schedule a few minutes within that 48-hour window to review his perspectives with the player prior to his meeting with management.

Third, with this added perspective and teaming, effective leaders then conduct the organizational appraisal and review session. The combination of the three culminates in an organization's positive and constructive approach to player development. This brings people together, instead of polarizing individuals within an organization.

The Appraisal Instrument. The success and effectiveness of the entire appraisal process comes down to how effective the appraisal instrument is at addressing the core trait and behavior issues needed for ultimate success in your specific environment. How often the official appraisals and impromptu appraisals occur also impacts the effectiveness of the process. All this impacts how effective the appraisal tool and appraiser will be at addressing successful habits, and those areas that may be causing some difficulties for a player (employee).

From this instrument, managers and leaders can develop players' potential for greater success and protect the organization against terrorists. Before you engage in your next appraisal process, evaluate the instrument that you use to determine whether it is a positive, focused tool, or sounds hard and negative.

For an instrument to be effective it should contain three primary sections for management and players to focus energies upon:

- A general ratings section where core performance issues can numerically be addressed and rated. This should have primary divisions (and then be further broken down as applicable for your environment into subsections), such as general performance, job performance and knowledge, adaptability and initiative, interpersonal relationships, communications skills, and supervisory factors (for management staff).

- An employee development action sequence plan where positives and areas for improvement can be addressed in an essay/editorial format. This section can be broken down into subsections as well to address specifics in your environment.

- A sign-off section with all appropriate players' signatures, indicating that the review has been conducted.

The length of your appraisal instrument should be the exact number of rating categories and pages necessary for you to measure any individual and any performance in any capacity she represents—to ensure improvement where necessary and success where critical. Any area that becomes a performance challenge for a person or a performance problem for management should be added to the instrument immediately. Remember, that which gets measured gets addressed!

Near the end of this chapter is an example of an effective employee performance appraisal form that incorporates the tenets presented in this section. You may want to make a copy of this form and utilize it directly with your team for developmental purposes.

Upward Feedback. Accelerate the growth and development of not only the team player, but also the leader of the team (whether he is the manager, supervisor, boss, and so on) through some sort of upward feedback system.

Growth can be accomplished by allowing, or even expecting, all members of a work group (team, department, organization, unit, and so on) who are direct responsibilities or reports to management-level personnel to utilize the same appraisal system to regularly evaluate and appraise the management team.

This process can be discomforting to some people and can actually lead to destructive behaviors and attitudes if not constructed in a positive, productive manner. Here are some safeguards to ensure peak performance:

- Each member of a team has the opportunity to participate in upward feedback sessions on a regular basis (just as often as self-analysis, peer reviews, and organizational appraisals occur).

- All members must sign the upward feedback instrument; if they don't sign it, the appraisal is void. It is easy to criticize another person anonymously.

- Just as with the other appraisal systems, areas noted as challenges and difficulties in the appraiser's notations for suggested action plans for future growth and desired success behaviors must follow a person. The intent of this tool is the development and growth of the leadership team, just as it is designed to develop the player.

- The upward feedback can be delivered in person or tendered for review by the party in question. Management can then meet one-on-one or as a group to brainstorm how to become more effective as a team and as the team leader.

Managerial Leadership Bible Lesson 12

Optimal performance by managerial leaders and from the members who comprise the team leads is continuously appraised, developed, held accountable, and grown for future needs and successes. Managerial leaders have multiple instruments that can be used mentally and physically to determine how best to assess the individuals they are responsible for, so as always to remain objective in their thorough analysis.

With these instruments, managerial leaders can deploy individuals as personnel assets and task projects to individuals accordingly.

The next pages reflect a template for performance appraisal utilized in my *Leadership Academy of Excellence* training series. If you want the template in electronic format, contact DrJeffSpeaks@aol.com and request it free of charge.

This sample personnel assessment is built off of best practice measurements from my clients and Fortune 100 firms over the past decade; recognizing the patterns most typically measured led me to this template. This can serve as a scorecard to performance; you can have general measurement areas that all members of an organization would be expected to achieve, and you can have situational- and positional-specific areas for measurement.

The assessment score is critical; I suggest simplifying the scores, as the more score options you provide the greater inconsistency there could be for how individuals are assessed. To me it is simple; either a person is doing the job she has been hired for or she is not in each measurement category. So the measurement is one of three options: (1) Meets the expectations for performance in each measurement; (2) Does not meet the expectations for performance in each measurement; (3) Exceeds the expectations for performance in each measurement.

One of the many responsibilities of a managerial leader is to grow and develop the human capital of her respective team and the organization overall. Providing someone wimpy measurements of any other score does an individual, colleagues, management, and the customer a disservice. An individual among the managerial leadership ranks who can't intellectually grasp this fact or wants to debate this fact has probably never signed the front of a check and is most likely not a leader.

Also, the annotated narrative comments section should be adjacent to each measurement category so specific KPI developmental comments can be made as you develop the assessment instrument from beginning to end. Keep in mind that the assessment instrument is a historical snapshot of the past to calibrate performance for the future.

Also, once you have customized the assessment instrument for your situational positional needs, this same form can be used in times of performance problems. While you may also do a deeper dive and complete a specific Performance Improvement Plan (PIP), it should also be wrapped around the facilitation of this instrument, and the obvious "does not meet expectations" would have to be attributed in appropriate measurement categories.

You can also benchmark the development and administration of your assessment instrument off of your trade industry and association templates, leaders within your industry, human resource professional services organizations, peer groups, and from common sense needs.

Anytime you start to have universal behavior or performance lapses, those may be situational clues of items that may not be on your assessment instrument and that may need to be added to future iterations and roll-outs. Remember, what gets measured get performed!

In designing your assessment instrument, do not be concerned whether your instrument has too few or too many measurement categories. It needs to be what it needs to be for the performance you need.

Think about it this way: The next time you get onto a commercial airline, would you want the pilots to have an abbreviated checklist of expected performance abilities of the plane, or would you prefer that they have as long of a list of checkpoints as necessary to ensure the safest, most proficient operation of that plan? The answer is obvious; so too should you in management have the appropriate depth of measurement categories necessary for peak performance of your people factors.

With the following template, notice how we have incorporated a modified version of the Managerial-Leadership-Coaching Engagement Model, also known as the SA Model, onto the top of the document so that your score of the player into the L-grid should be supported by the individual assessment categories and vice versa.

Performance and Development Assessment

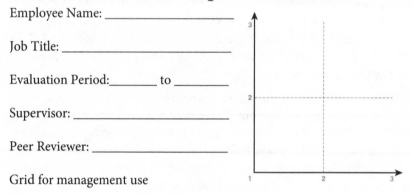

Employee Name: _____

Job Title: _____

Evaluation Period:_____ to _____

Supervisor: _____

Peer Reviewer: _____

Grid for management use

Part I: Goal Setting—What You Need to Achieve

List the 3-5 target goals, objectives, projects, or special assignments to be achieved or worked on in the next assessment period.

Part II: Review of Employee Job Description—What You Do

Review the employee's job description and make comments based on the defined areas of responsibility. What does the employee excel at? In what area(s) is more training or better performance needed? Be sure the entire job description is accounted for.

Part III: Behavioral Traits and Performance Factors—How You Behave

Following are behavioral traits and performance factors that are key to the success of the employee in his or her position. The following rating system will be used. Any line item marked "Needs Improvement" must have a plan of action toward improving the skill attached to this assessment. Line items marked "Exceeds Expectations" must include some examples of how expectations were exceeded. Please type "plans of action" and "exceeding expectation" examples in a different-colored font immediately following the specific trait or performance factor.

1. **Needs Improvement**—Consistently or occasionally fails to meet job requirements due to performance, behavior, or lack of knowledge in the case of the job or duty being new to the employee. Immediate improvement required to maintain employment.

2. **Meets Expectations**—Able to perform 100% of job duties satisfactorily. Normal guidance and supervision are required.

3. **Exceeds Expectations**—Frequently exceeds job requirements; all planned objectives were achieved above the established standards, and accomplishments were made in unexpected areas.

General Performance

Rating

Add a rating in the blank to the left and narrative notes to support the rating in the blank to the right. (This sample template has a short line to indicate the notes; in a real assessment, the notes would likely be detailed and longer.)

_____ **PUNCTUALITY**—Employee observes assigned work hours and adheres to them._____

_____ **ATTENDANCE**—Employee can be depended on to report to work regularly with few unplanned absences. Provides proper notification when absent. _____

_____ **POLICIES & PROCEDURES**—Employee understands and complies with company policies and procedures. _____

_____ **JUDGMENT & DECISION MAKING**—Employee effectively analyzes problems, determines appropriate action for solutions, and exhibits timely and decisive action; thinks logically.

_____

_____ **DEPENDABILITY**—Employee can be depended upon to apply him/ herself to tasks, use time efficiently, follow instructions, and carry out assignments to completion. _____

_____ **PROFESSIONALISM & WORK HABITS**—Employee demonstrates pride in the job and conducts self in a professional manner; identifies with the mission of the company. _____

_____ **INITIATIVE**—Employee accepts and/or volunteers for extra responsibilities beyond normal job duties in order to improve self. Employee monitors projects independently and follows through appropriately.
_____

_____ **DRESS**—Employee's workplace attire is professional (business casual as a minimum). When onsite at an official organization event or onsite at a company, employee's dress is professional and matches the expectations of the client. _____

_____ **WORK SPACE**—Employee maintains a professional, neat, and operational work space. _____

Job Performance and Knowledge

Rating

_____ **QUALITY OF WORK**—Employee demonstrates accuracy, neatness, and thoroughness in performing job duties. _____

_____ **QUANTITY OF WORK**—Employee demonstrates ability to meet required work output without sacrificing quality; ability to manage several responsibilities simultaneously. _____

_____ **SENSE OF URGENCY**—Employee demonstrates a sense of professional urgency in meeting job responsibilities and interacting with others. _____

_____ **JOB KNOWLEDGE**—Employee possesses and demonstrates necessary knowledge and skills to accomplish job duties. Uses experience effectively to enhance work performance. _____

_____ **TIME MANAGEMENT & ORGANIZATIONAL SKILLS**—Employee demonstrates ability to effectively plan, organize, and prioritize work; demonstrates effective use of time management practices; completes tasks in a timely manner and meets deadlines without sacrificing quality. _____

_____ **TRAINING & SELF IMPROVEMENT**—Employee utilizes what is learned in training; makes an effort to obtain on-the-job training and to improve skills and knowledge for advancement and improved performance. _____

_____ **ONGOING TRAINING & SELF IMPROVEMENT**—Employee seeks continued opportunities for additional learning and training; makes an effort to obtain on-the-job training and to improve skills and knowledge for advancement and improved performance.

_____

_____ **ADAPTABILITY**—Employee adjusts with ease to changes in duties, procedures, supervisors, or work environment. Employee accepts new ideas and approaches to work; responds appropriately to constructive criticism and suggestion for work improvement.

_____

_____ **CREATIVITY/INNOVATION**—Employee demonstrates new and creative ideas in carrying out job duties and makes constructive suggestions for seeking new and improved procedures.

_____

_____ **SELF-MANAGEMENT**—Demonstrates good self-discipline. Has the ability to forecast needs and opportunities and proactively exercises abilities to capitalize on those opportunities. Has the ability to be productive (not just busy) to attain continued profitability and productivity. _____

Interpersonal Relationships and Communication

Rating

_____ **ATTITUDE**—Employee demonstrates cooperative attitude with fellow employees and a willingness to share responsibilities as part of the team; displays a positive attitude toward work and fellow employees. _____

_____ **RELATIONSHIP W/ SUPERVISOR**—Employee responds positively to supervision, direction, and constructive criticism.

_____

_____ **DEALING W/ THE PUBLIC**—Employee demonstrates tact and patience in dealing with others. Relationship with clients is firm but fair, positive, decent, and respectful. Promotes good public relations and works effectively with teammates, clients, and vendors alike.

_____

_____ **WRITTEN COMMUNICATION**—Employee demonstrates a high level of competency in written expression, including reports and correspondence; uses grammar and syntax correctly and expresses ideas clearly and succinctly. _____

_____ **VERBAL COMMUNICATION**—Employee demonstrates competency in oral expression and listening; expresses thoughts clearly; listens and understands oral instructions and information, and actions reflect that understanding. _____

_____ **OPEN COMMUNICATION**—Employee interacts with peers and supervisors in such a manner that good rapport is maintained with the company; follows established chain of command.

_____

The following section is for employees in a *Customer Service & Sales* role.

Rating

_____ **RELATIONSHIP BUILDING**—Employee has made routine contact with Centers-of-Influence (also known as advocates, allies, and champions) to make sure our company's name is top of their mind and to ensure the manager has a pulse on market trends and issues that sales reps are facing. _____

_____ **LEAD GENERATION**—Employee has worked to grow his/her market share through additional market contacts since last assessment period. _____

_____ **SELLING PROCESS**—Employee understands the selling process and has worked to ensure effective selling is taking place and that the skills of him/herself and others have been elevated since the last assessment period. _____

_____ **MAINTAINS A CHAMPION SELLING ATTITUDE**—Employee demonstrates, promotes, and exudes a positive selling attitude and motivational beliefs. _____

_____ **PHONE MANAGEMENT**—Employee manages calls efficiently and meets expected inbound and outbound call volumes.

_____

_____ **DATABASE MANAGEMENT**—Employee keeps contact files updated and current and documents thoroughly what he/she has done with each contact. Call back dates are maintained and current.

_____

Supervisory Skills

This section to be completed only for those who perform supervisory functions within the company (in addition to the previous sections).

Rating

_____ **UNDERSTANDING OF DUTIES**—Supervisor understands the duties, functions, and responsibilities of her management position and the role she plays on the team; understands the mission of the company and adequately represents position of management.

_____

_____ **LEADERSHIP SKILLS**—Supervisor demonstrates leadership qualities by setting an example of excellence and dedication for subordinates to follow; motivates subordinates to perform duties to optimum level of abilities. _____

_____ **EFFECTIVE SUPERVISION**—Supervisor manages subordinates effectively to maximize their performance and produce the desired quantity and quality of work; exerts authority when necessary.

_____

_____ **ORGANIZATIONAL SKILLS**—Supervisor demonstrates effective use of organizational skills to keep department and subordinates working in a cohesive and organized manner; good knowledge of all aspects of work of department. _____

_____ **RELATIONSHIP W/ SUBORDINATES**—Supervisor encourages an open door policy with subordinates; deals with all in a fair and impartial manner. _____

_____ **INTERPERSONAL SUPERVISORY SKILLS**—Supervisor demonstrates effective interpersonal relationship practices with peers, subordinates, and management, so as to foster good communication within the department and company; effectively and properly uses the chain of command. _____

_____ **STAFF**—Supervisor is accessible to his/her staff and others during work hours and beyond (when emergencies arise). He/she has regular team briefings, meetings, and communication as appropriate. Supervisor effectively promotes the improvement and development of staff and subordinates through formal training sessions, coaching, and other activities. _____

_____ **SELF DEVELOPMENT**—Employee demonstrates a proactive behavior in searching out job-appropriate skills training (books, articles, audio, video, live classes, and so on) in the past assessment period to elevate his/her competency level to share and guide the team to greater successes. _____

_____ **BUDGET RESPONSIBILITIES**—Supervisor has a firm grasp of the budgeting process and how to analyze and use the data to impact the profitability of his/her division. _____

Personal/Professional Development

This section addresses specific personal/professional developmental commitments for the next measurement assessment period.

PROFESSIONAL DEVELOPMENT—To better develop and grow professionally overall within your organization, I plan to _____

POSITIONAL DEVELOPMENT—To better develop and grow my positional/job/rank effectiveness, in the areas of technical and professional capabilities/proficiency, I plan to enroll in the following programs, classes, webcasts/seminars, distance learning, certifications, programs, books to be read, journals to subscribe to, and so on. _____

PERSONAL DEVELOPMENT—To better develop and grow I plan to _____

Signatures

Supervisor: _____

Date: _____

I have been advised of my performance ratings. I have discussed the contents of this review with my supervisor. My signature does not necessarily imply agreement. My comments are as follows (optional).

Employee Signature: _____

Date: _____

Review Questions

The review questions accompanying each chapter or section are designed to assist you in achieving the learning objective stated at the beginning of each chapter. The review section is not graded; do not submit it in place of your final exam. While completing the review questions, it may be helpful to study any unfamiliar terms in the glossary in addition to course content. After completing the review questions for each chapter, proceed to the review question answers and rationales.

1. Quality measurement is the price of:

    A. Tradition

    B. Playing the game

    C. Nonconformance

    D. Playing by the rules

2. Using a _____ as a planning device is fast, explosive, and exceedingly thorough.

    A. Outline

    B. Growth wheel

    C. Calendar

    D. To-do list

3. One of the major destructive points for businesses and managers is when they force themselves into a _____ that doesn't take the specific environment into consideration.

    A. Mission statement

    B. Work schedule

    C. Computer system

    D. Measuring system

4. Annual employee evaluation is the best way to track employee performance.

    A. True

    B. False

5. Before the appraisal session, be sure you are using consistent and _____ tracking and measurement systems or tools for the entire team.

    A. Objective

    B. Subjective

    C. Personalized

    D. Simple

6. The sole purpose of an appraisal or appraisal tool is to:

    A. Scare employees straight

    B. Enhance player development and growth

    C. Determine pay raises

    D. Justify employee dismissal

7. An additional problem to an improper review is that it takes an employee as much as six months to recover from such a review.

    A. True

    B. False

Review Question Answers and Rationales

Review question answer choices are accompanied by unique, logical reasoning (rationales) as to why an answer is correct or incorrect. Evaluative feedback to incorrect responses and reinforcement feedback to correct responses are both provided.

1. Quality measurement is the price of:

    A. Incorrect. In traditional management, quality was not managed properly and led to company downfalls.

    B. Incorrect. To truly change any part of your organization, you need to be able to measure it and create a new game.

    C. **Correct. By being flexible and ready to adapt to your company's needs you are not conforming to standard business practices.**

    D. Incorrect. This book is all about creating new rules, and that is what quality measurement will help you do.

2. Using a(n) _____ as a planning device is fast, explosive, and exceedingly thorough.

    A. Incorrect. An outline can sometimes be tedious and the format can require many pages of text instead of one.

    B. **Correct. Also known as "clustering" or "brainstorming," this technique gets to the heart of matters and organizes quickly.**

C. Incorrect. A calendar should be used a planning guide for dates, not ideas.

D. Incorrect. A to-do list may be a product of a growth wheel, but it will not establish the things "to do."

3. One of the major destructive points for businesses and managers is when they force themselves into a _____ that doesn't take the specific environment into consideration.

A. Incorrect. Mission statements are usually much broader than the specific company's line of business or product, so they often do not take the company environment into consideration.

B. Incorrect. A work schedule can be changed and, therefore, is not a major destructive point.

C. Incorrect. Software can make any computer system adapt to your needs and is therefore not a major problem.

D. Correct. A tool is only useful if it is used in the proper context. If you are measuring the wrong things, you will not learn how to make your company more efficient.

4. Annual employee evaluation is the best way to track employee performance.

A. Incorrect. In today's business world, annual evaluation is not sufficiently regular. Frequently scheduled evaluations are necessary to track performance.

B. Correct. To maximize growth, employees need immediate feedback, not just once a year.

5. Before the appraisal session, be sure you are using consistent and _____ tracking and measurement systems or tools for the entire team.

A. Correct. All members of the team must be judged by the same standards.

B. Incorrect. If you let personal opinion get in the way of judgment, then it will inherently be biased.

C. Incorrect. Personalized measurement would be unfair for extremely productive or unproductive employees.

D. Incorrect. As you can see from this chapter, there are many ways to create measurement systems, and designing them may not be simple.

6. The sole purpose of an appraisal or appraisal tool is to:

   A. Incorrect. Scaring employees or idly threatening dismissal will cause a total breakdown in communication.

   B. Correct. Appraisals should not instill fear or conflict.

   C. Incorrect. One of the goals of employee development could be a pay raise, but appraisals should not be done for only that reason.

   D. Incorrect. While an appraisal may be part of a dismissal documentation, there are other processes that need to be documented.

7. An additional problem to an improper review is that it takes an employee as much as six months to recover from such a review.

   A. Correct. This is why reviews must be done correctly and frequently.

   B. Incorrect. This lengthy recovery can lead to a great deal of hostility toward management and other employees, potentially turning a transmitter into a terrorist.

13

Powerful Steps to Convert Negativity to Positive Outcomes

Difficulty and negativity is a perception of a reality. How you view a reality impacts what you will experience emotionally, psychologically, and physically. And it is how you respond (not react) that determines your effectiveness and happiness.

—**Jeff Magee**

Learning Objectives

After completing this section of the course, you will be able to counter and even eliminate negativity in the professional sphere.

Challenge, change, conflict, confusion, communication cracks, and confrontation can all contribute to levels of tension, frustration, difficulty, and bottom-line negativity. When negativity develops in a professional environment, it can lead to paralysis and stagnation of an otherwise effective team. Working to counter and even eliminate negativity in the professional sphere, or being able to control and effectively deal with negative stimulants when they do arise, is necessary for both management personnel and players alike.

Think about it. How many times have you heard negative comments or voices? How many times have you heard one in your own mind, talking to you about something or someone that led to inner stress and anxiety for you? When this happens, reflect on how much time is being taken from productive causes, inwardly manifesting additional negative thoughts. All the while productivity suffers, and personal health pays the price.

If you find yourself in similar situations, or observe that members of your team become unfocused due to challenging or negative stimulants, as the lead player on the team, accountability has to start with you to stimulate some positives. Consider how negativity in most forms can impact a player's and thus an organization's performance and proactiveness. A few recent case studies have shown:

- Roughly 80 percent of adults in America viewed themselves as having "low self-esteem." (1990s Gallup study commissioned by Reverend Robert Schuller.)

  The more one is subjected to negativity and stimulants that do not reinforce one's positives, the lower one's self-esteem may be. The lower the self-esteem, the lower one's peak performance (refer to Chapter 9, "Nine Tactical Steps to High-Impact Leadership").

- How you view stimulants directly impacts individuals and team inter-action effectiveness. Harvard University reports in a 1990s study that immigrants to America in the 1990s (specifically) have 4.1 greater odds of becoming millionaires in their lifetimes than those born and raised in America! Why?

The answer is easy. It is reflected in how a person views stimulants. Are they roadblocks and challenges, or opportunities and fortunes? The answer lies in the eyes of the experienced participant.

So how does management focus energies on a negative situation or person and work to convert that unpleasantness into a positive situation or person? Stimulating a change in behaviors follows a three-step interaction process. You can accomplish these conditioning steps in a number of ways (we present 22 strategies and high-impact tactics). It does not really matter which way you choose; what does matter is that whatever course of action you pursue, first reflect upon these steps and address each one at a time before progressing to the next subsequent step.

A violation of any one of the three basic and primary steps impacts each outcome and could lead to greater negativity and frustration.

Before you can convert a negative to a positive, follow the three-step sequence or formula for lasting impact and results. Each step can be involved or simple. It is a subjective response, depending upon what management is faced with, and which alternatives are being exercised as one's management style at a given time. Consider:

Awareness. First you must create an atmosphere conducive for the parties involved to even want to interact and have dialogue toward a solution or resolution. This is done by first working to ensure the other party sees a need, a problem, or a possibility for something better or greater. This is the phase of the interaction where you noncombatively address the "what" and "why" factors to motivate the other party to see why she should even listen and participate in the interaction.

Interaction. Now you can progress to a level where the parties involved can begin to workshop ideas for the intervention, action plans for resolution, and steps for forward progression: the how-to plans. This is the phase where you address the "how" factor of the progression forward.

Commitment. Commitment only occurs after the first two steps have sequentially been addressed, with the involved parties signing on to accountability behaviors and applying themselves toward a more constructive and positive future. This is the phase of the interaction whereby all participants know the "when" factor of the engagement.

There will be times when you have authority to maintain the control powers to stimulate positive change through the utilization of these strategies and tactics. There will also be times when you cannot stimulate the change you want. In those situations, the best course of action is to manage the challenge.

> *Because some people just live to be bitter, ugly, and negative, the reality to managing away many difficult situations and confrontational people is to select from one of four basic interaction options, and recognize when doing nothing may be your most explosive intervention action plan of all!*
> —**Jeff Magee**

There are two extreme behavioral patterns one can experience when engaging a poor performer or negative and difficult person, a person who is destined for a conflict or all-out confrontation. You can select an action plan that allows you to shine as a leader, or you can barge straight onward and increase the odds of ending up as a loser!

To work through conflicts and confrontations and determine a logic-based, response-driven *best course of action (BCOA)* every time, consider a lesson learned from today's Generation X/Y. The Gen-X'ers and Y'ers have made famous the sign of raising their left hands in an upward direction, with the index finger pointing upward and the thumb pointing outward in the fashion of a large letter "L." This is their universal sign to represent "loser."

In management, this same symbol could be interpreted as an L-grid. By visualizing this L-grid, or in some instances even graphing this out on a sheet of paper to plot multiple players or situations, you as a manager or leader have the ability to instantly lead your own behavior away from that of loser and toward that of continuous leader. This new instrument born out of the L-grid becomes your action engagement model. By plotting a variable from low to high on the vertical axis, and the same on the horizontal axis, you are directed powerfully to your BCOA.

The Methodology of the Action Engagement Model for Resolution. To measure and determine how best to engage to resolve, solve, manage, eliminate, avoid, or cope with negative, difficult, and confrontational situations or people, consider how you would measure the situation or person on the grid (see Figure 13.1). The vertical axis represents how you would score the level of reality control of a given variable. The horizontal axis represents the level of impact for better/change variables. Now, within the grid, visualize both axes as if they were numbered, 1–10. With 1–5 representing unacceptable or negative scores and 5–10 as acceptable or positive scores, you can now score individuals and situations against this model.

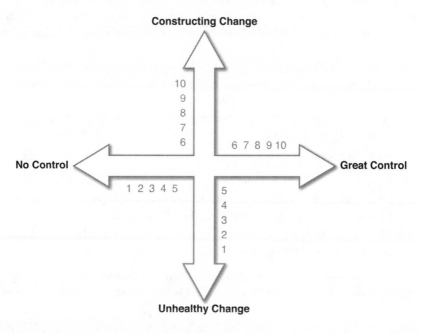

Figure 13.1 Action Engagement Model

Now if you really want to address conflicts and confrontations for resolution, determine in which quadrant you would land the next time you feel compelled to engage either a person or situation. Within the action engagement model grid, there are four basic quadrants from which you can guide your best course of action plans.

The Best Course of Action from the Action Engagement Model L-grid.
To determine exactly what to do, decide whether you have or do not have control in reality over the person or situation on the vertical axis line (low on the line means "no," and high on the line means "yes"). After that measurement determination, decide using the horizontal axis whether, if that person or situation were addressed, it would be a positive impact or constructive, healthy change (low on the axis line means "no"; high on the line means "yes"). Your course of action in fast-tracking how best to address conflicts and confrontations is follows:

1. **Bottom-left quadrant** placement reveals that your BCOA here is to "shut up" and walk away. This quadrant represents items of no control and no impact, so don't invest your time and energy!

2. **Top-left quadrant** placement reveals that your BCOA is to "drop it" and leave it alone; no one but you cares, and it does not matter!

3. **Bottom-right quadrant** placement reveals that while "it" matters, you have no control over it, so your BCOA is to determine who does have influence and control over it and work to influence him or her to address it.

4. **Top-right quadrant** placement is for those people and situations that should be on your "to do" list," as you have control and the impact would be worth the engagement.

Based upon whichever quadrant you find yourself in, this action engagement model directs you to design immediate action plans.

To look backward at the last series of conflicts and confrontations that consume one at home and in business, and to recognize the percentage of time invested in them according to the four quadrants of the action engagement model, may be alarming. Time spent on the bottom-left and top-left quadrants is a percentage of time lost.

As a managerial leader, one must maintain control at potentially volatile times, and gauge all actions in a manner so that one may stay on the right-side quadrants. This is the best investment of a managerial leader's time.

There are more than 22 powerful conversion strategies (extrapolated from *Enough Already: 50 Fast Ways to Deal With, Manage and Eliminate Negativity at Work and Home*, by Jeffrey Magee, Brown Books Publishing, $12.95) to implement when you are in either the lower-right or upper-right quadrants of the model. Here are just some:

- **Avoidance**—When you feel a negative situation about to develop or a negative conversation about to start (based upon prior experience and knowledge), simply walk away from it. If you are not a willing participant with a negative person and don't take part in the interaction, there can be no negative encounter. Don't get sucked into negative zones.

- **Don't argue**—It takes two to debate and argue. If you're not a willing, active participant, it becomes difficult for the other party to continue his disruptive behavior. When a conversation moves from issues and performance toward people and personalities, it is time to end it, as an individual's emotions when he is wounded lead to significant tensions in professional environments. Convert these oral situations into both oral and visual conversation by immediately writing the issues down on paper, so you can navigate the conversation and all parties toward the black-and-white issues, not the sidebar argumentative topics.

- **Isolation**—There are two ways this can be interpreted. First, maintain your distance from those people or situations over which you have no control, and that you know to be negative. Keep yourself isolated from them and focused upon other activities. (Idle time gets everyone into trouble in the face of negativity.) Second, in certain situations, a person may be negative, have a bad attitude, or pose difficulty, yet his presence is needed for other reasons. Therefore, isolate him from other players. Keep the player focused and busy at what he does best; don't allow idle time to interact with other players on a team. Remember that negative people can become toxic to a productive organization. You may need to interact as both manager and counselor with these people, should the negativity in them persist.

- **Garner prior support**—Identify your positive support network—those who will benefit from change or something new or different that you are enacting—and interact with them prior to interfacing with the entire team. Gain support from your transformers (refer to Chapter 2, "Five Mission Statements for Ultimate 'New View' Success") and strategically use them to motivate others.

- **Linkage**—Identify key factors in your position and in that of the other party. Link an aspect of the two together to establish common ground and connection of the two positions. This tends to diffuse otherwise seemingly differing views and positions held by individuals and stimulates a higher degree of interaction for a mutually desirable outcome. It becomes difficult for a combative or negative person to remain so on a winning team when you are tying elements from everyone's positions together. It also becomes difficult to keep pointing the finger of blame or guilt at other people when there are at least minimal elements of linkage among the parties' positions. Linkage is a powerful strategy that allows you to interact successfully with others.

- **Double standards**—By using double standards, you can sometimes illustrate hypocrisy and present an alternative point of view. For example, consider the double standard society has with regard to actions exhibited by men and women.

  A man can be assertive in a professional environment and be viewed as assertive. If overly assertive, he may perhaps be viewed as aggressive, pushy, or even overbearing. Yet if a woman is assertive in a professional environment, there is a good likelihood she will be seen not as aggressive, pushy, or overbearing. She will be viewed as a b_ _ _ _ (double standard)! By illustrating your position in this way, you can assist the other party in nonconfrontationally seeing another viewpoint.

- **Assign 100 percent accountability**—An explosive strategy for converting a consistently negative stimulant (your terrorist from Chapter 2) into a more participatory player on the team is to prepare your actions ahead of time. The next time a player challenges your positions, merely allow him the pleasure of assuming 100 percent accountability for that task or project he professes to be the expert on, on which he has been challenging you or other players. Assign this accountability, with no strings attached and walk away.

- **Visualized statement required**—Another powerful technique for defusing negative persons is to request or recommend that when they challenge a position or statement you have asserted, they in turn take their perspectives and ideas and write each down on paper with the associated rationales. Once written down, the two parties should get back together to discuss them logically and calmly. Players who merely like to challenge others will quickly back off from instigating negativity and tension, if they learn that in response the other party is not going to participate in a verbal bashing match, but will engage in dialogue once all is written down.

- **Cost-benefit analysis**—Conduct a survey or study to illustrate in black and white the costs and benefits associated with a position, task, or project that may cause controversy. Thus all parties will have documentation, not allegations, on which to base decisions. Costs can be measured in player, environmental, and physical factors.

- **Identify distortion(s) and immediately examine**—When a negative statement, distortion, or embellished statement is made that is misleading and may cause further negativity, immediately stop an interaction and examine that individual factor to determine and educate all parties as to reality and factuality. If you ignore a misstatement and allow it to go on and on, there will have been far too many of them made to be able to effectively go back, sort through, and deal with each. Take each as it comes and as you first hear it. If you are consistent in your behavior here, the negative person will eventually learn that her behavior doesn't work with you. And you will see a change in her.

- **Objections**—Have the most vocal objector state his position in advance. If you know there may be a colleague at a meeting who is opposed to you or your position, and that he will eventually challenge you, put him on notice and turn the environmental conditioning factors around.

  For example, immediately after presenting your idea, turn toward your perceived negativist and ask him for feedback. What are his feelings as to what you have just said? At this point, you have merely asked a nonconfrontational question, and peer pressure is on your side. This is because as you ask the question, everyone in the room will be looking toward the colleague you asked.

- **Breathing pattern adjustment**—When confronted with a challenging and/or negative situation or person, you may experience a change in your breathing patterns. You may feel a shortness of breath, tight shoulders, tense limbs, and a tight forehead, resulting in a headache. Whether this happens in a meeting situation, on the telephone, in traffic, or after leaving a face-to-face encounter, take a couple of minutes (two to three will work) to control and adjust your breathing patterns. First, force yourself to inhale every breath through your nose in this time period. Second, exhale each breath through your mouth. By changing your normal pattern to this sequence for a few minutes, you will relax psychologically because this pattern relaxes you physiologically. In a relaxed physical state you can regain control of your emotions and stimulate your logic track.

- **Avoid challenge words**—Work to remove words that may stimulate additional anger or negativity in combative or negative people. Words that cause confrontation with others are words, such as *however, you, but, opinion, think.*

- **Use ownership words**—In dealing with people, whether you know them or not, replace challenge words with ownership words. These are words that don't stimulate any negativity or challenge when heard by others. In essence, these words make it appear that you are pointing a finger at yourself and not another person. They are words, such as *we, us, team, I, feel.*

- **Go one-on-one in private**—With persistent, challenging players in an organization, you may choose to meet one-on-one in private (see Chapter 9 for counseling ideas) to address the differing positions that you and the other parties have. This may be uncomfortable for you as a manager but may be an educational experience for both you and the other persons involved.

- **Stimulate a conversation**—There are six effective and quick ways to initiate a conversation with another person in a nonconfrontational manner. There is an adage, "The one doing the talking and the one who talks first loses." This could lead to a confrontation with another person if you are face-to-face and no one wants to talk for fear of losing. However, you can control a conversation while at the same time not dominate it.

  The fastest way to motivate the other party to open up and talk, so you can direct the interaction toward agreement and proactiveness among the players involved, is to start off your statement with WHO, WHAT, WHEN, WHERE, WHY, and HOW. These six words alone are powerful openers. Remember: W, W, W, W, W, H!

- **Three up**—When someone disagrees with you or another player, don't argue and don't defend your position (that is what he expects and it leads to confrontation). Request that the challenging player provide three alternatives to what he disagrees with. You may find a new and more effective solution, or you may nonconfrontationally communicate to the other players: put up or shut up!

- **Demand an alternative: Three Times**—Another explosive technique to convert a routine negativist into either a transmitter or transformer is to halt conversations when someone else disagrees with you. Move the conversation in a new direction, using the six words presented earlier, to gain another alternative or a nonresponse. Demand this alternative at least three times before you allow the conversation to proceed, and before you let the other player off the hook.

For example: "What do you feel we should do?" If they have a non-response, don't proceed. Stay right on that question for a second try. "Really, what do you feel we could do, if this idea isn't realistic?" After another nonresponse, ask one final or third time: "No, really, what do you feel we could do?"

- **Relocate**—Remove the task or issue at hand that causes the tension. If giving XYZ to player A causes trauma every time, remove that item to another player. In essence, relocate the negativity to another, where it will not be seen as a negative. Or relocate the issue and challenge from your accountability to another player or team/committee to deal with. Relocate the problem entirely (see additional examples and strategies as outlined in Chapter 9 in the "#4: Delegation Dynamics" section).

- **Empathy**—Another powerful diffusing strategy for increased interaction effectiveness is to acknowledge the other person's position. Empathy means acknowledgment; it does not mean that you agree or disagree with another person's position. Most challenging or negative people on your team have learned throughout life that to get acknowledged, they have to be difficult for a prolonged period of time. If you acknowledge them immediately, it throws them off their mental track and puts you directly into control.

- **Blend with the challenging player**—Look for a position she has asserted that you can live with, and join up with her. Your merging is least expected and also serves to neutralize her for successful interaction and subsequent conversion.

- **Increase your "VAK" (visual, auditory, kinesthetic) communications**—As you interact with players in stressed environments or challenging and unpleasant situations, you should work to communicate each message through all three channels (see Chapter 10, "Improving Interactive Communication") to eliminate any misunderstanding. Communicate each thought and signal through visual, auditory, and kinesthetic channels.

Converting negatives to positives is possible. Don't run or hide from negativity—face it head-on for success!

Managerial Leadership Bible Lesson 13

Anyone can complain, and everyone has learned how to be negative. An effective managerial leader has learned not to engage challenging, negative, and difficult people head-on. Rather, engage them by blending your energies and actions with theirs in such a way that you then involve them in a solution or resolution.

By actively using the engagement L-grid model in this section, you will ascend to great levels of success with your team and through your team.

Review Questions

The review questions accompanying each chapter or section are designed to assist you in achieving the learning objective stated at the beginning of each chapter. The review section is not graded; do not submit it in place of your final exam. While completing the review questions, it may be helpful to study any unfamiliar terms in the glossary in addition to course content. After completing the review questions for each chapter, proceed to the review question answers and rationales.

1. What does the bottom-left quadrant of the L-grid signify?
    A. Items with great control and no impact
    B. Items of no control and no impact
    C. Items with no control and great impact
    D. Items with great control and great impact

2. The "isolation" conversion strategy has two meanings.
    A. True
    B. False

3. *However, you, but, opinion,* and *think* are all _____ words.
    A. Open
    B. Thoughtful
    C. Sympathetic
    D. Challenge

4. There are six effective and quick ways to initiate a conversation with another person in a nonconfrontational manner.
    A. True
    B. False

5. Empathy can also be described as:
   A. Acknowledgement
   B. Sympathy
   C. Ignoring
   D. Being right

Review Question Answers and Rationales

Review question answer choices are accompanied by unique, logical reasoning (rationales) as to why an answer is correct or incorrect. Evaluative feedback to incorrect responses and reinforcement feedback to correct responses are both provided.

1. What does the bottom-left quadrant of the L-grid signify?
   A. Incorrect. This is the upper-left quadrant.
   B. Correct. These items should be left alone.
   C. Incorrect. This is the bottom-right quadrant.
   D. Incorrect. This is the lower-right quadrant.

2. The "isolation" conversion strategy has two meanings.
   A. Correct. You can either isolate yourself from a situation in which you have no control or isolate an individual who is causing a negative situation.
   B. Incorrect. Depending on the situation, you may need both or just one of the meanings.

3. *However, you, but, opinion,* and *think* are all _____ words.
   A. Incorrect. These words do no open further communication.
   B. Incorrect. These words do not take other people's ideas into consideration.
   C. Incorrect. These words do not suggest a sharing of feelings.
   D. Correct. These words negate other people's ideas and show you are not listening to them in the first place.

4. There are six effective and quick ways to initiate a conversation with another person in a nonconfrontational manner.

   A. Correct. These ways correspond to earlier discussions of WWWWWH.

   B. Incorrect. According to the text, most confrontations are about these six questions.

5. Empathy can also be described as:

   A. Correct. Empathy is recognizing someone else's position.

   B. Incorrect. Sympathy is feeling bad for a person's position.

   C. Incorrect. Ignoring is the opposite of empathy.

   D. Incorrect. Empathy does not refer to being right, but to recognizing someone else's position.

14

Speed-Reading Personalities, Negotiating Win-Win Outcomes, Building Alliances

In life you get what you negotiate for, not what you want or deserve.
—Dr. Chester L. Karrass

God's gift to us is life. Our gift back is how we live that life. So ask yourself, What am I giving?
—Les Brown, Jr.

Learning Objective

After completing this section of the course, you will be able to understand the tenets of basic personality style indicators, power negotiation, and how to forge alliances for organizational survival.

To effectively pull together resources and lead people of differing need levels and perspectives, managerial leaders need to possess or understand the tenets of basic personality (or social) style indicators, power negotiation, and how to forge alliances for organizational survival. Your ability to practice, in essence, negotiation jujitsu becomes critical to leadership effectiveness in building alliances and coalitions, and recruiting advocates and champions of your cause.

First, view negotiation as the art of interacting with differing need levels and interests of individuals who, for the most part, have similar end goals, merely different views on how to obtain those results. You have to navigate those differences to attain organizational and personal net results. So what is negotiation? Think of it in the following terms:

- It is a process.

- It involves posturing and positioning.

- It is a well-planned-out series of events, actions, strategies, and tactics.

- It is a learned skill level.
- It involves artfully designed questions.
- It is verbal and nonverbal language/powerful body language.
- It is a psychological process.
- It involves give-and-take (gambits) actions.

The key factors of an effective negotiation process involve and focus efforts on four key elements:

- Attack the *issues or problems* and never the people representing them.
- Handle *interest* and not positions.
- Brainstorm mutual *options*.
- Rely upon *objective* standards and criteria to be used.

Setting a solid foundation from which to negotiate is critical to effective negotiation and successful outcomes. The power of your negotiation process comes down to two approaches. What you do before the process—strategy—and what you then become capable of doing during the negotiation—tactics—dictates your negotiation strength, position, insight, and ability to finesse the interaction toward mutually acceptable outcomes that address each party's true need levels.

Start by asking yourself what the attitude is among the players involved in the negotiation process. If the attitudes are neutral-to-positive, you can expect healthy, productive interactions and dialogue. However, if some of the players have negative attitudes, effective leadership suggests that the initial focus needs to be either on neutralizing (conditioning) those negative players' attitudes, or on eliminating those players from the dynamics of the interaction or group. Otherwise, they can easily become terrorists (see Chapter 2, "Five Mission Statements for Ultimate 'New View' Success," for more on the subgroups in life) and sabotage your efforts and plans.

Before the Negotiation Process

Consider the following points and how they relate to you and your positioning. Each of the subsections has a powerful impact on your planning process, and thus impacts your ultimate effectiveness once face-to-face in the negotiation process.

There are specific commonly shared traits of effective negotiators, and many experts believe that some of these include the following:

- Ability to plan and organize the process effectively
- Realization that negotiation is always interactive and incorporates give-and-take situations
- Ability to think clearly under pressure
- Desire to acquire additional knowledge and skills
- Command of good verbal ability and listening skills
- Understanding of how "gambits" work
- Possession of personal power and practice of the skills everywhere
- Study of the process continually
- Ability to perceive and exploit power points
- Ability to be persistent and maintain patience

There are multiple levels of need that all parties involved in a negotiation are seeking to have addressed and met. These need levels can be broken down into two categories. An effective negotiator attempts to identify these before entering into a negotiation process with another party. The two need levels are minimum acceptable needs and maximum desired needs.

By identifying your minimum need level, you can focus your efforts on when it is best for you to walk away from the negotiation process and not be taken advantage of. And in reverse, if you can identify what the minimum need level of the other party is prior to a negotiation process, you know how much bargaining room or leverage you have, and therefore, what the other party's walk-away point is.

These two need levels allow you to measure the negotiation and bargaining process. Remember, knowledge and information are critical to the process. The more you have prior to the actual interactions, the better you will be able to prepare and strategize your moves, presentation, offers, and tactics.

In preparing your negotiation and positioning yourself for maximum interaction and leadership, consider the entire process in three basic modules: before, during, and after. Also, realize that three primary components impact your negotiation: the situation, the timing, and the players or people involved. I call this simply the *STP Factor* of the negotiation process:

S **Situation** attests to the fundamental need levels of the central personalities involved. From this awareness, the situation then progresses to the status quo and desired outcome for each party.

T Timing deals with the level of perceived or actual urgency by the stakeholders involved. From this understanding, timing moves into the realm of time needed for the engagement and process.

P Players deals with the simple or complex involvement of personality (or social) styles, their needs levels, agendas (or hidden agendas), the people necessary to execute the desired intervention, and what they are all buying into in the agenda.

The more you know and understand the STP Factor, the better off you will be in the actual negotiation process.

These elements all assist you in preparing your best course of action (BCOA) and your best course of interaction (BCOI) in the negotiation process—turn traditional hindsight into desired foresight!

Along with this prenegotiation activity, effective leaders also identify the dynamics of the personalities participating in the negotiation process and play to each specific personality's requirements.

There are endless ways to measure and determine a personality (social) style or type. The number of personality measuring models and instruments available to management and organizational leaders seems infinite. Given your own abilities in determining a personality style, the following matrix is merely another tool you can reference to do it, at a given point in time.

A managerial leader many times must be able to make an instant observation and assess a situation and the people involved to determine operating personality style in an individual or specific instance. The ability to speed-read another person allows the successful managerial leader to tailor her behavioral approach, communication intervention style, and the manner in which to engage a person, based on any one of the six different managerial leadership intervention styles.

Therefore, the answer from this personality matrix and its acknowledgment further assists you in preparing your interactions, and also has a great impact on how you may or may not approach and interact with another individual. Make allowances and adjustments to your style, based on what another personality style indicates you need to do to maximize your efforts with it.

Basically, personality falls into one of the four primary personality zones, based on environmental factors and one's beliefs at any given time. A person may evolve in and out of several different styles or zones in any given day. While most people do have a dominant style from which they operate more than 51 percent of the time, situations can cause them to temporarily evolve into a secondary zone.

Change the factors and a person's primary personality may also temporarily change. In plotting a person, visualize a simple "plus sign" as the matrix of the model to be used (see Figure 14.1). Always plot the vertical axis first and then the horizontal. The vertical axis line in this instrument represents the level of the person's comfort zone, from more task-oriented at the top to more people-oriented at the bottom. The horizontal line measures one's "energy zone," from a slow orientation on the left to a more fast orientation on the right.

Vertical-line observation clues in speed-reading someone's personality style:

TASK = More formal in actions and comments, prefers structure for performance, not as social or communicative. The farther upward one's actions reflect these types of descriptors, the farther up the vertical axis line you would plot a person—and thus make the mental or physical dissection mark.

PEOPLE = More informal and flexible, more outgoing, communicative, and social in nature. The farther downward one's actions reflect these types of descriptors, the farther down the vertical axis line you would plot the person—and thus put the mental or physical dissection mark.

Horizontal-line observation clues in speed-reading someone's personality style:

SLOW = Means this person is more methodical, analytical, process-driven, data-oriented, calm, and patient, and it takes a lot to unnerve him. The farther leftward one's actions reflect these types of descriptors, the farther to the left on the horizontal axis line you would plot the person—and thus make the mental or physical dissection mark.

FAST = Means this person is more assertive, outgoing, aggressive, and impatient; it does not take a lot to upset her or cause her to explode. The farther rightward one's actions reflect these types of descriptors, the farther to the right on the horizontal axis line you would plot the person—and thus put the mental or physical dissection mark.

From those two plot makers you have determined (the vertical and the horizontal axis), you can now speed-read a person and decide in which of the four zones he falls, and to what degree in that zone or quadrant, based upon your educated guesstimate from the two marks and where they intersect when graphed together. Based upon where you assess yourself to be at the same time as your interaction with the person, you can then determine what adjustment to make to move from your personality style toward his for best interaction effectiveness.

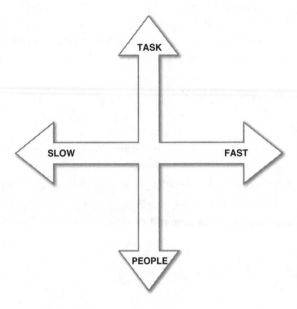

Figure 14.1 Reading a personality

As you identify your or another person's personality style based on the chart, note that it falls into one of the four zones or quadrants. A person's personality style gives you tremendous insight into how she may think and feel, given your interactions and the negotiation process.

The styles for each zone can take on many names or titles. Gauge each one in the following categories.

1. **Top-right zone/quadrant** = the driver or type A personality style. These persons are typically very driven and energized, fast-paced, bottom-line oriented. They tend to be at peak performance when by themselves and not held accountable for others' actions and productivity. They focus on what things mean to them and how they will impact their fast-paced plans toward their goals. Get directly to the point with these people. Change doesn't always bother them, and they

are fast to adapt to new environments or needs. They tend to be auditory communicators.

2. **Bottom-right zone/quadrant** = the coach or performer personality style. These persons adapt quickly to new environments, tend to be focused toward others' needs levels, and seek action, fun, and interaction with others. They tend to focus on getting others involved and don't mind being held accountable for others' actions. They don't mind group activities and will consider how things impact others in decision making. They tend to be kinesthetic communicators.

3. **Bottom-left zone/quadrant** = the amiable or blender personality style. They tend to be involved with those around them. They don't like the spotlight placed on them and are sensitive about the needs of others. They tend to be cautious and reserved about change and adapt slowly to changing environmental concerns. These people can be productive players and for the most part blend into the environment about them and follow the flow set by others. They tend to be kinesthetic communicators.

4. **Top-left zone/quadrant** = the critical thinker or analytical personality style. They may (not always) pose the greatest challenge in an interaction. These personalities need significant data and facts to support any change or new position/proposal. In the negotiation process, they keep the presentation and conversation focused on issues, not on feelings or personalities. These players tend to focus in great detail on the status quo and analyze how the norms of the right now meet needs. Therefore, they scrutinize any suggestion of change for how it will impact people or organizational dynamics. These players tend to be at peak performance when left alone and don't like the spotlight or having to participate in large situations. They tend to be visual communicators.

By identifying your personality style and those of the other people that you encounter in interactions or in negotiation cycles, you can gain a better understanding of how to manage behaviors for desired outcomes. Management attempts to control personality styles and behaviors, while effective leaders utilize this new information concerning personalities and lead the interactions and players to desired outcomes by first managing their own behavior to interact with others from their perspectives.

Understanding one's own personality assists in the negotiation process in other ways as well. Body language is critical to gaining additional insight into the process. Each signal is another in a series of subtle clues that further assists you in directing the interactions toward your desired minimum and maximum need levels. Having determined what another person's personality style is or may be in that given environment, you can then identify more efficiently their nonverbal signals and body language, and gauge what those may mean to you as you interact, speak, and so on in the negotiation process. Therefore, preparation now meets interaction.

During the Negotiation Process

Consider all the advance work and how it can come together for a successful interaction. Whether you are going one-on-one or engaging in a negotiation process consisting of multiple individuals, the effort made in advance of negotiation directly impacts your performance during the actual negotiation. The process is similar in structure to that of the evolving organizational structure outlined in Chapter 5, "Five Differing Organizational Structures and Levels."

The negotiation process is a cycle and has to be managed, while the personalities need to be led through this maze. To minimize the time spent in level or cycle two, prepare effectively for level one. This enables you to effectively interact in levels three and four. After every negotiation action, invest time in level five to ensure future successes. The negotiation levels or cycles are

- **Cycle One = Begin**—The startup stage activates.
- **Cycle Two = Defend**—Conflicts and confrontations arise.
- **Cycle Three = Blend**—Status quo time, and typically where most time is spent maintaining the norms.
- **Cycle Four = Transcend**—Where peak performance and significant progress take place.
- **Cycle Five = End**—Wrap up and final analysis effectively happens here. (Refer to Chapter 5 for a greater explanation of the five cycles.)

To maintain control during the negotiation process, design and follow an agenda of key or core issues and points to be addressed, to maintain and attain your minimum and maximum need levels. You can utilize an agenda like the agenda manager, as presented in Chapter 9, "Nine Tactical Steps to High-Impact Leadership." This system allows you to focus on the purpose of the negotiation during the process, attain that objective(s) in the amount of time allotted, and assists you in maintaining your negotiation power positions.

During the negotiation process, maintain a position of power over and among the other players involved. A number of positions afford you the necessary power to maintain the leverage advantage and authority in the interaction. Consider throughout the process (before and during) what type of power you hold in comparison to the other participants in the negotiation. The more power positions you hold, the more likely you are to command respect and authority throughout the interaction. Successful leadership and management of the negotiation process incorporate multiple positions of power.

There are 11 such core positions in a negotiation process. Reflect upon each, and identify among the players involved in the process (with the four core personality types/personality zones), which powers are held by which personalities. Work to maintain your power positions; definitely draw upon them during your interactions to maintain control and to enable yourself to work toward your minimum and maximum need levels.

Power positioning can be attained in many ways. An effective negotiator maintains and grows power in both traditional and nontraditional ways. Consider your position of power and how you can attain additional powers. Power sources come from:

- Personal power
- Professional power
- Influence power
- Legitimacy or reputation power
- Commitment power
- Knowledge power
- Experience power
- Competition power
- Courage power
- Bargaining power
- Time and effort power
- Age and background power

These are just some of the sources of power that can be drawn upon to navigate your interactions. The actual activities of the negotiation process, referred to as tactics, draw from your position of strength (power). Consider some of the following tactics for interacting with others to manage the interaction and enable you to obtain a successful outcome.

Fractionate. Take the core issue and break it down into individual and smaller component parts for discussion and agreement. Take the negotiation process one step at a time. This is an especially effective technique when disagreements arise. It also helps in moving the conversation forward one manageable step at a time.

Nibbling. When an ambitious agenda is placed before you, take one piece at a time and work on it. Address and resolve one issue or point at a time; then move on to the next. Nibbling can also be used when you want to attain more than your minimum need level. You can nibble your way through the agenda and toward your maximum need levels and wants.

Mini-Agreements. Work toward attaining as quickly as possible as many mini-agreements from the agenda issues as possible. From these you can then successfully work your way toward desired outcomes. The more mini-agreements attained, the more options afforded you. Should your interaction reach a point of difference of position or opinion, back up to your last place of agreement.

Linkage. Work to tie parts of your positions into parts of the other parties' positions. This linkage works to reduce tensions and positions of opposition.

Walk-Away Zone. By pre-identifying that point in the negotiation where you are better served by walking away than staying engaged, the other party many times will make significant concessions to get you back to the negotiation table.

Ask for Higher Authority. When you reach a stalemate in the negotiation process with the other player, you may be able to instill life back into the process by asking to continue it with a different person of higher authority. Change the players and sometimes you can change the situation.

Use Provoking Questions. Rely upon open-ended and strategically designed questions to get the other party talking and working toward your desired directions in the negotiation process. The fastest questions that can lead toward this result are *Who, What, When, Where, Why,* and *How.*

Invent Options. When there seems to be a breakdown in the discussion and negotiation points, make up alternatives or options with which the parties involved can work.

Qualify Concessions. Should you want to concede a position or point to the other party, always make sure that you qualify the concession, so the other party realizes you are offering something. Only then can you use that concession strategically later in the relationship or process.

Stall. Sometimes the other party may be pushing for a decision or commitment. A little stall for time may make him a little uncomfortable, and his discomfort may give you further indication of what his position is. Don't offer a decision quickly; use the stall to reinforce your position or your last statement/offer.

Use a "Bogey." A trial offer or idea can also afford you insight into the other person and her need levels. At periodical intervals in the negotiation process, offer up to the other party some little bogeys or offers to gauge her position and receptiveness.

The negotiation process is a series of interactions and decisions, all of which impact the next interaction and decision. Managed correctly, the process can always be a win/win, fair/fair outcome.

After the Negotiation Process

Invest private time after every negotiation to determine what took place before and during it that impacted the outcome. Mentally and if appropriate, physically, make notes (reflect upon your agenda, the players involved, and so on) about the entire interaction, so future interactions of a similar nature will be managed even more efficiently.

> When passions and emotions are electrified, resolving a conflict is practically impossible...to find a logical means of engaging the parties and focusing energies away from that which perpetuates negativity and increased conflict, and toward resolution, is a critical must. Look for a template for success at this point!

—**Jeff Magee**

The management and leadership giants of the past 50 years talked of the high percentage of business and technological advances that have occurred in the past century as a result of conflicts and change-necessitated issues. Each has led to a need to negotiate new realities. Businesses have invested more dollars in conflict-resolution training in the past decade than in any other soft-skill training topic, mostly due to personality implosions, no partnerships or alliances going into interactions, and a lack of understanding of how to negotiate toward amicable outcomes for all parties involved.

Sometimes no matter what you do, becoming engulfed in a conflict and confrontation with others is going to be a business reality. In these emotionally electrified environments a controlled and systematic approach to conflict management and resolution is necessary.

The following describes a powerful Anatomy of a Conflict matrix that will aid you in facilitating a dialogue with others. This model assists to ensure that all parties' interests are revealed and addressed, if in fact the aim by all parties is to reach an acceptable final resolution.

Step One—Basic Information Identification

Visualize, or when appropriate, draw a large plus sign on a piece of paper, white board, flipchart, and so on. This plus sign matrix creates four quadrants, guides the conversation to determine the core data necessary from each, and aids in avoiding the temptation to defend or challenge any specific quadrant. Step one is to first get the basic information on which everyone is at odds out in the open.

- Let the vertical axis line represent the difference between the left side, representing you and your needs, and the right side, representing "them" and their needs.
- Let the horizontal line represent the difference between position statements (the "what" one wants or needs) above the line and interest statements (the "why," also seen as one's motivators, what one has initially identified as needing) below the line.

With this model or template, visualize the top-left quadrant as quadrant 1, the top-right quadrant as quadrant 2, the bottom-left as quadrant 3, and the bottom-right as quadrant 4. Thus, quadrants 1 and 3 deal with "you"; quadrants 2 and 4 deal with the "other party."

At any point in this due diligence dialogue, if a quadrant is unknown or unclear to you, as the facilitator to conflict resolution, that is the quadrant attention needs to be directed toward.

Step Two—Scale of Flexibility

As you listen to the information revealed in step one (quadrants 1 through 4), listen for what each party initially purports to be seeking. Then work to see what other levels of acceptable resolutions there may be, without asking any party to make concessions. This range of acceptable resolutions is their *Scale of Flexibility*.

For example, if you had to fly from one city to another, arrived at the airport in time for the last flight out, and were told there was only one seat remaining, would that meet your minimum need level? If that seat were a middle seat, last row, would it still meet that need? On your Scale of Flexibility, there would be a wide range of other—and gradually better—acceptable resolution answers.

Step Three—Common Ground

As an outgrowth of all the information that surfaces through step one and step two of the Anatomy of a Conflict model, some sort of common ground between the two sides can be attained.

This is where you begin to reach a lasting and sustained resolution and closure. By identifying the common ground among the parties involved, the sides can now move away from their obvious differences back in step one, when everyone was initially only focused on her own position statements, and can concentrate on similarities. From here resolution is within reach, and as a leader you can aim everyone's energies toward shared successes.

As a leader, your ability to facilitate healthy dialogue at the height of personality differences recognizes the need for alliance-building. Your ability to aim interpersonal energies in the direction of fact-based, issue dialogue, not personal attacks, is critical.

As the reality of the business workplace today and tomorrow takes on an ever-changing complexion of gender, race, culture, and beliefs, we can add into this mix ever-colorful personality styles. The making of a powerful success story is present and so, too, is the making of one great implosion.

Leaders today face potential conflict and confrontation situations as a norm, given the ever-growing diverse generational segmentations, cultural differences, and passions that individuals bring to the workplace. Resolution through viable action plans leads to greater productivity and profitability, which all leaders must attain to be viable both today and tomorrow.

Managerial Leadership Bible Lesson 14

Everything in life is about negotiation. We negotiate big-ticket items and engage in deals with the people we live with. An effective managerial leader in an organization today must be able to speed-read both one's own personality, situation, social style, and those of the other person(s). The ability to know how to flex your persona with theirs to become a constructive blender of personality traits helps the managerial leader to tactically engage and attain success in alignment with the vision and goals of an organization, in both the short term and long term.

Review Questions

The review questions accompanying each chapter or section are designed to assist you in achieving the learning objective stated at the beginning of each chapter. The review section is not graded; do not submit it in place of your final exam. While completing the review questions, it may be helpful to study any unfamiliar terms in the glossary in addition to course content. After completing the review questions for each chapter, proceed to the review question answers and rationales.

1. If you can identify what the _____ of the other party is prior to a negotiation process, you will know how much bargaining room or leverage you have.

    A. Minimum acceptable needs level

    B. Maximum acceptable needs level

    C. Minimum desired needs level

    D. Maximum desired needs level

2. What STP factor attests to the fundamental need levels of the central personalities involved?

    A. Timing

    B. Players

    C. Situation

    D. Promises

3. By plotting an individual's personality style between Fast/Slow and Task/People on a grid, you are _____ their personality.

    A. Accepting

    B. Controlling

    C. Ignoring

    D. Speed-reading

4. During the negotiation process, maintain a position of _____ over and among the other players involved.

    A. Prestige

    B. Power

    C. Neutrality

    D. Observer

5. Managed correctly, the negotiation process can always be a win/win, fair/fair outcome.

    A. True

    B. False

Review Question Answers and Rationales

Review question answer choices are accompanied by unique, logical reasoning (rationales) as to why an answer is correct or incorrect. Evaluative feedback to incorrect responses and reinforcement feedback to correct responses are both provided.

1. If you can identify what the _____ of the other party is prior to a negotiation process, you will know how much bargaining room or leverage you have.

    A. Correct. If you know the minimum a party will accept, you can at least negotiate that much for them.

    B. Incorrect. Without a minimum, you do not know how low you can go in negotiations.

    C. Incorrect. Desired needs are in addition to acceptable needs and therefore come after acceptable needs have been met.

    D. Incorrect. Desired needs are in addition to acceptable needs and therefore come after acceptable needs have been met.

2. What STP factor attests to the fundamental need levels of the central personalities involved?

    A. Incorrect. This deals with the urgency of the matter being negotiated.

    B. Incorrect. Players are personalized needs of individual members that are found after establishing fundamental needs.

    C. Correct. From this awareness, the situation then progresses to the status quo and desired outcome for each party.

    D. Incorrect. This is not a factor in the STP process.

3. By plotting an individual's personality style between Fast/Slow and Task/People on a grid, you are _____ their personality.

   A. Incorrect. This process is not about accepting someone's personality.

   B. Incorrect. While speed-reading may give you insight into someone's personality, it will not let you control them.

   C. Incorrect. In fact, speed-reading is the opposite. You are trying to discover their personality, not ignore it.

   D. Correct. This process can allow you to size someone up quickly to handle any situation.

4. During the negotiation process, maintain a position of _____ over and among the other players involved.

   A. Incorrect. Someone with a good reputation may not make a good facilitator.

   B. Correct. Power is essential to gain leverage and command respect and authority.

   C. Incorrect. You may be one of the parties negotiating for something.

   D. Incorrect. You must be actively involved in the negotiation.

5. Managed correctly, the negotiation process can always be a win/win, fair/fair outcome.

   A. Correct. Using the proper skills and techniques, you and the other party can leave a negotiation satisfied.

   B. Incorrect. Although from your current viewpoint this may seem impossible, using the techniques in this chapter can make it a reality!

15

Putting Together a Winning Management Game Plan

If you're not fired with enthusiasm, you will be fired with enthusiasm!
—**Vince Lombardi**

When a mind is allowed to wonder and wander, creativity is allowed to grow and alas, anything is possible. Don't self-restrict; be open, and allow yourself to grow with and for others.
—**Jeff Magee**

Learning Objective

After completing this section of the course, you will be able to describe essential qualities for a manager and the best way to utilize these skills.

The management advantage for future success starts with the understanding and use of techniques designed in *The Managerial Leadership Bible* and gives you a leadership advantage.

Management effectiveness is both an art and a science. Three key characteristics must be present for effective management players to develop into effective leaders. The Gallup organization conducted a study of key factors sought in management and by leaders positioned to guide others. The poll determined that three factors were universally sought:

Likeability must be present in the person.

Believability in the person and his position is crucial.

Persuasive skills in interacting, communicating, and managing others must be present.

Consider how you measure up to these national benchmarks for management excellence. Ultimately, management and leadership must realize that it is a process, whereby (you, I, we) attempt to influence the behaviors of others. Once you start this process, there is no stopping or turning back. The commitment moves you forward.

As you measure your self-development and management growth with the ideas mapped here, consider this book a resource for present and future interactions. This chapter is a map of the alternative management process to organizational success. You can adopt these steps in your present management paradigm and use them to assist you in making appropriate paradigm shifts for greater success and productivity.

This map can be applied to your working environment and to the specific players on your team in many ways. Sometimes management finds it easier to manage in the same traditional ways, regardless of effectiveness. Managing is not a matter of right or wrong, good or bad. It is a matter of effectively utilizing yourself and the resources around you in the wisest fashion. Once a resource is used it cannot be retracted.

For others at the management level of an organization, putting together a game plan for action or response to a concern is difficult. Putting a game plan together should not be difficult, merely a step-by-step encounter. Management is not an exact science, yet all around the professional market there are examples of successful management players and leaders, as well as numerous examples of walking nightmares in management. Remember, there are always alternatives to how you manage people for increased success and persuasion.

With the ability to interact with, manage, and inspire others to greater levels of accomplishment, a manager evolves into a leader. Consider what your management alternatives can be, and how you can best interact and inspire others.

To gain the leadership advantage, you must realize that all six of the managerial leadership styles detailed in this text, in part, make up the effective leadership qualities and attributes of a winning leader. The ability to put a workable management game plan before others and see it through to completion also incorporates leadership. Leaders are not born, nor does someone else create them. Leadership comes from inside a person, when that person understands the five different mission statements of the organization that she serves stewardship in. Also that leader has solid values and strongly believes in something. Then the leadership and take-initiative abilities come to the surface. For some, these leadership flashes are irregular events, while for others these flashes are channeled, harnessed, and directed systematically for success on a regular basis.

The Managerial Leadership Bible presents what others would undertake as a college degree or in a seminar environment, and allows an individual of true mettle to recognize that all six of the management styles (teacher, manager, mentor, counselor, disciplinarian, coach) comprise the differing attributes of a successful leader. A leader has to realize the time and place to utilize a specific management style (or in essence when to wear which management hat) and whether or not a capable player exists on a team. Take this leadership style one step further.

A leader must know when to interact with a player or group to encourage, inspire, adjust attitudes, and push others (coach); when to strategically and surgically interact with a challenge or threat, and deal positively with or remove others from the environment (counselor or disciplinarian); how to establish a framework, set foundations, design structure, initiate training and educational systems, and establish protocol (manager or teacher); and when to guide, encourage, share with, and subtly motivate others to successful outcomes (mentor).

Leadership involves having and understanding the mission vision of that organization's purpose: understanding the holistic picture and how everything comes together for the ultimate needs, desires, and expectations of an organization and the overall good of the players. The inward flashes and core flame that burn toward leadership are rooted in something more significant than words, desires, mission statements, and visions—within one's unique, individual spirit and spirituality.

Leaders are guided by an inward energy and cause (spirit). It is this energy that propels one toward greatness. Vaclav Havel (playwright, dissident, prisoner, and then president of Czechoslovakia) speaking before the U.S. Congress made these reflections on democracy and leadership:

> As long as people are people, democracy, in the full sense of the word, will always be no more than an ideal. In this sense, you, too, are merely approaching democracy uninterruptedly for more than two-hundred years, and your journey toward the horizon has never been disrupted to a totalitarian system....
>
> We must all learn many things from you, from how to educate our offspring, how to elect our representatives, all the way to how to organize our economic life so that it will lead to prosperity and not to poverty....
>
> The salvation of this human world lies nowhere else than in the human heart, in the human power to reflect, in human meekness,

and in human responsibility. Without a global revolution in the sphere of human consciousness, nothing will change for the better in the sphere of our being as humans....

It is the fundamental factor in the movement of history. Spirit is. Consciousness is. Human Awareness is. Thought is. Spirituality is. Those are the deep sources of freedom and power with which leaders rise and people can be led to move boulders and create change!

Leaders are people who recognize that consciousness precedes being. Leaders hold the unusual power and ability to project their views and shadows, in essence, on others. Leaders take responsibility for establishing and creating the conditions in which people operate and live. These conditions start first from what is going on within the leaders and their minds. Inward activity guides leaders' actions outward. How people manage the inward forces impacts how leaders use the six management styles and come across to others. This impacts how others therefore follow leaders and whether people conspire and work toward the downfall of their leaders.

There are warning points to effective leadership as well, and they validate the need for effective leaders to aggressively utilize the six core management styles outlined. One of the most important elements of all managerial leadership is to move beyond just knowing what business you are in and where you want to participate in the market, or create a market; it is making sure every participant knows how they fit into your master plan—vision. A singular way to do this is to craft meaningful, real-time yet evolving job descriptions/expectations profiles for every organizational diagram person or need—no matter how they horizontally or vertically interlink.

As discussed in Chapter 1, "Ground Zero, All Factors Being Equal," these must also be connected to and serve a legitimate role in your:

1. **Strategy**—The where we are going and why factors
2. **Operations**—The who, when, and what factors
3. **Tactics**—The how factors

Job Description/Expectation Profile Document

In building your winning team, it can be an architectural exercise of what positions are necessary to stand up your business. From that exercise, each position you identify must have an interconnected purpose to the positions laterally and vertically to it. For each position on the organization chart or diagram, you must scope the job description or job position expectations in great detail. The drill of designing in real-time thorough job description/ expectations profile serves you in many ways, including but not limited to the following:

- For an individual's role within the organization.

- For the on-boarding process overall (posting a position vacancy, application process, interviewing, vetting, and potential offer letter and ultimate hiring on-boarding process)

- Any performance review (probationary, monthly, at anniversary, or mandated official dates) will be benchmarked directly against the job expectation description.

- Any Performance Development Plan (PDP) will be benchmarked directly against the job expectation description.

- Any Performance Improvement Plan (PIP) will be benchmarked directly against the job expectation description.

- Career-pathway coaching will be benchmarked directly against the job expectation description.

- Succession management, development, and planning will be benchmarked directly against the job expectation description.

- Evaluating individuals objectively against their job description and the Player Capability Index for appropriate on-boarding needs to ensure success.

- In the development of any operational, organizational, divisional, positional handbook or training manual; the job description should support any training need, and all training needs should support the job description.

It could be said that leaders exist only to serve their followers. In the 1970s, Robert K. Greenleaf, a former management researcher for AT&T and management philosopher of the twenty-first century, introduced a concept that has been slow to catch on, but in today's business climate, evidence abounds of its actuality—like it or not!

Greenleaf and the Robert K. Greenleaf Center for Servant-Leadership in Indianapolis, Indiana, offered an essay titled "The Servant Leader." Its premise is that leaders exist to serve their followers, and that the followers grant their leader their power and allegiance in response to their servant nature.

Servant leaders embody unique traits and qualities. Among them are seven core characteristics, according to Greenleaf:

1. Leaders are servants first to the team, and assist it to attain its true peak performance levels.

2. Leaders articulate goals to all players within and outside the organization.

3. Leaders inspire trust among and with others.

4. Leaders know how and why to listen to others, internally and externally.

5. Leaders are masters of positive feedback in directing and counseling others to greater accomplishments.

6. Leaders rely on foresight and allow themselves time to counsel and coach themselves to greater actions.

7. Leaders emphasize personal development and that external problems must first be solved inwardly. It is the inward that leaders have 100 percent control over and that merely influences the external forces. Deal with, manage, and change yourself first to stimulate positive changes in others around you.

Given these seven guideposts for leadership and the concept of a leader as servant, leaders must also realize that philosophies must be subject to the environment. Adjustments are always necessary for success. Practitioners of Greenleaf's ideologies abound.

The Managerial Leadership Bible presents both strategic and tactical aspects of improved managerial leadership greatness at every level within an organization. These servant-leadership guideposts parallel many of the aspects presented throughout this book.

Leadership among others and within you is the embodiment of following the six core management styles. There are times when you will be a manager or teacher of actions, a mentor to yourself and others, a counselor or disciplinarian for difficulties and challenges, and a coach of encouragement and attitude adjustments, to attain success, happiness, and harmony.

Leaders and management must also realize that the players on their teams today and those added in the future come already designed and, for the most part, perfected with personalities, attitudes, and behavioral patterns (habits). As effective managers and leaders today, they have to rely on alternative techniques for managing interactions at different times with these different people for success. As discussed earlier, management also has to understand that every management action and decision impacts people in both immediate and future time frames. Every action, in essence, conditions those around you positively or negatively.

Authors David Sadker, MD, and Myra Sadker, PhD, studied the conditioning factors of people from the earliest formal settings and found that many leaders unknowingly condition negatively. The Sadkers, in their book *Failing at Fairness*, studied children from first grade through high school graduation and found that early interactions with a person can impact long-term performance. For example:

- Children measured for self-esteem factors in first grade measured differently by graduation. First-grade boys measured themselves 80 percent positive overall. Girls measured themselves overall 67 percent positive. By graduation, high-school boys measured themselves 74 percent positive, while high-school girls measured themselves 32 percent positive!

- This early-stage conditioning impacts self-view and performance at later dates. How do you condition people now for later performance? Teachers in the national study identified how they conditioned boys positively and girls negatively, without realizing they were even doing so. For example:

    - Little boys receive more positive feedback and stroking for participation and response in classes than little girls.

    - There is greater male recognition than female acknowledgments in interaction situations.

    - Seating arrangements and leadership positions favored boys over girls in early years. Not because boys were more often correct, but more because boys answered faster than girls, and in our fast conditioning as a society, we play into the speed trap.

Gaining the leadership advantage requires the ability to alternate management techniques and strategies, just as the teachers in the Sadker study realized that they (and you) could fall victim to habits that can ultimately prove devastating to an organization and player development. For an organization to develop, player focus must continually be on the people equation for ultimate results to be positive.

Management's thrust is to solicit and stimulate the ability of its players to willingly cooperate with one another (people factor = P) to attain desired results (R). People participation leads to greater commitment. Commitment leads to success!

Visualize a scale used to measure weights with a large letter "P" on one side of the scale and a large letter "R" on the other side of the scale. One side will always weigh heavier than the other, and thus overinfluence outcomes, unless a strongly focused managerial leader surfaces and works objectively to keep the two emotionally balanced. Logic is only allowed to be the variable that weights one more than the other, thereby directing calculated decisions, whether liked or not.

Management using this scale analogy needs to maintain focus and practical balance between the people factor (P resource) and the needed results (outcomes or R factor). Management personnel have to be able to intertwine these two factors for organizational effectiveness and ultimate efficiency of all resources. Traditional management can obtain compliance from the players within it and not obtain commitment. With the management alternatives outlined in *The Managerial Leadership Bible*, management can now work to attain commitment, not just compliance, from players. The balance of the two main factors (people and results) coincides with the seven key factors that the Greenleaf Center sets forth for effective leadership management.

The Managerial Leadership Bible is a subjective plan of action with personal and professional models for guidance. Internalize those points that can help and adopt them into your lifestyle. Those points not relevant at present in your life can be set aside for possible future consideration. Lead yourself to success!

Creating Reengineering Laboratories

In this state of constant change, flux, chaos (for some), and rapid-fire innovation, the ability of leaders and management personnel to explore ideas, test techniques, and liberate fellow colleagues is critical to overall development (key organizational development principles—OD) and long-term success actions (key strategic planning processes—SP).

Reengineering suggests that individuals and groups take a new look, a fresh look, a different look, an alternate look at what needs to be done or what a group has a mission to be doing—not from a perspective of right or wrong, but from that of determining if what is being done is still needed. This observation, analysis, and interactive group discussion is based on the notion of whether there may be a more strategic approach to one's mission statements, and what an objective look would provide. For reengineering to exist and have any degree of success, senior management must authorize and give ownership to the ideas and objectives.

The creation of a reengineering laboratory suggests that a group of people such as an individual department, organizational division, a specific government agency, and so on, be tasked with a specific objective and empowered to address the task/challenge and attain results. From these results, measurement can then take place; from the final analysis objective decisions can be made for the best course of action (BCOA) of entire organizations.

To create a reengineering or experiment laboratory within an organization, a few common denominators need to be present:

- All participants/members must have a vested interest in the objectives and be held mutually accountable.
- All participants/members must have a common sense of being together.
- All participants/members need to want to be a part of this new group endeavor.
- All participants/members need to be willing to put forth the effort required for this new and different endeavor.
- All participants/members need to have access to the resources required to fulfill their challenge or task.
- Models for successful interaction and decision making need to be provided to participants in the beginning, along with any tools that can enhance their interactions for greater success.
- Participants brought together to interact within this special function should also be a cross-mixture of players from the organization, department, or agency.

In initiating an environment for creation and re-creation, laboratories need to be led by visionaries and sustained with energies and support mechanisms. Laboratories need to be measured by accomplishing or working toward the initial objectives and goals, not by existing standards and measurements utilized within an organization, department, or agency. Laboratories also should be free of the threats and challenges being faced by everyday employees and management personnel.

Laboratories for reengineering can be applied along human resource department/development (HRD) traditional organizational lines of growth by being tasked as organizational development (OD), strategic planning (SP), or changing culture (CC).

Laboratories, in essence, become zones of experimentation and challenge. Participants tasked with specific objectives should be free from traditional organizational hierarchy and protocol, free to explore any and all realistic and viable options to attain desired outcomes within these test environment zones. Participants start at ground zero and explore both the status quo and alternate options or routes to greater levels of success through new ways and means. When a laboratory concludes its initial tasked assignment, the players should be able to communicate to participants within and out of the larger associated group, organization, department, or agency exactly what took place within the laboratory setting.

Sustained organizational success depends on an organization's ability to meet and beat market needs. An organization's ability to better predict how to meet those needs and be in an action mode, not a reaction mode, puts it in a better position for success. That level of success can be attained through effective utilization of reengineering laboratories. Senior management must always task them to inwardly reflect upon what is presently being done; to play with present procedures, machinery, systems, technology, people abilities, and people dynamics; to attempt to see whether there are ways to tweak existing structures and people for greater efficient use of valuable resources.

Taking the concept of the reengineering laboratory one step further or closer into the implementation phase includes an atmosphere whereby managers can maintain a constant and never-ending laboratory experiment. Players should be charged with consistently looking at what is being done and exploring ways by which efforts can be better directed, and resources more efficiently used, toward goals and objectives.

Example: Action Plan

As a managerial leader, if you are serious about creating a new and lasting atmosphere of continual improvements, then create a system to harvest ideas from every player, to increase revenue, to increase productivity, or to save revenues. Place a significant bounty on such a program to draw out the most explosive ideas from your team; consider a 10 percent commission or bonus paid to any individual or group of individuals whose ideas can be implemented and that yield revenue generation.

An alternative to traditional organizational dynamics and management is to establish an environment whereby departments and agencies become reengineering labs, where organizations become complete multilayered labs of constant experimentation with what does and does not work. The human and nonhuman factors are always pushed to peak performance, all participants are held accountable for their actions and results, and those players hold one another accountable for participation and results. This multilayered laboratory experimentation approach causes growth, success, and opportunity.

In establishing your laboratory environment, consider what your team's objective is and what makes your team uniquely different from any competitive force in the marketplace. Focus on your competitive advantages, and in your laboratory ensure that those advantages are not lost or watered down to a minimum.

In converting a department to a reengineering lab, or in establishing and designing a special and strategic group of players for such a lab with a specific cause, with the authorization to experiment for a better net result, consider the Reengineering Laboratory Method. This method serves as a starting difference between success and failure.

In following the principles of the leadership alternative, this method allows management to empower a team with the "what" and "why" of a cause or need and instills into the participants the power to determine the best "how" for the game plan designed. When participants create their own "hows," it is the same as entrusting them to establish their newly designed best course of action (BCOA). Greater results are always achieved when players are involved in the "how" to do things.

This method serves as a valuable part of the establishment of an effective reengineering laboratory or team by using the following components of an action plan:

- **Four psychological decisions**—In every overall decision-making process (for example, buying decisions that a person may make), the human brain processes data and directs final judgments to be made after processing four independent factors. Once the brain has resolved and answered the questions dealing with the technical aspects of the topic (purpose) and the analysis is complete, it can process the second decision. The financial decision impacts what costs are associated with this decision. The third decision focuses upon the user, and how the judgment impacts those people directly associated with the outcome of the decision. Will it be resisted? The final decision rests upon the decision maker's approval of the overall idea. Will this person mentally cheerlead the decision and coach others through any potential problem areas within the decision process?

- **Time**—There must be a timeline or time frame established prior to initiation, and all players must be aware of it. How much time will be allowed for participation and when are these time blocks reserved?

- **Purpose**—The purpose or objective of this team's assignment needs to be clearly communicated at the beginning. Make sure that you or management has spelled out what this lab is to produce or explore.

- **Strategies**—Outline these within the lab. The net result of the lab should be to present a (possibly new) primary strategy and, always, contingency (backup) strategy plans.

- **Resources**—Always study resources allocated to the lab, so failure cannot be attributed to lack of materials and resources in the lab environment. Whether the resources are people, monies, machinery, technology, and so on, within reason, ensure that your lab is suitably equipped. Also make sure that players not directly involved with the lab experiment are aware that those in the lab have authorization for said resources.

- **Deadline**—Establish a deadline at the beginning of the lab assignment, so all players are clear as to when their activities are to be concluded.

- **Players**—Make sure that when a reengineering laboratory is being established, the players coming together to make up the team are compatible and have a common reason to be there. Make sure that those you choose are from the necessary cross-section of your team and organization to ensure the highest level of creativity and success while in the lab.

Reengineering labs are a fact of the future of successful organizational dynamics, a powerful way to ensure success and growth and to increase players' ownership and participation levels in the organization. By looking inward to your own players for answers, serious challenges and threats can be easily and cost-effectively resolved for future power. The concept of reengineering laboratories for achievement and organizational advancement can be utilized in many ways. Management can create these labs within the overall organization, managers can create them within their own areas, and departments and players can even utilize the reengineering concept on specific projects for which alternative answers and solutions may be desired. The labs are places from which creativity can grow. When only one person is utilizing a lab concept, it therefore allows for inner synergy (of the two sides of a person's brain).

From a psychological perspective and powerful behavioral motivator basis, true reengineering labs are the new-wave teams, the peak performers, and can thus be sustained if management and leaders focus on nine intrinsic team motivating factors. These factors by which participants within teams assume ownership and increase their level of commitment and synergy are the following:

- **Choice**—Players must be able to choose what they do and participate in; that is, "These three tasks need to be addressed and completed this week. Go for it." As opposed to: "These three tasks need to be taken care of. Tom, you take number one; Susan, you have number two; and you take number three!"

- **Decisions**—Players must be free to evaluate and make their own decisions free of vertical approval before acting.

- **Feedback**—Whether positive or negative, all feedback must be presented immediately in a positive manner and with solutions. Every decision, for example, that a player makes brings with it additional ramifications and decisions. Thus feedback needs to be immediate every time and be resolved mentally and agreed upon by all parties involved before any further action takes place. Feedback = action plan.

- **Challenge**—The activities and involvement that participants are faced with must always have some degree of challenge (personally or mentally). The human machine is motivated by challenge; without challenge players become stagnant, may procrastinate, and are complacent.

- **Competition**—This must be a present and looming factor. Three laws of nature can motivate players: one, we compete against something else; two, we compete against someone else; three, we compete against ourselves.

- **Creative solutions**—Players must be given autonomy and held accountable for designing their own solutions. Players assume greater ownership of their own ideas and solutions to tasks, and thus pursue them with greater energy levels.

- **Ownership**—Players who own their work become motivated and energized toward their future and that of the group—whether that group is a reengineered lab, team, or anything else! Empowerment builds personal ownership.

- **Accountability**—Ultimately, every player in a group must be held 100 percent accountable for her actions, efforts, and participation levels. Players are held accountable for their actions as well as of those players around them—peer unity.

- **Education**—Learning is the turbocharger to intrinsic teaming. Continued hard- and soft-skill education development is the lifeblood to sustained growth and success.

Reengineering labs also allow people and organizations to look at and even consider testing ideas and actions that others may be using with success but at present are foreign to your organization. This also allows assigned players the opportunity to rethink what is going on and what you are all about, to determine whether any course corrections are necessary for survivability.

Management also draws upon all four management styles when interacting with reengineering labs and the players within them. For the most part managers find themselves effectively operating as coaches with these teams of the future, via the management/team control model in Chapter 4, "Six Alternative Managerial Leadership Intervention Styles," and the relationship of the players' span of control—whether it lies with management or with those on the team (or department) of today.

The objective or purpose of *The Managerial Leadership Bible* is to increase player participation and net results, while at the same time reducing the active role of management personnel in the traditional daily activities of the player(s). This turns traditional organizational layers or bureaucracies, where the thinking was reserved for upper management and the action was placed on the lower levels (thus, entry level, mid-management, and rank-and-file workers), into a new age educational and empowered environment.

In this new environment, traditional management evolves into more of a leadership-management position and role. Vertical management is pushed to a state where each player is now accountable for his own level of thinking and action. Individual players and teams are now charged with and allowed to learn (through both adaptive and survival-based learning) and evolve with independent thinking and action (if so desired). Management now assumes the appropriate style (hat) necessary at any given time to attain peak performance.

As *Fortune* magazine recently said, "The most successful corporations will be something called a learning organization.... The ability to learn faster than your competitors"; thus, developing your people will be the new success factor. *The Managerial Leadership Bible* is designed to enable managers and leaders of today to survive for tomorrow. These ideas are held as disciplines and maps for immediate application and results with other people. This is not a fad approach to management, as Total Quality Management (TQM) was in the 1980s and early 1990s, and Lean Management/Lean Six Sigma was in the 2000s. Tom Peters, of *In Search of Excellence* fame and a major management thought leader of the past 40 years, and others reference the staggeringly high statistics attributed to the failure rates of organizations of the last two decades of the past century, and the continuation of that trend in the first two decades of this century (large and small) that underwent TQM or Lean Six Sigma–oriented management philosophies and changes.

Along with Peter's statistic that one out of ten organizations undergoing TQM will survive, the late W. Edwards Deming (perhaps the leading authority in the world on quality initiatives and management) felt that a major reason for this was a shift in management thinking. Deming felt that nearly 98 percent of organizational success was centered on basic changes in how people were treated and how they think. The focus must be upon the systems within organizations, and allowing the thinking to take place at the proper level. Management must make a shift in how it operates, from the straight manager role to more of leader-manager.

All management and leadership strategic planning and actions must aim toward the support and growth of this factor. All interdepartmental or inter-team actions should also support and reinforce both the individual's and group's development of said factor. Analyze the level of commitment that each has toward this factor, and what each does to ensure planned and structured growth in it on a daily, weekly, monthly, quarterly, and annual basis.

Think of this leadership alternative as "Get-out-of-their-face management" and "Get into increased net results management." What is the actual yield that your present management and leadership styles (*The Managerial Leadership Bible*) produce? Could some of these alternative ideas, strategies, and tactics assist with your future growth and direction? This is the foundation of leadership today and for tomorrow.

Managerial Leadership Bible Lesson 15

Building that winning team as a managerial leader is dependent upon your ability to execute strategically and tactically with flair, finesse, and power. The team you lead is hungry for a leader; the world awaits a leader. We have manufactured a planet full of operational managers who lack vision, mission, purpose, and resolve. To lead a team to greatness, a leader must know what greatness looks like.

Review Questions

The review questions accompanying each chapter or section are designed to assist you in achieving the learning objective stated at the beginning of each chapter. The review section is not graded; do not submit it in place of your final exam. While completing the review questions, it may be helpful to study any unfamiliar terms in the glossary in addition to course content. After completing the review questions for each chapter, proceed to the review question answers and rationales.

1. Ultimately, management and leadership must realize that leadership excellence is a process, whereby (you, I, we) attempt to _____ the behaviors of others.

    A. Describe

    B. Change

    C. Correct

    D. Influence

2. Leaders are people who were born that way and use their natural talents.

    A. True

    B. False

3. A leader must know when to interact with a player or group to encourage, inspire, adjust attitudes, and push others when he is being a:

    A. Coach

    B. Mentor

    C. Teacher

    D. Disciplinarian

4. Leaders are _____ first to the team, and assist it to attain its true peak performance levels.

    A. Servants

    B. Disciplinarians

    C. Friends

    D. Observers

5. Every management action and decision impacts people in both immediate and future time frames.

    A. True

    B. False

6. Traditional managers can attain compliance from their workers, but not:

    A. Interest

    B. Commitment

    C. Loyalty

    D. Love

Review Question Answers and Rationales

Review question answer choices are accompanied by unique, logical reasoning (rationales) as to why an answer is correct or incorrect. Evaluative feedback to incorrect responses and reinforcement feedback to correct responses are both provided.

1. Ultimately, management and leadership must realize that leadership excellence is a process, whereby (you, I, we) attempt to _____ the behaviors of others.

    A. Incorrect. An observer could do that.

    B. Incorrect. A leader cannot force people to change.

    C. Incorrect. Discipline is only one function among many.

    D. Correct. At best, that is what a leader can hope to do: influence others to success.

2. Leaders are people who were born that way and use their natural talents.

    A. Incorrect. Leaders acquire skills through reading and studying books such as this one.

    B. Correct. Leadership is a science and an art.

3. A leader must know when to interact with a player or group to encourage, inspire, adjust attitudes, and push others when he is being a:

   A. Correct. A managing coach supports his team.

   B. Incorrect. A mentor sets by example and educates.

   C. Incorrect. A teacher teaches the skills a coach will later encourage.

   D. Incorrect. While a disciplinarian may motivate workers to do their jobs, it is in a much more negative situation.

4. Leaders are _____ first to the team, and assist it to attain its true peak performance levels.

   A. Correct. Without a team, there would be no leader.

   B. Incorrect. Leadership is about enhancing, not punishing.

   C. Incorrect. Friendship can cloud some leadership responsibilities.

   D. Incorrect. Leaders must act, not watch!

5. Every management action and decision impacts people in both immediate and future time frames.

   A. Correct. This is why managers have to be so careful and organize their work into action plans and other formats described in this text.

   B. Incorrect. Remember the employees who took six months to get over a bad review?

6. Traditional managers can attain compliance from their workers, but not:

   A. Incorrect. You are more likely to get employees interested if you break from the norms of traditional management.

   B. Correct. A manager can make workers do what they want, but without giving them any ownership, they will not feel committed.

   C. Incorrect. With the contemporary high turnover rates of employees, it is apparent that traditional management does not instill loyalty.

   D. Incorrect. Love does not matter in this context.

16

Ensuring Your C-Force and E-Force Personalities Don't Sell You Out!

Everyone is not equal and should not be treated as equals.

Everyone should be treated with dignity, respect, and fairness.

When individuals within business attempt to play by the "equality card," the business will always lose in the end, and people will always lose in the final analysis—case in point of people that all feel they were equal to and above the standards and laws of the land.

—Jeff Magee

Learning Objective

After completing this section of the course, you will be able to describe C- and E-level personalities and handle them.

In a simpler time, traditional decision making within an organization, how individuals addressed the levels of risk, and even containing those levels used to be exact and predictable.

Historically within organizations, wise decision making was attained by adhering to defined procedures, protocols, and roles of responsibility and accountability. Individuals, divisions, departments, business units, institutions, agencies, and even regulatory entities have long since been conditioned to serve defined roles.

If you were to use a traditional business school organizational diagram and consider "all" the essential functional positions one would need for a successful organization, an ideal organization, or a lean organization, you would then recognize that every position in that diagram would fall into one of two distinct groups.

Each of these historical entities are what we today label as either:

- E-forces, defined as *entrepreneurial forces* in nature, charged with being cutting-edge, creative marketers, sellers, account builders, and acquirers. Thus these people were more risk players and were rewarded accordingly. Traditionally, they would be labeled on an organizational diagram as CEOs, leaders, R&D, sales, marketing, public relations, customer service, advocates, emerging market builders, and so on. Their compensation structure was tied to performance: the greater one performed, the greater the earning possibilities.

- C-forces, defined as the *control forces*, were fixed as the rules enforcers, regulators, auditors, actuaries, accountants, information technologists, and watchdogs of activities. Traditionally, these internal supports of an organization would be labeled on an organizational diagram as CFOs, COOs, CIOs, controllers, legal, auditors, accountants, regulators, administrators, and management. External to an organization the C-forces would be the board, regulators, auditing companies, industry policing associations, elected government leaders—Congress and the president—shareholders, and even the media.

The internal players within an organization were expected to be more in control and introverted in performance. Their compensation was predetermined and typically limited.

The battle was over decisions made and executed by these traditional roles of players. Each E-force and C-force player was predictable in his actions, and the neverending push and pull between these forces drove organizational decision making, growth, expansion, regulation, and maintenance of business transactions.

And the power of the players within either the C-force or E-force category typically drove a decision, and determined how a managerial leader would draw upon them for operational needs.

As a managerial leader, make sure when you build your team, delegate tasks to individuals, or assign responsibilities to a position, that the C-force is held by a C-person; and likewise that an E-force position is held by an E-person. If you have a C-person in an E-position, or vice versa, the expected performance output may be jeopardized or even bastardized. In building your structure, ensure that subsequent backup positions or safety devices deployed to ensure organizational integrity are being staffed appropriately.

Many business implosions happen most often because a position was staffed by the incorrect lettered (C-force/E-force) personality, and/or all the subsequent checking devices or other positions were also inadvertently wrongly populated.

The judgment of an aspiring leader, whether at an entry-level, junior-level, field, or executive senior-level position, is directly influenced first by whether she is by nature a C-person or an E-person, not primarily on whether she, as steward, is in a C-force or an E-force position.

Traditionally, it was expected that equal input would be sought before making a decision. Traditionally, it was also expected and (typically) delivered that individuals would stay within their realms of standard operating procedure (C-force and E-force people acted like C-force and E-force people).

Organizations historically avoided many of the extraordinary decisions being made today, many of which can subsequently be seen as having direct linkage to future organizational trauma. And in many sad instances between 2000 and 2004, the world business stage saw implosion after implosion. Most of these occurred because traditional C-force and E-force players did not execute their jobs from the category they were tasked into, and expected to operate outwardly from, by the board, the CEO, and consumers.

To better understand the even greater constraints that these two sets of decision makers assume, consider that any individual decision being made by either a C-force or E-force player is comprised of four intrinsic subdecision phases (parts, steps, or ingredients).

Within the realm of the E-force and C-force, these four core functions to a sound decision were traditionally assigned to the appropriate players. Many times the oversight of any one of these four potential "veto" stakeholders caused the increased risk associated with the decision-making process.

Whether you are engaged in critical self-thought or interacting with others, every overall decision has these four subdecisions. These four are especially noticeable when one makes decisions in environments or situations perceived to have an element of risk associated with them.

The subdecisions are critical stakeholders in the process and implementation of risk management decision-making protocols. Therefore, the four core stakeholders for any decision that need to be rallied and converted into advocates or allies are as follows:

1. **Financial** stakeholders, who scrutinize the decision from the perspective of what risks are associated with it financially—traditionally C-force players, and compensated in a structured and limited manner.

2. **Technical** stakeholders, who scrutinize the decision from the perspective of what risks are associated with it, and thus what it will or won't deliver—traditionally C-force players, and compensated in a structured and limited manner.

3. **User/implementer** stakeholders, those individuals who implement the decision, who are typically concerned for how they will embrace, respond, or react to it, based upon their perceived level of risk associated with adhering to or avoiding the decision. Traditionally E-force players, and compensated in a more performance-based production manner with high-yield capability.

4. **Advocate/champion/coach** stakeholder, that person (or your internal voice, at times) who may not have a direct influence on a decision, but who can brief you on how to engage the other stakeholders to gain allies. This internal voice may be what pushes you to buy something on impulse that you later develop buyer's remorse for, when you reflect upon it from the vantage point of one of the other three stakeholders' perspectives.

Engaging the four core stakeholders as allies simply involves the identification and engagement of each subdecision.

Other factors that influence which force an individual might evolve toward are age, gender, culture, race, education, and background of experience. People traditionally followed defined migration patterns in their work selection and thus their decision-making style; that would drive their risk tolerance or risk aversion.

Organizations used to be structured in such a manner that the way in which divisions of labor were established for decision making was defined.

These roles were further reinforced by individual personality styles. The personality style of a division, business unit, department, or regulatory entity would be much the same.

Traditionally, these forces were aligned to ensure that the highest level of integrity for decision making within organizations existed. Individual social or personality styles were tied to these force categories as well. It was a sure bet that the analytical and amiable personalities would most often evolve toward the C-force positions, while the driver/type A and the expressive personalities would typically be the E-force players.

Keeping both the historical E-forces and C-forces in alignment was and should continue to be the responsibility of:

- Boards of directors, with appropriately assigned individual board members assuming authority/auditing/command-and-control capacity to each core operational functional area of an organization.
- Outside regulatory entities that the board and organization could employ to keep both in check.
- Government regulatory entities.
- And ultimately, the shareholders, voters, and media, as further watchdog operatives.

As a managerial leader, your level of effectiveness is directly linked to your historical C-force or E-force orientation. To maximize your effectiveness as a managerial leader, make sure that your structural positions are populated accordingly, and that your center-of-influence advisors are proportionately staffed with representatives from both the C-population and the E-population.

Managerial Leadership Bible Lesson 16

Old rules of organization structure are gone, and the new ones are here. And with these new rules, we seem to be in a constant state of flux. As a managerial leader today, one must be able to recognize that the functioning positions in an organizational structure may be occupied by individuals with conflicts to resolve to facilitate their functionality.

To ensure greatness, the effective managerial leader realizes what the output of an organization must continually be to *wow* the customer (end user), and what that of the employees (the delivery mechanism of what customers receive) must be. The players and customers must be appreciated, valued, and happy. Then the shareholder value will right itself. With this mind-set, the new managerial leader must ensure that the C-positions and E-positions are in fact occupied by C-people and E-people in the organization.

Review Questions

The review questions accompanying each chapter or section are designed to assist you in achieving the learning objective stated at the beginning of each chapter. The review section is not graded; do not submit it in place of your final exam. While completing the review questions, it may be helpful to study any unfamiliar terms in the glossary in addition to course content. After completing the review questions for each chapter, proceed to the review question answers and rationales.

1. E-level forces are the unmotivated people who want an organization to stay the same.

    A. True

    B. False

2. In traditional management, decisions were made through a _____ between E-forces and C-forces.

    A. Negotiation

    B. Tug-of-war

    C. Discussion

    D. Contract

3. As a managerial leader, ensure when you build your team, delegate tasks to individuals, or assign responsibilities to a position, that the C-force is held by a C-person.

    A. True

    B. False

4. Most business implosions occurred because traditional C-force and E-force players did not execute their jobs from the category they were tasked into, and expected to operate outwardly from, by the board, the CEO, and consumers.

    A. True.

    B. False

Review Question Answers and Rationales

Review question answer choices are accompanied by unique, logical reasoning (rationales) as to why an answer is correct or incorrect. Evaluative feedback to incorrect responses and reinforcement feedback to correct responses are both provided.

1. E-level forces are the unmotivated people who want an organization to stay the same.

   A. Incorrect. E-level personalities are entrepreneurial and cutting edge.

   B. Correct. Neither level contains unmotivated people.

2. In traditional management, decisions were made through a _____ between E-forces and C-forces.

   A. Incorrect. If there were negotiations, one side would have to lose power, so compromises were made at best.

   B. Correct. It was the push and pull of these opposing forces that made business decisions happen.

   C. Incorrect. These decisions were a power play and not always calm.

   D. Incorrect. Contracts aren't relevant to this concept.

3. As a managerial leader, ensure when you build your team, delegate tasks to individuals, or assign responsibilities to a position, that the C-force is held by a C-person.

   A. Correct. Otherwise performance would be jeopardized.

   B. Incorrect. People work best in positions that align with their personalities, not against them.

4. Most business implosions occurred because traditional C-force and E-force players did not execute their jobs from the category they were tasked into, and expected to operate outwardly from, by the board, the CEO, and consumers.

   A. Correct. Thus the importance of identifying which individuals follow which force.

   B. Incorrect. If employees are not aligned with their basic personality forces, how can they function properly in an organization?

17

Gutless Leadership, the Deadly Sins That Erode Performance

It is easy to do what those around you want and like; it is far easier to do the easy and less challenging thing that those around you would like.

It is far more difficult to take a stand when the right and necessary thing to do is not in favor with those around you!

The gutless leader is the leader who is led by opinion polls and is less educated!

—**Jeff Magee**

Learning Objective

After completing this section of the course, you will be able to describe the symptoms of failing leadership for further understanding and avoidance.

I magine that you are flying a super commercial airliner. The combined energies of many people make this feat possible. As the pilot, you lead a team of individuals. Their combined energies determine whether your flights meet with success or devastating failure. You are actively aware of every task and actively participate in most of them. From the time the plane sits at the gate until you take it up to 10,000 feet in the air, you have your finger on the pulse of operations.

When the plane reaches its cruising altitude, which comprises the majority of the operational time aloft (30,000 feet issues), most pilots begin to relax. They pay less attention to tactical operational controls and task-oriented actions. The tendency is toward more of an autopilot mode, with a system in place that can be engaged for the remainder of that flight. This allows the pilot to look out over the horizon to ensure that the performance level is maintained. With this kind of foresight, she can ensure that they arrive at the intended destination in the most efficient manner possible.

As a performance-based individual you, too, are much like a pilot. You encounter situations that require your active participation in the tactical aspects of your responsibilities (0 to 10,000 feet issues). Then there are times when you morph into strategic activities (the autopilot, or 30,000 feet issues). Most individuals spend too much time at the operational tactical level and too little time at the strategic planning level. This is the cause of ineffectiveness and an overall lack of success.

Most individuals, whether at home or in business, seldom reach a cruising altitude of true greatness. Instead, they get caught up in the 5,000 feet issues. These include the following: bickering, passive-aggressive behavior, cliché warfare, destructive alliance building for self-serving purposes, implementation of hidden agendas, conflicts, confrontations, problematic personnel behaviors, and egos that bar individuals from being leaders and encourage bureaucracy and kingdom building.

Unfortunately, there is no shortage of gutless leadership. Today the papers are filled with and evening newscasts play out a steady stream of examples of corporate executives who sell out their businesses or constituents.

Such managerial leadership sins are seen as organizational and institutional cancers that can be traced to the absence of or bastardization of seven core ethical fibers.

These actions, or behaviors, eat away at the performances of great people. These leadership sins act as deadly poisons. If they are not dealt with early on, they erode performance. Once these sins become norms, they produce poor results and gutless leadership. Some early warning signs of poisonous acts include the following:

- Abdication of self-responsibility
- Abdication of accountability
- A sense of entitlement that elevates one above standard operating procedures (SOPs) and/or laws
- A sense that one is owed (tenure, seniority, rank, title) due to his station in life
- Excusing away low, poor, substandard performance as acceptable

As detailed in the research for *Coaching for Impact: Leadership and the Art of Coaching* (by Dr. Jeffrey Magee and Dr. Jay Ferraro, Brown Books

Publishing Group), it is revealed that sustained performance effectiveness is demonstrated through specific and consistent behaviors. These behaviors were observed in more than 1,000 peak performers (managerial leaders, executives, entrepreneurs) throughout the business place and are influenced, or guided by, specific, self-evident principles or rules. These shared rules culminated in a Performance Code of Ethics. They protect against venomous behaviors that are managerial leadership sins, eroding true performance achievement.

Recently, *CFO* magazine reported a Gallup/UBS survey that featured some "trust busters" among employees: "Fifty-four percent say they believe most corporate executives are honest and ethical; 59 percent say they aren't worth what they're paid."

Self-effacing cancers that lead an individual to gutless leadership can be avoided. Consider these seven ethical guideposts as your Performance Code of Ethics to determine your next course of mental and physical action:

1. **Competence** is aggressively committed to in the development of your necessary skill set; it is the only way to be competitive in the marketplace. Leaders recognize that their true differentials in the marketplace are human capital and their skill assets. *Training* magazine, August 2002, reports that in a university study of employees over a 25-year period, those who engaged in ongoing skill development training and opportunities increased their finances. On average, they earned 25 percent more than their colleagues.

2. **Accountability** cultivates strong networks within your organization/business for greater community.

3. **Integrity** is driven by constant vision, goals, and objectives. It must be consistent with your overall code of ethics. It must be common knowledge that your actions will be consistent, whether your grandmother is in the room or not.

4. **Professional responsibility and duty** to the dictated organization/business expectations is crucial.

5. **Respect for rights and personal dignity** of others helps us gauge actions according to this standard to ensure that individuals are not expected to choose between dignity and personal gain.

6. **Commitment to the other person** is a beacon for the other's vested interest.

7. **Social responsibility** is fostered via a sense of commitment to the community where you live and work.

These seven ethical standards serve as benchmark behaviors for managerial leadership greatness. Adhering to these performance codes kills any potential poisonous behaviors. The simple execution of these standards prevents such behaviors from arising, preemptively stopping any environments that would sustain them. Personal leadership ethics serve as powerful combatants against destructive actions, whether personal or professional.

Managerial Leadership Bible Lesson 17

True managerial leaders do not wait to determine what their core beliefs and actions will be. They resolve to operate from a definite set of values, core beliefs, and these drive their every action. In essence, effective managerial leaders of tomorrow will operate from a clear set of organizational and professional ethics.

Review Questions

The review questions accompanying each chapter or section are designed to assist you in achieving the learning objective stated at the beginning of each chapter. The review section is not graded; do not submit it in place of your final exam. While completing the review questions, it may be helpful to study any unfamiliar terms in the glossary in addition to course content. After completing the review questions for each chapter, proceed to the review question answers and rationales.

1. Excusing away low, poor, substandard performance as acceptable is a symptom of:

    A. Gutless leadership

    B. Apathetic leadership

    C. Lazy leadership

    D. Micromanaging leadership

2. The ethic of _____ is aggressively committed to in the development of your necessary skill set; it is the only way to be competitive in the marketplace.

    A. Accountability

    B. Integrity

    C. Competence

    D. Commitment

3. True managerial leaders do not wait to determine what their core beliefs and actions will be.

    A. True

    B. False

Review Question Answers and Rationales

Review question answer choices are accompanied by unique, logical reasoning (rationales) as to why an answer is correct or incorrect. Evaluative feedback to incorrect responses and reinforcement feedback to correct responses are both provided.

1. Excusing away low, poor, substandard performance as acceptable is a symptom of:

    A. Correct. This symptom can lead to a deadly poison that can erode businesses.

    B. Incorrect. Apathy suggests that leadership doesn't care. In this example they do care, but only to cover up problems.

    C. Incorrect. Such leadership is not necessarily lazy, but could be planning a more harmful deed.

    D. Incorrect. A micromanaging leader would be paying close detail to performance, not making excuses.

2. The ethic of _____ is aggressively committed to in the development of your necessary skill set; it is the only way to be competitive in the marketplace.

    A. Incorrect. Accountability is taking responsibility for mistakes.

    B. Incorrect. Integrity is maintaining the reputation for being ethical and consistent.

    C. Correct. Competence is being fully versed in what you need to know.

    D. Incorrect. In this sense, commitment is to the work being done, not just competence.

3. True managerial leaders do not wait to determine what their core beliefs and actions will be.

   A. **Correct. This is what creates their integrity.**

   B. Incorrect. If someone else dictates a leader's core beliefs, then the leader is being a gutless leader.

18

Succession Planning and Exportable Skills

Because of a leadership vision vacuum, most organizations are thrust into chaos when leaders transition.

—**Jeff Magee**

Learning Objective

After completing this section of the course, you will be able to plan for the end of a leadership position or the transfer into another.

hould you invest in developing the skill set of your human capital and have it potentially leave you, or not provide it with continual skill development and have it remain?

As a managerial leader, the answer is simple. Continually developing exportable performance players for your organization is the ingredient that spells success and profitability. No matter which business one is in today, the continual need to refine and fine-tune individuals' core competency skill sets is a minimal must to be relevant tomorrow.

Recognize the value of an individual to your business as an asset, much like leading-edge technology, equipment, facilities, and market share. People are today's most valuable assets.

Every player within your organizational diagram (whether identified from a global perspective or within individual strategic business units, lines, divisions, departments, areas, and so on) must be seen as assets. They should be viewed as having unique skill sets that may have specific application to what they do, and these skill sets must also be observed for exportable application.

Tactical leaders continually ask whether they have created an atmosphere, culture, environment conducive for individuals to welcome, embrace, and seek out ongoing skill development (technical or nontechnical, degreed or nondegreed, certification or noncertification) that would then be exportable with them, should they need to make a career transition. Consider the following:

- Can an individual with her present skill set make a horizontal move within your organization and bring immediate value to her new team?
- Can an individual make a vertical move within your organization and shepherd others to greatness with his always-relevant skill set?

How exportable are you and those you lead based on unique skill sets, experience, and performance platforms?

Succession planning is more involved than what most understand. The "planning" is the macro architecture that allows you to examine your human capital and manage it as a talent against present needs and forecasted against future known and unknown factors (attrition management, retirement forecasts, market expansions, global market expectations, individual career pathways and position pathway needs, and so on). This exercise and the subsequent analytics and documents that may come out of this as work-product serve a more micro daily organizational and individual need in succession management and succession development as specific key performance indicators to ensure we live our plans.

As a tactical leader, you may need to work with other stakeholders within your organization to create an atmosphere in which everyone becomes fanatical about ongoing and continuous skill set development. Consider these questions to determine whether your organization has developed peak performers with exportable skills:

- Has the executive team willingly embraced skill development initiatives and defined career development pathways for everyone?
- Has the rhetoric of all influencers (management, unions, senior employees, and new hires) moved from excuses and naysaying to outright endorsement and instances where everyone welcomes and actively participates in ongoing training?
- Has the union leadership enthusiastically embraced any training opportunity to make any member/employee more valuable (and thus exportable) to his functionality?
- Is it the overall attitude of employees to welcome and hold one another accountable for the use of new skills, for continually increased efficiencies in everything that is undertaken within an organization?

A few years ago, a study by the American Society for Training and Development (today the Association for Talent Development) revealed that the amount of time organizations in America invest in training initiatives for their human capital was less than 2 percent of the annual employee work time each year. A true test for today's tactical leader is to correctly and continually provide the sequential skill improvement and enhancement necessary for each individual to do two critical things:

- Become the best she can be (present and future tense) at the task for which an organization has employed her.

- Attain his personal goals, whether within your organization or onward toward another place in his life.

Knowing whether employees have truly relevant exportable skills can be answered by this question: "If an employee on your present team were to leave you and go to another business unit within your organization or to a new employer, and you were now to consider hiring her, would she bring truly cutting-edge skills that could be immediately drawn upon to elevate the level of performance in the new environment?"

A player performing at peak levels of effectiveness is a sign that a great leader has invested daily, tactically, and wisely in that individual. A player who can take those skills, move onward, upward, or outward, and continue his reign of success is an even greater testament of greatness!

So let's explore tactical ways for you and all members of your leadership team to learn how to assess and deploy exportable skill sets, for organizational functionality and performance success.

The way organizations and leaders have been conditioned to manage and develop performers, work their bench of players, and cultivate future high potentials must be radically changed to be relevant in tomorrow's business world.

First, leaders should build a winning team of peak performers who functionally serve the organization's needs, devoid of personalities. To do so, think globally (big perspective on what the organization really needs, versus how it may presently look) and identify the essential functional positions necessary for the organization to survive (worst-case scenario) and thrive (best-case scenario).

Then, for every such position, design a master index of deployable skill sets required to facilitate that function for the organization. Add to that index what the enhancement skills should be to remain cutting edge tomorrow.

You can identify these essential attributes-behaviors-characteristics (ABC formula) for each ideal position and then find a player who matches.

There are several ways to evaluate exportable skill sets:

1. Ask the top players (present or past tense) in each identified position what they feel are the minimum requirements for someone to be a star in that given position.

2. Recognize what the leaders in each position feel would enhance the core responses, above and beyond what the occupants of said position have identified.

3. Recognize the essential ABCs for any key functions with which a particular position will be interfacing, internally and externally.

4. Reexamine existing criteria or profiles for each position. As most established criteria for such positions were designed to meet needs, those needs are often in the past tense. If not monitored, positions can evolve away from their primary purposes and begin to take on lives of their own!

5. As a benchmark for designing or retooling your skill set functionality, reference any trade association profiles, industry standards, or academic models determined to be critical to a position's core function.

In deploying appropriate skill sets for organizational functionality and performance success, continually ensure that the necessary skills are always cutting-edge and exportable, in the sense that any occupant of a position truly serves a purpose, his skills have a viable nature, and if he were to leave, the acquired skill set would be marketable. The idea is that if someone were to leave with the skill set, it would have application elsewhere, and a void of such a skill set in the previous organization would impact the overall effectiveness of that function. Many times, an individual with perceivably great skills leaves, and that loss has little real impact on what the position really entails!

For organizations with nonexportable talent pools, one can see many individuals in today's business world who occupy positions with skill sets that are outdated and unwanted. Often, one can glance inward and recognize the redundancies of functionality of individuals serving in jobs that no longer constitute full-time, wage-earning positions.

The legacy of a great managerial leader is the continued effectiveness of an organization when he is not present and long after the manager leaves the stewardship role of the organization. Thus, the drive to ensure that all players have real-time viable skills and allowing individuals to showcase their unique and powerful talents becomes the proof of exportable skill sets and exportable people assets contributing to the marketplace.

Managerial Leadership Bible Lesson 18

With a vision of where you as a leader are headed and focused on taking your team, you can determine objectively what true skill and talent assets are necessary to arrive at your market-driven destination. From this insight it is imperative that managerial leaders design their templates of objective skills and the means to enable individuals to attain and deploy them with vigor and unwavering commitment.

Review Questions

The review questions accompanying each chapter or section are designed to assist you in achieving the learning objective stated at the beginning of each chapter. The review section is not graded; do not submit it in place of your final exam. While completing the review questions, it may be helpful to study any unfamiliar terms in the glossary in addition to course content. After completing the review questions for each chapter, proceed to the review question answers and rationales.

1. Every player within your organizational diagram should be seeking _____ to be able to transfer within your company or move to another company.

    A. Ongoing skill development

    B. Trade secrets

    C. Agents

    D. Life coaches

2. A study by the American Society for Training and Development revealed that the amount of time organizations in America invest in training initiatives for their human capital is more than 50 percent of the annual employee work time each year.

    A. True

    B. False

3. A player performing at peak levels of effectiveness is a sign that a great leader invested daily, tactically, and wisely in that individual.

   A. True

   B. False

4. The way organizations and leaders have been conditioned to manage and develop performers, work their bench of players, and cultivate future high potentials must be radically changed to be relevant in tomorrow's business world.

   A. True

   B. False

Review Question Answers and Rationales

Review question answer choices are accompanied by unique, logical reasoning (rationales) as to why an answer is correct or incorrect. Evaluative feedback to incorrect responses and reinforcement feedback to correct responses are both provided.

1. Every player within your organizational diagram should be seeking _____ to be able to transfer within your company or move to another company.

   A. Correct. Therefore, you should make sure your company fosters continual training.

   B. Incorrect. This is a sneaky way to get a promotion.

   C. Incorrect. Most businesspeople would not need an agent to get a different job.

   D. Incorrect. A life coach might provide motivation but not the necessary skills for a transfer.

2. A study by the American Society for Training and Development revealed that the amount of time organizations in America invest in training initiatives for their human capital is more than 50% of the annual employee work time each year.

   A. Incorrect. In fact it was less than 2 percent.

   B. Correct. If only it were true!

3. A player performing at peak levels of effectiveness is a sign that a great leader invested daily, tactically, and wisely in that individual.

   A. **Correct. Your employees' exportable skills are a reflection of a good manager.**

   B. Incorrect. A player's performance cannot be based on personal merit alone.

4. The way organizations and leaders have been conditioned to manage and develop performers, work their bench of players, and cultivate future high potentials must be radically changed to be relevant in tomorrow's business world.

   A. **Correct. Throughout the course, the author demonstrates how changing ideas and methods of management can create successful and influential leaders.**

   B. Incorrect. This course emphasizes that deviations from traditional management are necessary.

19

The Trajectory Code Model

Being Trajectory Code proficient allows increased point C success and avoidance of derailment caused by point B behaviors.

—**Jeff Magee**

Learning Objectives

After completing this section of the course, you will be able to understand how everything you do affects strategy, operations, and tactics.

As an effective managerial-leader, executive, solo business entrepreneur, civil servant, association or lay-leader, you need the ability to apply the strategies, operational systems, and tactical habits as detailed in this book. They are critical for a competitive posture in the business marketplace of today and tomorrow. To attain a higher level of return on investment (ROI) in everything you do, understand this final model and you can apply everything in this book as overlays.

Think of a simple V diagram, which we will call the Trajectory Code Model (see Figure 19.1). We all start at point "A" (representing the starting point, such as a new day or project, new employee start date, or the launch of a new program) en route to our individual and collective goals, which are at point "C." Far too often, individuals and organizations get off track and mired in point "B": dead-end derailment behaviors.

Be deliberate and purposeful: Point "C"—defined as aspirations, goals, and objectives and measured by objective and specific key performance indicators (KPIs) and milestones—is created from your values that drive both your inward vision and outward mission statements (MAPS). These all become the building blocks of your culture. It is as one leaves point "A," the starting point, that, for a short period of time, actions and behaviors place you on either a trajectory toward point "C" or point "B." And it is at this starting point of the two pathways that you need to recognize that a mere 1% effort in any one way can influence the trajectory direction toward either point "C" or point "B."

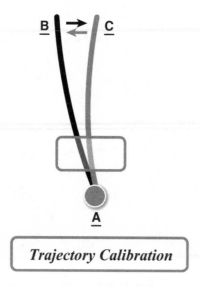

Figure 19.1 Trajectory Code Model

As a leader, you need to be able to extrapolate out at any point in the trajectory diagram and recognize that if you continue with what you are doing, it will take you toward point "C," and then continue with even greater conviction. However, if you recognize that if you continue it will take you toward point "B," then make an immediate strategic and tactical calibration adjustment to get you and your resources aligned with a trajectory pathway toward point "C."

Recognizing what those action or directives are as one leaves point "A" and being able to extrapolate forward which trajectory pathway line you will be sent down is critical to success, achievement, and sustained performance that matters.

In reality, what most people and organizations experience is best intentions when leaving point "A" (the on-boarding of a new employee, the starting of a new campaign or initiative, and so on), but unless there are mindful individuals, coaches, mentors, milestones for benchmarking, or systems in place to continuously evaluate or self-evaluate where one is at all times—on trajectory pathway "C" or "B"—one can evolve off track.

Think of the KPIs that keep you on pathway line "C"—en route to point "C" goals—as the GPS system for accelerated growth. As you go off course toward trajectory pathway "B," if you could easily recalibrate to pathway "C," then success could be more easily and often attained.

But once you evolve towards point "B" with no accountability mechanisms in place or individuals that care for accountability, it becomes your behaviors that keep working in the unwittingly point "B" trajectory. And over time this behavior becomes habit-forming, and habits become your personal SOP (standard operating procedures). At this level, it becomes engrained within you to operate and see things only from this dead-end trajectory, which in turn becomes your vested emotions. And your emotions cause you to believe that your way (SOP) is the only way and the best way. The early identification that you or someone is off course and heading down trajectory pathway "B" can be constructively engaged with coaching and mentoring, realignment of values, situational performance reviews applying the Player Capability Index model, counseling and disciplinarian sessions, and ultimately termination.

When you reach the dead-end pathway of point "B," the explosion causes defensive behavior, blame gamesmanship, and the necessary change to get from point "B" to point "C" seems far too overwhelming for most. And when a person or business unit finds itself at point "B," the perception is that the distance to point "C" is so great that this becomes an enhanced misuse of resources, and people find themselves in a conflict-resistance situation.

Now, imagine if, at the base of the Trajectory Code Model at point "A," we had people, systems, and tools in place to continuously ensure that we are making the simple and easy recalibrations necessary to ensure arrival at point "C." I call these easy adjustments the 1% factors. The intersecting and progressing ROIs that can be plotted into the pathway "C" trajectory, which never ends, are numerous. You ensure progression along pathway "C" by plotting onto that timeline KPIs, on-boarding processes, Performance Development Plans (PDP), and performance reviews applying the Player Capability Index model, milestones, mentors, and coaches, mission statements, cultural identifiers, and more.

When you operate from a greater understanding of the trajectory diagram and an understanding of the historical to present state influencers upon yourself and others within the base circular area, known as your trajectory code, then you can manage and forecast human behavior more accurately and facilitate simple 1% change calibrations to attain greatness. Consider the new ROI vocabulary that your trajectory code can drive through the greater understanding of the content from this book:

1. **ROIntellect**—Now demand that you continuously enhance your mental DNA and draw deeply from within to always showcase the best of you and others.

2. **ROIndividual Initiative**—Now imagine that your trajectory "C" line was paved with support systems and people to allow you to deliver on ROI #1, so you and others freely gave 100%, 100% of the time, and accepted nothing less from everyone in your space.

3. **ROInterpersonal Relationships (leverage multiplier)**—Now imagine you could have 100% presence of mind to be able to leverage 100% of the people you know and could motivate others to do the same in pursuit of rrajectory point "C."

When one has clarity of point "C" with clearly defined language that guides every action, it can become a common DNA thread that units people of like cause, mind, or goal with one another, and the cumulative energies can be overwhelming. And that would spell real ROI of any capital you get to work within!

Effective managers, leaders, and executives understand that their legacy comes from trajectory pathway point "C" accomplishments and beyond.

Glossary

This is a glossary of key terms with definitions. Please review any terms you are not familiar with.

60-Second Power Vacation™—This is one of the most powerful ways to refocus your mind and body for greater energy and sustained success in professional (and personal) environments.

Action Memo®—Allows the player needing management interaction to take a traditional auditory conversation or problem and convert it into a visual communication interaction.

attitude—Our mind-sets, beliefs, self-talk, self-affirmations, inner-voice dialogues we occasionally have.

Attitude and Ego Management SAFETY Model—The descending six levels of maturity (6. Youthfulness 5. Territory Security 4. Enlargement of Fiefdom 3. Friendship Factor 2. Association & Integration 1. Security & Safety) are applicable to both the individuals you interact with and groups as a whole. Similar to Maslow's Hierarchy of Needs psychological association model, this model expands upon that from an organizational dynamics viewpoint.

autocrat—A person invested with or claiming to exercise absolute authority.

benchmarking—A tool of measurement whereby one identifies what is perceived to be the best in a market (whether a product, service, employee performance, and so on), and then uses that data to gauge one's own performance. This enables management to determine many important factors.

bureaucrat—An official who works by fixed routine without exercising intelligent judgment.

countdown—Technique to gain control over emotionally piqued anger; pick a number (try 100) and begin counting down toward zero. By immediately and consciously focusing your mind off a challenged stimulant and toward something else, by the time you reach zero, you will more often than not have calmed yourself down and gained needed self- and management control for a more efficient interaction with others.

cross-functional team—Designed on a need-to-be basis, comprised of only the task-functional appropriate individuals from within and outside an organization. Decision making is structured, with subject matter experts on the team owning their areas of specialty, and with authority limited or conditional to the situation.

DNA of dynamics—The new view of organizational culture and climate.

FIST FACTOR® (Mental Board of Directors)—The conditioning factors that hold the greatest impact and shaping power over us and our potential are tied directly to our hands.

Grief Cycle™—A theory that states that for most players (transmitters and terrorists), the reason it takes so long to get to the blend, and ultimately to some degree of a transcend, level is that many get caught up in opposing anything out of the norms of the organizational flow and society (are change-averse)—regardless of the merits. The steps of the cycle are Denial, Resistance, Commitment, Exploration/Investigation.

horizontal movement—A transfer within a company from one department or position to another without a promotion.

huddle—A brief meeting that requires no sitting and allows for exchange of documents and information much more quickly than a regular meeting.

interactive communication—Communication in which the parties involved are interacting with positive signal transfer, and each is equally assuming 100 percent accountability for the signal exchange.

management team—Designed for intermediate decision-making powers on the front line and throughout an organization. These individuals have been elevated into official managerial leadership and have assumed official managerial, supervisory, legal, ethical, formal, structured, and mandated roles and responsibilities as such. They have decision-making authority up to completion of needs, and serve to manage and monitor workflow for an organization.

micromanagement—To manage or control with excessive attention to minor details.

Mind Mapping or Growth Wheels—Powerful techniques you can utilize to increase your comprehension of written materials.

mini-agreements—During a negotiation session, work through the agenda items one at a time and work to obtain an agreement on each individual issue, as to what it is and what will be done jointly to resolve it.

mission statements—A brief description of a company's fundamental purpose that articulates the company's purpose both for those in the organization and for the public.

Negativity Action Index™—An L-grid model to mentally assess a potential engagement with a perceived challenging or negative individual to ensure the best tactical approaches are best deployed.

Optimal Decision Point (ODP©)—The point at which the highest and most realistic level of value is obtained from decisions.

paradigm shift—The notion of a major change in a certain thought-pattern—a radical change in personal beliefs, complex systems, or organizations, replacing the former way of thinking or organizing with a radically different way of thinking or organizing.

Performance Code of Ethics—Ethical standards that serve as benchmark behaviors for managerial leadership greatness.

permanent team—Designed out of a need that appears to be a new norm. Thus additional roles, responsibility, and authority are conditionally given to these individuals for those items that fall within the domain of the new permanent team charter or mandate.

Peter Principle—The theory that eventually good, competent people will be promoted up and out of their realm of ability and into places of complete incompetence!

positive center of influence (COI)—Colleagues, mentors, advisers, associations, networks, and the FIST FACTOR.

private isolation time—Every key manager knows the value of isolation time. Whether this time is used for work, brainstorming, and reflection, or merely self-time, insist upon regular isolation time for yourself each day to enable you to maintain control and focus.

punch list—A listing or chart of each issue addressed, with the status of each. The status should include action to be taken, date initiated, who initiated it, date to be completed, who is accountable, and comments.

RAFT—The four power questions for managing and eliminating paper stacks from your life:

> **R = Refer:** Can I refer this item to someone else?
>
> **A = Action:** Does this need my action?
>
> **F = File:** Does this need to be filed?
>
> **T = Toss:** Can this be recycled or tossed away?

SA (skills/attitude) Model—First, assess the skill level (knowledge, education, training, skill set...) on the vertical axis from low (score as a zero) to high (score as a ten), with the middle area (score as a five) representing the difference between acceptable and unacceptable skill levels. Second, assess the attitude level (desire, motivation, willingness, ownership, acceptance, demeanor, attitude...) on the horizontal axis from low (zero) to high (ten), with the middle area (five) representing the difference between acceptable and unacceptable attitude levels.

self-directed team—Designed here to be independent and free flowing from a traditional organization hierarchy, with clearly assigned roles, responsibilities, and authority to facilitate the team's mandate. Individuals work with one another to get the job done, hold one another accountable, and assume all levels of liability for their decisions and actions.

self-meeting—Some private time after a meeting to focus on what happened and what the next steps are.

SMART Formula™—A formula for effective negotiation.

> **S**=Communication needs to be specific.
>
> **M**=Your interaction needs to be measurable.
>
> **A**=Attain an agreement.
>
> **R**=Discussion is realistic, reasonable, and reachable.
>
> **T**=Establish the time frame.

STOP Formula™—A map to follow when discussion gets bogged down. With this formula you can work to maintain and make decisions issue oriented, not personality oriented.

> **S** =Stop and see the issue.
>
> **T** =Target (analyze) the positives and negatives.
>
> **O** =Organize your options (solutions).
>
> **P** =Pick and proceed with an option.

STP Factor™—A negotiation process that describes the three basic components of a negotiation:

> S=Situation
>
> T=Timing
>
> P=Players

temporary team—Designed to address a specific need that is typically not a normal event and has a limited life cycle. Once addressed, this team disbands and does not assume a new, longer lasting life cycle. Thus decision-making powers are conditional, temporary, and may rotate among actual individuals and vary from what they would otherwise have within the organization.

terrorists—These people are often seen as the negativists or complainers, not as the devil's advocates (someone who actually has a viable alternative); they fight change for no real reason. They just don't like the idea because the idea wasn't theirs. These individuals are sometimes corrosive to your team; they are your pessimists, naysayers, criticizers, and condemners, and they live to torment and terrorize forward-moving contributors to the world. They can find fault with anyone and anything.

traditional (old-school) management—A pyramid structure that begins with front-line workers and entry-level positions at the bottom of the pyramid (typically closest to daily realities and customers). Mid-level managers and supervisors are in the middle (typically facing daily operational issues and becoming removed from the daily pulse of reality). Finally, senior-level managerial leaders or executive-level functionaries are at the top (typically concentrating on the future direction of the organization and industry and, unfortunately, extremely removed from the actual daily realities of the front line).

transformers—These are often seen as the proactive and positive members of a group, and who have strong convictions and high levels of self-esteem. These personnel can be cultivated as strong allies and advocates for you. With them on your side, they will bring the transmitter/follower subgroup into your corner.

transmitters—Eighty percent of any group who will tend to perpetuate the status quo it is directed to accept and support. They work and perform based upon what the influencers have conditioned them to do. These people are also known as followers.

vertical movement—Transfer in a company that involves a promotion.

work group—Designed as a collection of individuals necessary to task facilitation with limited low-level decision making authority. Traditionally found within most organizations, where individuals work toward a common goal with no tangible final decision-making authority.

Index

A

B

C

I

I-ACT (Immediate Action
Correspondence Turnaround),
190-191
ideal all-star player profile, 216-218
identifying transformers, 143
Immediate Action Correspondence
Turnaround (I-ACT), 190-191
incentives, 134-141
  guidelines, 138-139
  incentive idea bank, 136
  self-assessed motivators, 139-141
individual initiative, 344
information identification (Anatomy
of a Conflict matrix), 296-297
initiating conversation, 279
integration, 130
integrity, 329
intellect, ROI (return on
investment), 344
interactive communication, 273
  accountability, 210-211
  communication pyramid model,
  202-204
  customizing for receiver, 209-210
  ensuring message is received,
  204-205
  ensuring message is understood,
  205-208
  explained, 201-209
  interacting with difficult
  personalities, 168-171
interpersonal relationships, 344
intervention styles. *See* alternative
management styles
interviews, 224-231
inventing options, 294
investigation, 73
isolating difficult personalities, 168
isolation, 276

J

job description/expectation profile
document, 223-224, 304-308
job sharing/rotation, 227-228
Johnson & Johnson mission
statement, 17

K

Karrass, Chester L., 285
Kelly, Gary, 23
kinesthetic people, communicating
with, 210
Kissinger, Henry, 69

L

laboratories for reengineering, 308-315
leadership
  alternative management styles
    coaches, 52-59
    counselors, 50-51
    disciplinarians, 51-52
    empowerment, 64
    explained, 43-46
    *Management/Team Control
    Model, 60-64*
    *Managerial-Leadership-Coaching
    Engagement Model, 52-59*
    managers, 46-48
    mentors, 48-49
    table of, 45
    teachers, 48
  attitude, 33-34
  communication. *See* communication
  FIST FACTOR, 33-39
  gutless leadership, 327-329
  hiring decisions. *See* hiring process
  management game plan, 301-304
    *benchmarks for management
    excellence, 301-302*
    *job description/expectation profile
    document, 304-308*

N

negative participants. *See* difficult players

negativity, converting to positive outcomes, 271-280

Action Engagement Model, 274-275

BCOA (best course of action), 273-274

conversion strategies, 275-280

Negativity Action Index, 171-173

negotiation, 285-286

Anatomy of a Conflict matrix

basic information identification, 296

common ground, 297

scale of flexibility, 296-297

follow-up activities, 295-296

key factors, 286

negotiation cycles, 292-293

personality assessment, 286-287

power sources, 293

preparing for, 286-292

STP Factor, 287-288

tactics, 293-295

traits of effective negotiators, 286-287

neutralizing difficult personalities, 167-168

new management model

characteristics, 4-5

illustration, 3-4

Next Generation, 64

nibbling, 294

nonconfrontational solution emails, 180

nonverbal signals, 206

notepad management, 171

notes

Agenda Manager System, 179

growth wheel note-taking technique, 245-246

meeting notes, 150

visual notes, 169

O

objections, overcoming, 278

ODP (Optimal Decision Point), 160

"old school" management styles, 1-10

The One Minute Manager (Blanchard), 72

one-on-ones, 170, 279

operation levels. *See* organizational levels

operations, 2

Optimal Decision Point (ODP), 160

options, inventing, 294

organizational levels

Begin

characteristics, 114

managerial leadership hints, 115-117

Blend

characteristics, 115

managerial leadership hints, 118-119

Defend

characteristics, 114

managerial leadership hints, 117-118

End

characteristics, 115

managerial leadership hints, 120-122

explained, 69-74, 113-114

Transcend

characteristics, 115

managerial leadership hints, 119-120

organizational mission statement, 17-18

outcomes, negotiating. *See* negotiation

ownership

ownership words, 168, 208, 279

player ownership, 313

P

transmitters (followers)
  communication with, 105
  cultivating, 116
  mentoring, 118
two-minute warning, 146-147
type A personality style, 290

U-V

user/implementer stakeholders, 322

VAK (visual, auditory, kinesthetic)
  communications, 280
venting, 168
vertical movement, 92
visual aids, 207
visual notes, 169
visual people, communicating with, 209
visualized statements, 277
vocabulary style changes, 74-75
  challenge words, avoiding, 168,
    278-279
  ownership words, 168, 208, 279
voice mail, 188

W

walk-away zone, 294
Wandell, Keith, 23
Welch, Jack, 7
What's In It For Me? (WIIFM), 207
What's In It For Us? (WIIFU), 207
winning player profile, 216-218
work groups, 161
workflow charts, 157
workload liabilities, 148
write-ups, requesting
  after delegation, 158
  from meeting participants, 149

X-Y-Z

Yoshida, Sidney, 8
youthfulness, 132

Zappos mission statement, 23